D1500300

THE
MEDIAEVAL UNIVERSITIES

THE
MEDIAEVAL UNIVERSITIES

BY

NATHAN SCHACHNER

NEW YORK
FREDERICK A. STOKES COMPANY
PUBLISHERS

FIRST PUBLISHED 1938

PRINTED IN GREAT BRITAIN BY
T. AND A. CONSTABLE LTD.
UNIVERSITY PRESS, EDINBURGH

To my daughter

BARBARA

Contents

Preview

THREE all-embracing institutions characterize the Middle Ages—the Church, the Empire, and the University. Of these the first two were derivative; only the University was peculiarly a mediaeval invention.

The Catholic Church was a heritage from the declining days of the Roman Empire, when the Bishop of Rome was but one of many bishops of equal rank and weight. By reason of a series of historical accidents, the superior shrewdness and energy of the Roman pontiffs, and the happy discovery, at a most propitious moment, of the forged decretals of the pseudo-Isidore, the Papacy became the head and front of Catholicism.

The Church moulded and dominated the mediaeval scene with a completeness that is unexampled in the history of the human race. No one, from the humblest peasant to the most powerful prince, was immune from its control. From birth, with its attendant formulae of wedlock and the baptismal font, through a life punctuated by confession and the payment of inevitable tithes, to the last absolution and the masses to speed the errant soul through purgatorial fires, the most Catholic Church kept a diligent watch over the eternal welfare of its charges.

Nor did it confine itself to things of the spirit. There were wily and ambitious Popes in those days, and Innocent III was the wiliest and most ambitious of them all. It was he who brought the Papacy to heights of political power and influence at the beginning of the thirteenth century, and enforced submission to its most arrogant claims. It may be that in the hurly-burly of the market-place certain small spiritual values were permitted to languish, and the seeds of discontent sown for future burgeoning in the bloody upheavals of Lollards and Hussites, and the ultimate Reformation. But that is

1

running slightly ahead of our story. At the turn of the thirteenth century the Church was an authentic Colossus, straddling Western Europe.

The Empire, the second great institution of the Middle Ages, likewise struck its roots in that earlier and greater Roman Empire. In fact, it was an attempt to recreate, or perhaps, more plausibly, to translate from its abhorred residence in the East, the august dominion of the Caesars. It may be that Charlemagne was tricked into receiving the coveted crown from the hands of the Pope, as he afterwards privately claimed, but in any event that grandiose laying-on of hands prepared the foundation for the future pretensions of the Papacy to the overlordship of the Empire. Later Emperors were to regret bitterly that slip on Charlemagne's part. "*What the Pope hath given, the Pope taketh away. Blessed be——*" etc. etc.

The Empire developed into the implacable foe of the temporal aspirations of the Papacy, but it was foredoomed to defeat. Its title was at all times vague and shifting, and during considerable periods it was wholly ineffective. Its dominions, aside from the private patrimony of the regnant Emperor, were those which his troops could conquer and hold; its feudal loyalties were doubtful, and subject to the absolving thunders of an antagonistic Church. Frederick II, greatest of the Emperors, "the first modern," went down to disastrous defeat before a combination of rebellious Lombard States and the Papal forces. Thereafter, the Holy Roman Empire which, according to Voltaire, was neither holy, Roman, nor an Empire, eked out a perilous existence until it dissolved in smoke in the very midst of the nineteenth century.

In the presence of these vast forces, it seems temerarious to mention the University in the same breath. Yet its influence on the Middle Ages and on modern times is certainly greater than that of the Empire, and if it does not approach the torrential flow of the Church, it helped quite measurably to mould that institution, its theology, its very policies. The University was the darling, the spoiled child of Papacy and Empire, of king and municipality alike. Privileges were showered on the proud Universities in a continuous golden stream; privileges that had no counterpart, then, before, or since. Not even the sacred hierarchies of the Church had quite the exemptions of the poorest begging scholar who could claim the protection of a University. Municipalities competed violently for the honour of housing one within their walls; kings wrote siren letters to entice discontented groups of scholars from the domains of their rivals; Popes intervened with menacing language to compel royalty to respect the inviolability of this favoured institution.

An astounding state of affairs, that strikes strangely on modern ears. For twentieth-century institutions of learning are but pallid simulacra of their lusty forbears. Their hold on religion is slight, their influence on politics even slighter, if we exclude the professorate of one T. Woodrow Wilson, and the recent tentative gathering of University professors in the so-called "Brain-Trust" of Franklin D. Roosevelt; cultural, scientific, and economic thought has a habit of slipping past the portals endowed by retired and repentant millionaires; a University degree is no longer a sure passport to worldly preferment. In fine, the Universities of today are but inconspicuous eddies in the vast currents of modern life.

Such was not the case with the mediaeval University. Originating at some time during the twelfth century, it sprang almost at once into a burst of effulgence that illuminated every nook and cranny of the mediaeval scene. Write the history of the great Universities, and you have an almost complete history of mediaeval thought and culture, of theology and philosophy, of legal and medical achievements. The proud Doctors of Paris disputed and philosophized, and the mediaeval world paused to listen; a Pope apologized humbly for daring to differ from them on a subtle point in theology when he, poor wretch, had never attained to the inestimable advantages of a University degree; the Bolognese Professors determined the course of European law for centuries to come; the Rectors of Paris, magnificent as kings in purple and ermine, sat in the Royal Council and claimed precedence over the greatest dignitaries of Church and State; when the good citizens of Oxford so far forgot themselves as to hang certain scholars, they learned to their eternal sorrow the power of an outraged University. From that fatal day almost, Oxford, the free town, independent, substantial, became but an appendage, a chattel of the University, having no exterior political life of its own, submerged in the greater entity.

Certainly these were no backwater institutions for turning out sleek bond-salesmen and unemployed lawyers. The life of the Middle Ages swirled around their impalpable walls; learning sat on a throne and was respected accordingly, if not deified.

It is a fascinating story, this one of the mediaeval Universities, as authentically indigenous to the mediaeval scene as that of their sister aspirations, the Gothic cathedrals; with their privileges and charters, their vast confluence of students from the farthermost reaches of the Western world; their inordinate dignity and fierce-held democracy, their turbulent, hard-drinking, riotous students; their bloody affrays, strikes, and secessions; and withal, their good hard learning and their soaring philosophies. A stupendous, variegated mosaic, to which the modern scene has no counterpart. The very names of those old Universities breathe a strange, nostalgic fascination: Salerno, Bologna, and Paris; Salamanca, Oxford, and Padua; Montpellier, Valladolid, and Prague; Angers, Heidelberg, and Upsala.

There was nothing like them in the ancient world. Greece and Rome, it is true, knew of the higher education, but it was not organized; there was no body of licensed Masters, there were no formal examinations, and no degrees blazoning to the world that their possessors had achieved a modicum of learning, and were competent to teach other thirsters after knowledge. Socrates paced the tree-lined walks of Athens with his pupils, arguing and searching; Protagoras, for a price, taught the subtleties of logic; the Romans had their public schools, but they formed no self-perpetuating guilds or corporations. These were truly mediaeval in spirit and origin.

The miracle of Greek thought and civilization paled into the more practical, uncreative culture of the Romans. The world of Southern and Western Europe was a civilized place. Learning flourished, manuscripts multiplied, magnificent codes of laws were enacted; certain of the citizenry lived orderly, secure, and gracious lives. The Roman Peace seemed perdurable.

Then, in the fourth and fifth centuries, the thin shell burst that hid the rotten core within. The long-withheld hordes of barbarians—Vandals, Goths, Huns, Franks, Saxons—poured in whelming floods over the defenceless riches of the Empire. By the sixth century Europe was a smoking wilderness; civilization seemingly extinct, manuscripts and monuments destroyed; the learning of the Greeks forgotten in a ruining world. The night of the Dark Ages had commenced.

Only in the Byzantine Empire of the East did civilization and culture perilously maintain themselves. For centuries it was cut off from the rest of Europe, keeping alive in somewhat pedantic fashion the learning of the past. Ironically enough, when later, much later, this precious lore began to trickle back from the Christian Empire of the East to the Christian nations of the West, it was through the filtering medium of infidels, Mahommedans, and Jews. Not until the capture of Constantinople by the Turks did the West receive the true, direct flood, and ere long the Renaissance was in full bloom.

From the sixth to the eighth century, Western Europe was a sea of darkness. All the safeguards—economic, legal, and cultural—of the Roman Empire were gone. Political divisions were broken down; each man seized what he could, and held on by sheer force. Petty rulers swarmed in profusion; robber barons built castles on inaccessible crags and laid tribute on the surrounding countryside; local wars were innumerable. Small wonder that there was no time for the leisured things of the spirit, the poring over ancient manuscripts, the pondering over imponderables. Here and there was a valiant spirit, cupping with numbed fingers the tiny flickering flame of enlightenment, striving vainly to protect it against the uproarious winds of confusion.

Yet through the welter of events the Church moved steadfastly, the one binding force in a centrifugal period. It exhorted and preached, it spewed forth missionaries with the flame of fanaticism in them, it bullied and intrigued, it organized and cemented, until the barbarian hordes, the savages with mighty thews and uncomplicated minds, rendered at least lip homage to Christianity. With that the Church was content.

It did not require that these newly converted Goths, Franks, Vandals, and Saxons should *understand* the esoteric and subtle doctrines of Pauline Christianity, of Nicean Creeds, and Augustinian neo-Platonism. A knowledge of the crude terrors of damnation, of the equally crude bliss that awaited the devout in heaven, a blind faith in the infallibility of the Church and its appointed ministers, the prompt payment of all tithes and levies: that was all that was necessary.

The Church was the only universal organization of the time. The spirit of other-worldliness became thoroughly indoctrinated; the preaching that the things of this earth were but passing evils to be endured for the sake of future eternal bliss an inevitable consequence. Accordingly more and more men withdrew themselves from the contamination of the world as a surer means of attaining that future. It was easier and more comfortable for many to contemplate their holiness together than to endure the rigours of solitary anchorage in a cave, so monasteries arose, to be institutionalized by Benedict, an Italian of the sixth century. His rule for monasticism spread until it became the formula for these retreats.

The Roman schools were defunct or moribund; there was

no education worthy the name. The Church frowned on secular learning. Whatever literature was extant was pagan in origin, hence tainted with the lure of the flesh and the devil. It served only to distract men's minds and instil uncalled-for doubts. To read and write meant to possess the ability to yield to temptation.

But some knowledge was essential, at least for its own clergy. There were the sacred books, the writings of the Fathers, the prayers, the rules of the Order, which it was necessary for a cleric to know in order to prepare the laity for salvation. So that in spite of itself the Church found itself compelled to take over the process of education.

Schools were formed in the monasteries for the education of the monks. The instruction was almost exclusively religious in character; bare bones to enable them to mumble their prayers and obey the rules. The legend that the monasteries during the Dark Ages were islands in a sea of darkness, radiating light and scholarship to a barbarous world, is a very pretty one, but it is not in consonance with the facts.

With few exceptions the monasteries were astounding repositories of ignorance, enamoured of the easy, slothful life, recoiling from any hint of secular learning as from the very devil. The legend of the exterior schools also dies hard. It was the exceptional monastery, like that of St. Gall, which provided for lay pupils some modicum of religious instruction; and to counterbalance this, there were many cloisters that disdained any form of school even for their own novices.

The bishops founded schools, too, in connection with their dioceses, but here instruction was limited to theology for the higher clergy. When, later, the study of grammar, that innocuously dry subject, began to creep in, the Popes banned it with exceeding promptitude. For to learn the rules, one must read sentences, and these sentences were taken from the early Latin authors, who were pagans. Insidious ideas might creep into the minds of the pupils droning over their tasks.

This clerical monopoly of learning made for far-reaching

results. It determined the course of Western thought for almost a thousand years; it canalized the very acute minds of the Middle Ages into fields of speculation from which they dared not escape; it set up the standards and interests of the Church as the limits beyond which knowledge must not spread; it predetermined all philosophy, all science, all social, political, and economic institutions. Back in the Dark Ages were shaped the moulds into which the mediaeval Universities were one day to be poured.

In the ninth century, with the coming of Charlemagne, a breath of fresh air blew across the face of Europe. This son of Pepin, usurper of the throne of the Franks, for some reason or other found time in the interim of his wars of religious conquest to discover a real passion for learning. He threw his Court open to scholars of all lands; notably those of Italy, England, and Spain. Here came the famous Englishman, Alcuin, greatest scholar of his day, to be master of the so-called Palace School.

This school was composed of the mighty Charlemagne himself, no doubt an unctuously humble pupil, all the members of his family, and the young nobles of his Court who desired to retain the royal favour. It must have been a pleasant sight to witness these rude young warriors, more accustomed to the heft of a heavy sword than to the delicate operation of a quill, bending over their tasks under the earnest admonitions of the venerable Alcuin and the more dreaded glances of their liege-lord; tracing clumsy pot-hooks, and learning the various parts of speech. If they muttered among themselves, history has left no tangible records thereof.

But far more important than this purely local manifestation was Charlemagne's insistence, probably at Alcuin's instigation, that the standard of learning among the Frankish clergy be raised to a decent level. To accomplish this he ordered the opening of schools for the education of future bishops and abbots, and decreed that every monastery and every cathedral must have its school. Primarily and originally his aim was purely ecclesiastical, to drag the clergy of his day out of their abysmal ignorance of the tenets of their own faith. But the movement spread beyond these narrow limits. Learning began to be appreciated somewhat for its own sake; the Latin classics and the Latin Fathers became the objects of study; manuscripts that had managed to survive the Merovingian Age were protected and copied, and the sky of civilization showed streaks of dawn. More, there appeared here and there schools for the instruction of a limited number of lay pupils in connection with the monasteries.

But, unfortunately, this earliest Renaissance did not long survive. True, Charlemagne's grandson, Charles the Bald, followed in his doughty grandfather's footsteps. The Palace School continued under the mastership of the first of the mediaeval philosophers, John the Scot. In the last years of the ninth century, however, the Frankish Empire, torn by internal dissensions, finally split asunder. The ensuing tenth century was an age of anarchy and bloodshed, rivalling in its gloom and general despair the sixth and seventh centuries of odious memory. The Palace School was deserted; the young nobles were fighting for their lives against the inflowing hordes of Saracens, Magyars, and Northmen. Learning was forgotten in the monasteries, whose abbots thought only of fat revenues in the wreckage of the world. This suited the fancy of the invading marauders, who gleefully looted the piled-up treasures. Monastery after monastery went up in smoke, the terror-stricken monks fleeing with what possessions they could carry on their backs. Perhaps a few snatched up a precious book in the anguish of their departure. Only in Germany, where Otto the Great managed to hold back the flood, did learning find a small resting-place. Once more there was darkness, clerical as well as lay.

But such is the elasticity of the human spirit that almost before the terrible invasions were over, learning began to revive. If it is necessary to place a date upon such a delicate and intangible event, one might well pick the year 1000, the millennial year, as the turning-point, when men's minds were occupied with thoughts of the second coming of Christ. Perhaps the relief felt by the devout at the fact that they were not to be catapulted prematurely into eternal bliss had something to do with it. Yet we must not exaggerate; there were stirrings even before that fateful day.

Here and there a monastery, a cathedral, had maintained a certain continuity. There were schools at Rheims, at Chartres, Angers, Tours, and Laon; the Benedictines of Cluny and of Bec were famous for what passed as knowledge in the tenth century. Odo (879-942) who taught at Cluny, Lanfranc (1005-1089) and St. Anselm (1033-1109) in the Norman school at Bec; Gerbert, "the greatest teacher of his time," who held forth in the Cathedral School at Rheims prior to 980, and Fulbert, the practical founder of Chartres (*d.* 1029), were all tipped with the authentic fire.

All life took an upward swing in the eleventh century. Comparative peace had descended on a war-torn Europe; Papacy and Empire were powerful units; nations were making their vague appearance; and toward the end, the First Crusade wrought the masses to a pitch of hysterical enthusiasm. The feudal order had become definitely fixed, making for a certain degree of security, and the towns, as political and economic units, were gathering strength. The true Middle Ages had begun.

CHAPTER II

Eleventh-Century Learning

THERE were two distinct lines of evolution in the intellectual progress of Europe, based upon a sharp geographical division. In Northern Europe—that is, Northern France, Germany, England, etc.—education had perforce devolved upon the Church. The only other ruling class, the feudal aristocracy, breathed a large contempt for crabbed manuscripts and even more crabbed thinking. Kings and towns alike were as yet but adjuncts of feudalism. As a result all learning had become tinctured with a purely ecclesiastical bias; the schools were connected with priestly institutions; the overwhelming majority of the pupils were clerics or novices who aspired to holy orders. Small wonder then that education bore a tonsured appearance and had a faint musty odour of holiness about it. Nor can we fail to understand why, when the great Universities took form and being, they fell inevitably under control of Pope, Bishop, and Bishop's man Friday, the Chancellor. The history of the Northern Universities is the history of a Homeric struggle to rid themselves of the incubus of Bishop and Chancellor, with complete success at Oxford, modified triumph at Paris and elsewhere, and pathetic failure in other places.

In Southern Europe, however—namely, Italy and to a lesser degree, Southern France and Spain—the shoe was on the other foot. Italy, the home of Mother Church, the incubator of the Papal hierarchy, feeder of Popes and Cardinals, was essentially pragmatic and secular in its outlook. It may be that too close propinquity to the lords spiritual made for something a little less than reverence. Education was emphatically not a matter of ecclesiastical interest and control. There were Church schools, of course, but they represented a minor current. The great Schools, which in a later century developed into Universities, were strictly lay institutions, run by and for laymen, and the predominant subjects were the practical and lucrative studies of Law and Medicine.

The old Roman laws, the old customs and traditions, had never wholly succumbed during the Dark Ages. There remained a thin thread of continuity from earliest days; the municipalities, vigorous and independent long before the Northern towns had dreamt of purchasing their freedom from their feudal lords, were perfect repositories for rising young lawyers; and the Italian aristocracy, unlike their Northern brethren, actually admired learning. A gentleman was permitted to skewer his enemy on the point of a sword and quote Ovid with equal grace. Nor had they the theological fanaticism of the more recent converts beyond the Alps.

Thus it was that Europe gradually drew into two camps: the North, with religious fervour, concentrating on theology, philosophy, and fine-spun distinctions; the South, with an eye to the main chance, on law, medicine, and the writing of letters.

Before proceeding to that great intellectual flowering known in history as the Twelfth-Century Renaissance, it would be well to take stock of just what knowledge was available to the man of the eleventh century, should he be willing to sacrifice home and family, wealth and possessions, and apply himself for years to the acquisition of knowledge.

It is almost impossible for the modern mind to visualize the paucity of that knowledge and the tremendous efforts required to attain it. The splendid intellectual and artistic life of Greece had been swept away without leaving a trace; its scientific achievements and speculations were completely unknown, save that the physicians had a garbled smattering of Hippocrates and Galen. As for its literature, Homer was a myth; the very names of Aeschylus, Sophocles, Euripides, Aristophanes, Pindar, Sappho, and Thucydides were as though they had never been. Even the language, for all practical purposes, was lost. There were no Greek manuscripts in existence in Western

Europe; those few adventurous spirits who achieved a modicum of Greek had travelled and studied in the Eastern Empire, in Syria, at the Court of the Abbasids.

Latin culture was in slightly less parlous straits. Latin at least was the universal language of the Church, of the Law, of educated men wherever they met. To this day doctors disguise their remedies under a plague of mediaeval Latin terms; judges interlard their decisions with mouth-filling Latin phrases. Not all the Roman monuments had succumbed to the disintegrating influence of the Dark Ages. The Forum and Colosseum were perpetual reminders of an earlier and mightier era; great walls, roads and aqueducts dotted all Europe. Roman Law had survived in various barbaric Codes, slightly mangled, it is true, and forced to perform strange tasks, but with quite legible outlines. Practically all Roman literature was extant, thanks to the diligent work of the Carolingian copyists. There were not many manuscripts, and most of them were hidden in scattered monasteries, but there were available a sufficiency at Bec, at York, at Chartres and Laon, for the truly diligent searcher. Except in such great centres, however, they were little studied or appreciated.

Practically all the knowledge of the age was based on the work of five unoriginal and for the most part inaccurate compilers of the fifth and sixth centuries. In those centuries of gloom and defeat there was no thought of pursuing novel investigations; only desperate attempts to salvage what each author thought valuable out of the funds of learning yet available. Of these Boethius (*c.* 475-524) was the most distinguished and competent. His compilations and translations in arithmetic, music, astronomy, and philosophy, notably of Aristotle, coloured the thought of Europe for ages to come. Isidorus (*d.* 636) was the next most influential. He attempted an encyclopedic rendering of the little knowledge still extant in those barbarous days. Martianus Capella (*c.* 424) was famous chiefly for introducing later times to the ancient divisions of the Seven Liberal Arts, into whose sanctified compartments the Middle Ages tried to force all learning. The others, Orosius (*c.* 416) and Cassiodorus (*c.* 490-585), were comparatively unimportant.

On this insecure and narrow base, then, was laid the super-structure of Western instruction prior to the twelfth century. No one had added to it since; no one had been interested in original inquiry, with the possible exception of John the Scot. In fact, the early mediaeval scholars and even a goodly number of later ones, felt more comfortable in the presence of a com-piler and interpreter of other people's thoughts than in the presence of the original thinker himself.

As for the meat of the matter, that was comprised within the rigid limits of the famous Seven Liberal Arts. Here they are, neatly catalogued: the Trivium, or Three, of Grammar, Rhetoric, and Logic; the Quadrivium, or Four, of Arithmetic, Geometry, Astronomy, and Music.

It was certainly not remarkable for a wide range of interests, and the content of each particular subject was exceedingly thin. For the most part only the Trivium had any particular potency. In Grammar there were certain technical rules to be learnt: for beginners, the textbook of Donatus; for more advanced students, Priscianus. Occasionally a daring teacher would add titbits of Latin classics, but the Church frowned heavily on such scandalous nonsense. Rhetoric was pure pedantry where it might have been an appreciation of style and artistry in writing. The treatises of Cicero and the elements of Roman Law were unintelligently studied, and the works of the Christian orators imitated. In Italy, however, Rhetoric still retained some of its ancient grace, and verses were shaped with some regard for the sense of poetry.

But it was Logic, or Dialectic, as it came to be known, that was studied with the greatest assiduity, becoming by the thirteenth century the all-engrossing passion of the time. The logical works of Aristotle were known in translation; Por-phyry's Introduction as Latinized by Boethius; and the several commentaries of Boethius himself.

The studies of the Quadrivium were a snare and a sham. Arithmetic and Astronomy, so-called, were mere means of calculating the date when Easter fell each year, so that the clergy might avoid the unforgivable sin of celebrating the Resurrection a day or two before time; Geometry was represented by a few of Euclid's propositions taken out of their context and propounded without proof; Music was a jargon of pseudo-Pythagorean numbers and Psalter and Church music.

There were also, of course, Philosophy and Theology. In early days these were inextricably entwined; only later did the invaluable aid of Dialectic disentangle them, not always to the complete satisfaction of the Church. Theology was naturally based on the Bible and the early Fathers; Philosophy on the logical writings of Aristotle and a fragment of the Timaeus of Plato in translation. More of Plato was derived from his influence on St. Augustine and the allusions to him in the works of his arch-enemy, Aristotle. With these rags and tags, the great game of Scholastic Philosophy had its inception, to proceed with enormous fervour until it burst of its own superhuman expansion in the fifteenth century.

It is true that by the eleventh century the curriculum of studies had enlarged a little, but how little may be seen by the course given at Chartres under the great Fulbert, hailed by Henry Osborn Taylor in *The Mediaeval Mind* as the finest range of studies of the time. There was considerably more reading of the classic Roman writers; to Astronomy were added the signs of the Zodiac and methods of finding the stars on Gerbert's Astrolabe; a few medical prescriptions were memorized in verse, a little law was learnt, and the Scriptures and the Liturgy were extensively studied. Otherwise all was almost exactly the same as in the heart of the Dark Ages.

It has been the fashion to account for the intellectual spurt of the twelfth century by attributing it to the Crusades, then the leading outdoor sport of European chivalry. As successive tides of Western soldiery swept over the ancient Byzantine Empire and the less aged Saracen domains, it was inevitable that the backwash into Europe should bring with it a rich silt of ideas from these superior civilizations, fertilizing and quickening the West into a great blaze of learning and speculation. The explanation is obvious, facile and only half true.

I am inclined to give the Crusades less credit for the twelfth century than is generally accorded them. True, they played their part—it would be idle to deny that—but their part was not so important as has been generally assumed. The Crusaders as a class were not receptive soil for the rooting of delicate intellectual seedlings. They were (1) feudal lords and knights, strong of body and weak of head, whose whole and fierce delight was in the shock of battle-axe on helmet, and the minutiae of their precious chivalry; learning was for snivelling shavelings; (2) professional men-at-arms whose intellectual outlook was even more limited than that of their masters; (3) criminals, outlaws, the idle, the ne'er-do-wells, the scum of every city and village and countryside, eager for blood and loot and the proclaimed absolution of the Church for all their murky pasts.

Certain things the Crusaders brought back with them: tons of plunder; soft-bodied Saracen concubines; filth and the germs of unfamiliar diseases that were to play havoc in the forthcoming centuries; ineradicable habits of luxury and splendour; and an acquaintance with other lands and other customs; but learning, the things of the spirit, were not in their baggage. These were not viable commodities. The scholars, the men of thought, had remained at home; they were clerics, not fighters.

The roots of the twelfth century struck much deeper. Historically there are no discontinuities. We have already seen that its predecessor, the eleventh century, had initiated the emergence from darkness. The same factors that were then in control were accelerating their effects. The Empire reached its climax of power and glory with Frederick II, *Stupor Mundi*,

the Wonder of the World; the Papacy, in the person of
Innocent III, topped the pinnacle of its spectacular climb in
the final years of the twelfth century; from that commanding
height there was only a down-grade for succeeding Popes;
the kings of Europe—and notably the King of France—
were gradually overcoming the centrifugal pull of anarchic
feudatories and laying the foundations for cohesive kingdoms;
the towns and the trade guilds began to acquire political
power; in Italy the cities had become practically independent
republics; commerce and trade were attaining notable proportions, accustoming the mediaeval mind to the notion of
wandering in other lands; emperors, popes, and kings, either
from an abstract love of learning, or for more devious reasons,
were vying with each other in the encouragement of scholars
and scholarship; and lastly, and possibly most important of
all, the rediscovery of the Pandects of Justinian in Italy, and
the translation of the complete Aristotle and his Arabic and
Jewish commentators, made at the command of Raymond,
Bishop of Toledo, poured their quickening fluids into the
veins of the century. It was in this age that the Universities
first began to stir and have their being.

Again, we must differentiate between Northern and Southern
Europe. The two threads of evolution diverged more and
more. Law and Medicine held their particular fascination for
the South: in Medicine, Salerno, and later, Montpellier, were
the great exemplars; in Law, Bologna became the fountain-
head and inspiration of half the Universities of Europe.
In the North the more subtle logic, philosophy and theology
overwhelmed all other studies, and Paris mothered a vast
progeny of Universities.

Let us consider Northern Europe first. During the eleventh
and twelfth centuries the monastery schools, with certain
notable exceptions, had become moribund, until finally they
faded out of the scene, and became a negligible factor in the
intellectual progress of the age, and of no importance in the
rise of the Universities.

The cathedral schools, on the other hand, increased and multiplied, attracting more and more outside students, until they became the most potent intellectual force in Northern Europe.

Rheims and Chartres, Laon and Tours, Orléans and Paris—these were the great centres to which students flocked from the far corners of Europe. At Chartres and Orléans, especially, the twelfth century brought with it a notable revival of classical studies. Under the guiding hands of great teachers, the far-wandering scholars were brought into fresh contact with the golden period of Latin literature, rolled sonorous phrases appreciatively on their tongues, and absorbed culture and the amenities of life.

In fact, for a while it seemed as though Humanism was to remain in the saddle, and that what is commonly known as the Renaissance would be anticipated by at least two centuries. One wonders what might have been the course of civilization and world history if the Paris schools had remained unimportant, if Abélard had not lived, if the "new" Aristotle had not been translated, and the Humanism that was the glory of Chartres and Orléans, Laon and Tours, had been permitted to grow and bear fruit. Fascinating speculations, but entirely profitless. Yet we must be thankful for this pleasant interlude before the dry bones of Scholasticism overwhelmed all else. It gave us men like Bernard of Chartres and John of Salisbury, who was the most notable student, the most catholic and broad-minded man, the purest Latin writer of his day. Of him, more anon. It was Bernard who sensed the philosophy of history:

"We are as dwarfs mounted on the shoulders of giants, so that we can see more and further than they; yet not by virtue of the keenness of our eyesight, nor through the tallness of our stature, but because we are raised and borne aloft upon that giant mass."

What was this Scholasticism, this passion for Dialectic, that overwhelmed the more fragile Humanistic studies, and caused Chartres to go into a decline in the middle of the twelfth century from which it never recovered, and turned Orléans later into a University famous only for its Law? To understand, we must go back to the unending metaphysical warfare between Plato and Aristotle concerning the former's doctrine of Ideas.

But let Porphyry, the Greek scholar and commentator on Aristotle of the third century, pose the question, the irreconcilable difference; because it was through him that the problem reached the Middle Ages and started the interminable disputes of the schools.

"Next," he wrote in the *Isagoge*, "concerning genera and species, the question indeed whether they have a substantial existence, or whether they consist in bare intellectual concepts only, or whether if they have a substantial existence they are corporeal or incorporeal, and whether they are separable from the sensible properties of the things (or particulars of sense), or are only in those properties and subsisting about them, I shall forbear to determine. For a question of this kind is a very deep one and one that requires a long investigation."

Sensible, modest man! Could he have read the future, he might have shrunk from tossing so casually into the stream of time this little paragraph, so innocuous-seeming, yet so packed with dynamite. Rashdall has stated that this passage has played a more momentous part in the history of human thought than any other passage of equal length in all literature. I am inclined to agree with him, possibly to go even further, and to say solemnly that it outranks, in causative influence, any passage of *any* length.

By this time no doubt those readers who are innocent of philosophical training, and who were therefore inclined to skip this short quotation from an obscure Greek, have gone back to the passage and re-read it with more care. Their bewilderment increases. What is all the hullabaloo about? It sounds innocuous enough; abstruse certainly, boring if the truth must be told. What possible effect could it have on the thought of an age, on civilization and practical affairs?

Yet, in fact, the controversy implicit in those few words coloured the whole vision of the Middle Ages, down to the very close of the fifteenth century; it was responsible for the rise of and the prevalent absorption in Dialectic, Scholastic Philosophy, and Theology, and for the decay of twelfth-century Humanism; it sired innumerable heresies, and brought worthy men into the ungentle hands of the Inquisition; much blood was shed because of it, and students rioted in the streets of the University towns; Church and State alike followed the endless controversies with anxious mien and alert restraint. Even to this day, the purlieus of philosophy echo to the belated noises of the great mediaeval conflict. The famous doctrine of Universals!

Stripped to essentials, it is purely a question as to whether or not general ideas or universals have a real existence in themselves, or whether they are mere words of abstraction invented by human beings for convenient speech, while the only reality resides in the particular, or individual. For example, let us take the word *man*. Here is a man, John Jones by name, whom you and I both know. He is a neighbour of ours; he is easily recognizable. He is white, has greying hair, a large nose, and false teeth. He walks with a limp, invariably wears blue serge, makes a noise when he eats soup, is kind to his children, and has positive opinions on total abstinence, the causes of the depression, and Greta Garbo. In short, an individual, unlike any other individual in the world, a unique thing in the history of the universe. That is obvious, you are likely to say; and so said the Nominalists, the champions of the individual, in the Middle Ages.

But there is another angle, another possible point of view. After all, retorted the Realists, who favoured the general, the universal, what is John Jones? A man, of course. A member of a class, a species, consisting of innumerable individuals like himself. Try to define John Jones, try to describe him to a stranger, without relating him to the common man, humanity, and see how unrecognizable he becomes. True, he has certain qualities, certain attributes, distinct from those of all other men, but when you dig down you find how few they are, how unessential to the real mannishness of him, how *accidental* they are. That is it; they are *accidents*; the real *substance* of John Jones is what he possesses in common with all mankind. Hence the universal, the *idea* of man, is the only reality; John Jones, the particular—poof—he is but a passing phantom, doomed to die and leave no trace, while mankind remains immortally enthroned in a crystalline heaven of ideas.

Not so simple after all, is it? There is much to be said on both sides, and during the Middle Ages, it *was* said. It occupied the thoughts of men almost to the exclusion of all else; the arguments pro and con, if laid end to end in fine type, would reach from here to Mars. What chance had the poor Latin authors, with their pastoral imagery and the placid flow of their verse, against the robustious rough-and-tumble of getting up in the schools and calling your opponent an ass because he did not agree with you on the burning issue of Universals, and proving it, with much subtle distinction and logical hair-splitting, to your own satisfaction, and the tumultuous stamping and whistling of your audience!

Note further how this hair-splitting led right back to the things that mattered most to the mediaeval man: his religion and his relation to Church and State.

John the Scot, Master of the Palace School back in the ninth century, started the ball rolling. He asserted that true philosophy and true religion were in perfect agreement, and therefore philosophy should be able to lead to the solutions of the moot problems of faith. The first part of his thesis sounded orthodox enough, but the second smacked suspiciously of something or other. For while his conclusions were well within the folds of the Church, he had forged a mighty weapon for future trouble. He had applied logic, the weapon of reason, to an examination of doctrines that had hitherto been held solely on faith. A most dangerous and explosive weapon!

Realism was in the saddle until the eleventh century. It best fitted in with the purviews of the Church. For the Catholic Church was an idea, was it not?—a sweeping generalization. Now if this idea had a real existence greater than that of the transitory individuals who composed it, if it were immortal and immutable, then it is easy to see why it must be obeyed and followed blindly by mere accidental mortals. A very superior doctrine, said the Church complacently. And Empire and feudal State agreed. For they, too, were general ideas, very tenuous and very wispy at times, and requiring a good deal of philosophic bolstering. And so said every institution that desired more authority and less questioning. No wonder the Middle Ages became horribly institutionalized; man became a joiner of institutions, a member.

Even the obscure doctrine of original sin was neatly solved by Odo of Tournai (*c.* 1092) with the aid of Realism. The human race, he said, is a universal, a real substance. The sin of Adam and Eve infected that entire substance for ever and ever. Uncounted generations of children are not creations of new substances, but merely different aspects of the one unique already existing substance. A dour doctrine, but wait a moment. Does not this fantastic mediaeval solution anticipate in so many words the very modern and scientific doctrine of heredity?

But there were catches, as the Church reluctantly discovered, and she was compelled to call in the services of her best doctors to undertake a politic clipping of wings. For a too enthusiastic support of the doctrine might lead to embarrassing, if logical, conclusions. If man were but a fleeting accident, and the idea of mankind the only reality, what happened then to the immortal soul of man? Surely it vanished! And the idea of mankind itself—is it not but a part of a greater and more all-embracing idea, and that in turn of a still greater one, until we come to—a single supreme essence for the entire universe? But that way lies Spinoza—and pantheism. Call that essence God, or anything you wish . . . the Church, with infallible instinct, realized the danger, and drew back. Exaggerated Realism would not do; Realism was of course the truth, but within limits.

The Nominalists never had a chance with Mother Church. The early proponents of Nominalism were too intellectually honest to withhold their fire as did the Realists; they pushed their logic to grim conclusions. For example, Berenger of Tours (*d.* 1088) actually applied Nominalism to the sacrosanct doctrine of Transubstantiation, thereby anticipating Wyclif by several centuries. He declared baldly that it was an affront to his reason to hold that the bread and wine of the mass were transmuted into the body and blood of Christ. They were individual realities, incapable of such juggling. The whole thing, he argued, was merely a symbolical ceremony. Thereby he raised a storm that threatened to overwhelm him.

The Realists retorted with his own weapons of reason. The "substance," the universal, of the elements of the mass was changed, they said, though the "accidents"—that is, the perceptions of smell, touch, sight, etc.—were seemingly unaltered. All Christendom leaped joyously into the fray. It became the burning issue of the day. The Church took a hand, and by her familiar methods compelled Berenger to retract. Thereby her honour was saved.

But there was to be no peace. A greater champion of Nominalism arose in the redoubtable person of Roscelin of Compiègne (*c.* 1050-1122). He taught his pernicious doctrines at Tours and at Loches, and for a time Abélard was his pupil. He outdid Berenger in daring and hardihood; transubstantiation was but a minor point; he went after much bigger game. He attacked the very foundations of the Church when he applied the keen probe of his intellect to that Holy of Holies, the doctrine of the Trinity.

If the three divine persons of the Trinity were one God,

he asserted, then all three must have become incarnate in the person of Jesus Christ, which is manifestly absurd. It is contrary to doctrine, and what is more important, contrary to reason. For if the Father, the Son, and the Holy Ghost were all three present in the body of Christ as he hung in agony on the Cross, then all three were expiating the sins of mankind, and heaven was tenantless. Therefore, he continued, the three divine substances must be three separate and distinct Gods, each an individual with his own peculiar substance.

The storm that Berenger aroused was nothing compared to this. Against Berenger the Realists could find arguments in their arsenal; here they were reduced to inarticulate cries of rage. For a while the Church seriously considered banning reason in the form of philosophy altogether from any consideration of the tenets of the faith. Later she actually did prohibit consideration of this particular doctrine of the Trinity and the Incarnation. In the meantime, following her usual procedure, she compelled Roscelin to retract. And ever after, Nominalism was suspect, a refuge for sceptics and doubters.

This, then, was the background of the great problem of Universals that occupied the schools for centuries to come. Scholasticism *per se* was merely the method of the schools: to wit, the application of Logic, or Dialectic, with its formal use of the syllogism, to the problems of philosophy and theology.

CHAPTER III

Abélard, Greatest of Teachers

SO that when the twelfth century opened, the problems were set, the weapons forged. Men's minds were stirred by the winds of these great discussions. Learning became something combative and fascinating. All over Europe young men, and older ones too, became restless and dissatisfied. They wanted to be in the thick of things, to hear from the lips of the protagonists themselves the details, step by subtle step, of these strange new arguments. This was the beginning of a hegira unprecedented in the history of the world. There had been mass migrations before, greater in extent and area, but never a one in eager search of knowledge. From the ends of Europe, from northernmost Sweden, from the plains of Hungary, from the dour fastnesses of Scotland, from Germany and England, from Bohemia and Sicily, from Ireland, Italy, and France, they poured in an increasing flood to the centres where learning was to be had, where they could literally sit at the feet of the great teachers and absorb wisdom. Travel was hard and dangerous in those days; the roads were choked with dust in the hot dry summers, thigh-deep in mud in the wet season, breast-high with snow in the winters; brigands and cut-throat soldiery infested the highways; and every few miles was an alien land, to whose inhabitants the foreigner was fair game. Yet undeterred the students traversed the length and breadth of Europe; the poor man trudging wearily on foot, knapsack on back, begging his way from hamlet to hamlet; the rich youth on horseback, with an armed servant in attendance; the more elderly rich man in a great bouncing carriage with a retinue of clattering retainers.

Nor did they stop with one teacher or one school. When they had absorbed as much wisdom as one could give, or they could safely hold, they pulled up stakes and wandered on to other schools, where other teachers had new pearls to bestow. John of Salisbury, that *parfait gentil knight* of mediaeval scholarship, gives a pleasant description of his wanderings, which will be quoted in a later chapter.

Now remember, thus far there is no hint of a University, of any organized institution of learning. There were the cathedral schools, of course, and they were mighty in the land in the early twelfth century; but their fame was due solely to the renown of the particular resident teachers. But the latter shifted from school to school with bewildering rapidity, and there were scores of free-lances who set up their teacher's chair anywhere, and the pupils gathered around them, even though it were in the market-place. For the students sought the man, not the school; where the man was, there was the school.

The man most responsible for this efflorescence of the human spirit, the teacher who did most to set the feet of mediaeval youth on the wandering paths of scholarship, was Abélard, the most fascinating and brilliant figure of the Middle Ages. He brought to perfection the Scholastic method; in the bitter argument of faith against reason he was the staunch upholder of reason; the University owed him a tremendous gift of gratitude, though it did not come into formal existence until two generations after his death; because of his presence Paris leapt into a position of intellectual pre-eminence that it was to retain for centuries to come; yet to most moderns his claim to immortality rests upon his love-affair with Héloïse, and its tragic, gruesome ending.

Abélard was born in 1079. A young Breton nobleman, he early evinced a passion for learning. He studied under the famous Nominalist, Roscelin, and was afterwards to repudiate his master. He wandered from school to school until finally he reached Paris. There, at the age of twenty, he sat before William of Champeaux, then at the height of his powers, the unquestioned despot of the Cathedral School of Notre Dame. No one dared to dispute his crude, exaggerated form of Realism until the young Abélard, handsome, witty, and eloquent, rose to puncture his pomposities with pointed questions and close-pressed arguments. The mighty William stared aghast at his youthful antagonist, heard the waves of applause beating up from the thronged spectators at each telling point, and departed from his chair in shame and humiliation. The King was dead, long live the King!

Socrates, William had taught, was purely an "accident" of the general substance "man"; there was nothing in Socrates that was not at the same time under the forms of Plato or any other man. Abélard retorted that if the species "man" is wholly and completely present in Socrates, then it must, in the nature of things, be completely absorbed in Socrates; hence where Socrates is not, "man" is not; and accordingly the substance "man" cannot be in Plato or any other human being. A veritable *reductio ad absurdum* that effectually took the wind out of uncompromising Realism.

In place thereof, Abélard set up his own teaching, which on examination proves to be a skilful compromise between Realism and Nominalism; very cautious and heedful of the suspicious eye of the Church. It attracted favourable attention; each man was able to read into it whatever he wished. Inasmuch as Abélard never elevated it to the dignity of a complete, rigid, and unyielding system, it was almost impervious to attack. A clever man, Abélard!

He taught a form of Conceptualism: that the individual alone had substantial existence; that the universal exists in the individual, and the common elements in diverse individuals can be abstracted by the mind. These mental concepts are not merely subjective, but correspond to an external reality. In other words, it satisfied both the Realist and the Nominalist, provided they were not too terribly in earnest, giving each considerable aid and comfort. And strangely enough, this middle view came to be generally adopted, giving a breathing-space to the problem of Universals.

The noise and clangour of the controversy resounded all over Europe. The trickling migration of students of former years grew to an overwhelming flood. Paris became the Mecca of thousands eager to be in at the death.

They took sides with infinite gusto. William thought better of his position, and did not resign his lucrative Chancellorship of the School of Notre Dame. Instead, he modified his stand on Universals to meet Abélard's frontal attack. In so doing he made it less open to assault, but only because it was wrapt in impenetrable obscurity. And naturally, being only human, and possessing the "universal substance" of wounded vanity, he resented bitterly what had occurred.

Abélard, flushed with triumph, and urged on by his throng of admiring disciples, decided to open his own school. In those free-and-easy days no licence to teach was necessary, as long as the fledgling instructor did not poach within the precincts of the Cathedral. But William had still considerable power by virtue of his official position, so Abélard moved his school to Melun, some thirty miles away; then to Corbeil, as being closer to Paris.

The battle was terrific; students swarmed to hear the new master's teaching; hastened to Notre Dame to hear what William had to say in refutation; ran the long distance back again the following day to hearken to Abélard's rebuttal. On the way, they met partisans of the other camp; words passed; blows maybe.

Then Abélard broke down. His health was bad, and he closed his school, going back to Brittany. A few years later he was back again, this time to teach under the official auspices of the Abbey of Ste. Geneviève in Paris. William had retired in the meantime to the monastery of St. Victor. Abélard shone in undisputed triumph. Yet, sickening perhaps of the heady wine of adulation, he suddenly decided to close his school again and study theology under the tutelage of Anselm at Laon.

As a dialectician and philosopher Abélard was supreme; in the more rarefied field of theology he was regarded as no more than a novice. But his intellectual audacity and daring knew no bounds. Even as he had bearded the mighty William when but a fledgling, he dared now to dispute with and insult the mightier Anselm, the acknowledged holder of "the sceptre of theology."

Listen to what Abélard himself says of this episode:

"So I came to this old man, whose repute was a tradition, rather than merited by talent or learning. Anyone who brought his uncertainties to him went away more uncertain still! He was a marvel in the eyes of his hearers, but a nobody before a questioner. He had a wonderful flow of words, but the sense was contemptible, and the reasoning abject."

Back went Abélard to Ste. Geneviève; the students flocked to him in greater numbers than ever; all Europe resounded with his praises. He was the orator and the clever logician *par excellence*. There seemed no limit to the heights to which he could rise; he was a cleric, and he was following the sure path of preferment to the highest offices within the gift of the Church.

Then, like many another man, he fell in love. This story of the love between Abélard and Héloïse has been called the greatest love-story in history, and possibly it is so, if we consider Héloïse alone. For Abélard's side of it was shot through with streaks of worldly caution, egoism, and petulant vanity that mar the smooth surfaces a little. Abélard tells the story in his *Historia calamitatum suarum*, an open letter abounding in complaints against his fate.

She was "not unfair, and her knowledge was unequalled," he says of this learned young niece of the canon, Fulbert. Finding her "not unfair," and thinking of this and that, Abélard took lodgings with her unsuspecting old uncle. "The old man being miserly . . . he eagerly entrusted her to my tutorship." Abélard rather naïvely marvels "with what simplicity he confided a tender lamb to a hungry wolf. As he had given me authority to punish her, I saw that if caresses would not win my object, I could bend her by threats and blows." They were not necessary. Love flamed between the famous scholar and his young pupil.

"The books lay open, but our words were of love rather than philosophy; there were more kisses than aphorisms; and love was oftener reflected in our eyes than the lettered page. . . . A passion so plain was not to be concealed; everyone knew of it except Fulbert."

But as Héloïse grew big with the fruit of their unlawful love, even the purblind uncle had perforce to open his eyes. He took steps; the lovers were separated; whereupon Abélard had Héloïse abducted, and a son was born. Abélard made the magnanimous gesture; he offered to marry her; she refused at first, pointing out that marriage would irretrievably ruin his brilliant prospects; fornication was regarded indulgently in a cleric, but lawful wedlock was fatal! Nevertheless, they were married secretly, in the presence of the uncle, who had evidently taken a hand in the proceedings. He was sworn to secrecy, yet he announced the marriage immediately. Abélard's career was about to crash in ruin. Héloïse rose to the occasion, and calmly gave her uncle the lie. There had been no marriage, she said; she was merely Abélard's light-of-love. Abélard, in the ecstasy of his fear and the thought that all his ambitious plans were threatened, hustled her off to the convent of Argenteuil, where she put on the garments of a nun.

Fulbert, reasonably fearing that his niece was being got rid of, took a terrible revenge. "Having (in Abélard's words) bribed my servant, they came upon me by night, when I was sleeping, and took on me a vengeance as cruel and irretrievable as it was vile and shameful. . . . In the morning the whole town was assembled, crying and lamenting my plight, especially the clerks and students; at which I was afflicted with more shame than I suffered physical pain. I thought of my ruined hopes and glory, and then saw that by God's just judgment I was punished where I had most sinned, and that Fulbert had justly avenged treachery with treachery. But what a figure I should cut in public! how the world would point its finger at me! I was also confounded at the thought of the Levitical law, according to which I had become an abomination to the Church."

The Middle Ages had no place for a castrate; soprano voices were not yet in demand in the Catholic Church, nor were there in Western Europe seraglios to guard. Overwhelmed with misery, Abélard became a monk at the Abbey of St. Denis, and Héloïse a nun.

As a monk he continued his lectures, and abated not a jot of his former personal attacks on rival dialecticians and theologians. Indeed, their bitterness was rather exacerbated by the thought that his opponents were now better physically endowed than he. He lashed out right and left with a new venom; even the sanctuary which he had found was not spared. He tore to tatters the cherished theory of the monks, that their monastery had been founded by St. Denis. Such ingratitude merited his expulsion by the indignant monks. Enemies sprang up on all sides. His book *De Unitate et Trinitate divina* was condemned to be burnt as heretical by the Council of Soissons.

He withdrew, in the bitterness of his soul, to a lonely heath not far from Troyes, where he built himself a hut with his own hands. His life seemed over.

But now occurred an authentic miracle. The students of Paris, hearing of his refuge, deserted the schools, the masters, and the fleshpots of the capital, and swarmed out into the wilderness. A flourishing community sprang up overnight; Abélard found himself restored to power and glory. Such was the fascination of his personality, the brilliance of his teaching, the hunger of the early mediaeval student for knowledge.

Abélard had learnt nothing, and forgotten nothing. He renewed his excoriating attacks on his enemies, and in so

doing, raised against him one mightier than all the rest—
Bernard of Clairvaux, later to be sainted for his die-hard,
stick-in-the-mud attitude on theology, and the savage
vehemence with which he defended it.

The storm was too terrible. Abélard bowed to it and fled
to a monastery in Brittany, where the monks, regardless of
the alleged heresies of their famous refugee, promptly elected
him their abbot. Then, almost as promptly, as he indiscreetly
unfolded his doctrines, they tried to murder him, and Abélard
fled for his life, this time back to Paris. The students flocked
around him as enthusiastically as ever, but his chequered
career was rapidly nearing an end. That grim gaunt hound
of orthodoxy, Bernard, the saint-to-be, had smelt blood. In
1141 the Council of Sens, at his instigation, condemned
Abélard again, this time in no uncertain terms. Had there
been an Inquisition functioning at the time he would have
been burnt at the stake. As it was, he retired to Cluny in
disgrace, his wings clipped, there to die the following year,
a broken, prematurely old man. Héloïse, the nun, outlived
him by years, a meek, obedient wearer of the veil, renowned
for her charity and good works.

Thus ended the strange, fascinating, tragic history of the
greatest man of his time, a curious mixture of vanity and
passionate devotion to learning, of showmanship and acuteness of intellect. He reared no monumental system of philosophy, nor was his solution of the moot problem of Universals profoundly original, yet he influenced the thought of
the Middle Ages to a greater degree than any other individual
up to the time of the Angelic Doctor himself, St. Thomas
Aquinas.

It was Abélard's method, rather than his content, that was
revolutionary. In him, Logic, the epitome of the syllogism,
as exemplified in such of the Logical Works of Aristotle as
were then known, came to complete fruition. He set Reason
upon a throne in realms where Authority had hitherto been

the only guide. Everything, he insisted, must prove amenable to the active processes of the mind, to the rigorous following of major premise, minor premise, and conclusion; even the sacrosanct articles of theology. Nothing was immune from his method; he must understand in order to believe.

A very dangerous and radical doctrine. To be sure, John the Scot, Berenger, and Roscelin had enunciated somewhat similar theories before—the two latter with more explosive effect than Abélard—yet it was he who put them into general circulation. The budding minds of Europe sat at his feet, felt the intellectual stirrings of his discourse, and went forth to fertilize a waiting age. The method of Scholasticism was born; Dialectic overbore everything in its path; men argued, with sweeping generals, more modest particulars, and triumphant soaring conclusions. It was a fascinating game, this one of formal argumentation, with its rigid unyielding rules; and Abélard was its prophet.

We cannot be certain that Abélard did not accomplish more harm than good, even though unwittingly. For in the eyes of his disciples anything that was not amenable to analysis by syllogism was a waste of time, sterile, beneath contempt. And inasmuch as art, literature, natural phenomena, and the delicate nuances of beauty, are outside the realm of Logic, they became unworthy of consideration by vigorous, sharpened wits, eager for wordy battle. So it was that Abélard, who knew and appreciated the Latin orators and poets, who could quote them to apt purpose in the course of his lectures, was partly responsible for suppressing the resurgence of learning in the twelfth century.

There is another side to the picture, of course. Never again was respect for authority, the abject grovelling before the early Fathers of the Church, to have quite the force which it had before Abélard's day. True, he did not impugn the established verities of the Church; he accepted them implicitly. He himself bowed before the weight of authority, but—he must understand what it was that authority stated. He would not take any other man's interpretation on faith, not even if it were that of the Church. If the authorities were in conflict, the conflict must be resolved, and the dogmas harmonized. He expressed a naïve confidence that reason would never overthrow authority, and in his hands it did not; but the way lay clear for future iconoclasts, not as tender or as timorous as Abélard.

It is difficult at this late day to discover just what were Abélard's private thoughts in the matter. Publicly, he disavowed his teacher Roscelin in disassociating the Trinity; he refused to follow Berenger all the way in reducing Transubstantiation to a symbol; he followed carefully the accepted path. Yet he was too acute not to see where reason was leading him. In his innermost mind there must have been certain articles of faith that he doubted; that could not be accepted. But Abélard was a man of the world, and an ambitious man to boot. The plums of the Church were hanging temptingly just within his reach; he knew the inevitable thunders that would follow any slightest sign of heresy. So he yielded, and waited for the preferment that never came.

For Mother Church, and Bernard, that watch-dog of orthodoxy, were wiser than he thought. They penetrated the sham and the disguise, they saw with awful clarity where such doctrines, if extended, would inevitably lead. To Bernard the technical heresies for which Abélard was finally convicted did not matter so greatly; what mattered was the pernicious doctrine of Reason in the courts of Theology. To accept the dogmas of the Church because they were reasonable was just as reprehensible as to disavow them for being unreasonable. The principle was exactly the same.

The explosive possibilities of his method may best be seen in his most famous work, the *Sic et non*, "Yes and No." In the Prologue to this book he sets forth his plan of action:

"Wherefore we decided to collect the diverse statements of the holy Fathers, as they might occur to our memory, thus raising an issue from their apparent repugnancy, which might incite the readers to search out the truth of the matter, and render them the sharper for the investigation. For the first key to wisdom is called interrogation, diligent and unceasing. . . . By doubting we are led to inquiry; and from inquiry we perceive the truth."

He then proceeded to propound 158 specific articles of the Christian dogma. After each accepted article of faith he set in parallel what the sacred Fathers, the not-to-be-questioned authorities, had to say on that particular point. It was a revelation to an authority-loving and authority-quoting age. For the parallels were deadly in revealing the confusion that reigned in the ranks of authority; the diverse, apparently irreconcilable statements on practically every one of the 158 fundamental tenets.

Abélard was like that mythical character of Mother Goose lore, little Jack Horner. He, too, stuck his thumb into the forbidden pie of theology, pulled out an astonishing series of contradictions, and then, with innocent face and gesture, waved them aloft for all to see—and to explain. For, note this, while elsewhere he proclaimed that the Fathers were always right, that Reason would prove them to be so and could reconcile their seeming differences, here he made no slightest attempt at reconciliation. He left the glaring discrepancies, so to speak, dangling in the air.

His disciples were many, those influenced by his methods innumerable. The most famous of the former was Peter Lombard, afterwards to become Bishop of Paris. His *Sentences* were regarded as only a little less authoritative than Aristotle and the Bible, those twin peaks of authority in the Middle Ages. He, too, set up the conflict on theological questions, but, in despite of his master, he solved them by a nice balancing of authorities, by ingenious distinctions and subtle differentiations. Once the true path was found, it was to be followed unquestioningly. Lest this seem quaintly mediaeval to the modern reader, let him turn his inquiring eye upon our present-day judiciary. They, with as great a show of subtlety and of naïve distinctions, compose as great differences in the decisions of defunct judges, to the satisfaction of their own consciences, if not always to that of the hopeful suitor for a mythical justice.

So, too, did Gratian, the Italian, give definitive form to the Canon Law. And so, too, later, were Albertus Magnus and St. Thomas Aquinas, favourite and beloved sons of the Church, to apply the methods of Abélard to a reconciliation of Aristotle, the Pagan Philosopher, and Christianity. The Universities of Northern Europe may logically regard Abélard as their intellectual forbear, for their whole existence was coloured by his use of Dialectic, and they, too, were favoured children of the Papacy. Thus did the Church appropriate the very weapons that seemed at one time most dangerous to her continued existence, and utilize them for her own good purposes.

CHAPTER IV

The Decline of Humanism

WHAT was the state of learning in Northern Europe during Abélard's time and the generations of the twelfth century that were to follow? There were thousands on thousands of students; what was their intellectual fare?

In the first place, there were the few books of Aristotle known as the Old Logic. Abélard knew these, but so did John the Scot centuries before. Only about the time of John of Salisbury, in the middle of the century, did the Latin translations by Giacomo of Venice of the hitherto unknown books of Aristotle's Organon, to be hailed as the New Logic, reach the scholars of Northern Europe. Aristotle, the metaphysician, the scientist, the seeker after natural causes, was still completely unknown. It remained for the thirteenth century to reveal him and to set him up as a veritable divinity.

Yet Abélard and his pupil, John of Salisbury, were not restricted in their studies to Aristotle or to Logic. They knew and appreciated the classic authors; they possessed the broadly humanistic point of view; culture was a thing of the spirit, not merely a recommendation to remunerative employment; Chartres and Orléans were flourishing centres of enlightenment.

But other followers of Abélard saw and admired only his supernatural skill in the handling of Dialectic and Theology, and forgot that the master knew and loved other things as well. The finding of the New Logic added fuel to the argumentative fires of the time, and John laments in later years the triumph of Logic over the beloved studies of his youth. By the time the Universities emerge, toward the end of the century, Chartres, the school of letters, was declining, Orléans was fast becoming a law school, and the fresh liberal culture of the twelfth century was already submerged in a formalized, professional curriculum that was to hold its own right up to the late Renaissance. It sounds paradoxical, but it is true, that the Universities were never to have that broad attitude toward learning they possessed before their formal inception.

The finest period of scholarship in the Middle Ages was when John of Salisbury travelled leisurely from one end of Europe to the other, sitting before all the famous teachers of his time, pondering and savouring what he learnt, reading the ancients with delight from well-conned manuscripts, writing the purest Latin of the mediaeval era, unmarred by the barbarous jargon of a later day. For twelve years he studied and taught the while. Life was good to the scholar then.

But the craze for disputation, the contempt for his beloved classics, were already crowding the schools of Paris. By 1149, the end of his period of student life, he was viewing them with alarm. The Scholastics were in the saddle and riding hell-for-leather. John wrote his *Metalogicus* as a protest, but it was in vain. The spirit of the age could not be turned by one man or any group of men.

Nevertheless, the *Metalogicus* is a fascinating book, that should prove of exceeding interest to modern readers. In it, besides taking up the cudgels for "Grammar," he includes autobiographical detail, especially of his travels in search of learning, and gives us the finest description of the life and studies of a scholar of his day.

"When as a lad," he writes, "I first went into Gaul for the cause of study . . . I addressed myself to the Peripatetic of Palais (Abélard), who then presided upon Mount Saint Genovefa, an illustrious teacher and admired of all men. There at his feet I acquired the first rudiments of the dialectical art, and snatched according to the scant measure of my wits whatever passed his lips with entire greediness of mind. Then, when he had departed, all too hastily, as it seemed to me, I joined myself to Master Alberic, who stood forth among the rest as a greatly esteemed dialectician, and verily was the bitterest opponent of the nominal sect.

"Being thus for near two whole years occupied on the Mount, I had as my instructors in the dialectical art Alberic and Master Robert of Melun (that I may designate him by the surname which he hath deserved in the governing of schools; howbeit by nation he is of England): whereof the one was in questions subtil and large, the other in responses lucid, short, and agreeable. For they were both men of sharp intellect, and in study unconquerable. . . . Thus much for the time that I was conversant with them; for afterwards the one went to Bologna and unlearned that which he had taught; yea, and returned and untaught the same; whether for the better or no, let them judge who heard him before and since. Moreover, the other went on to the study of divine letters, and aspired to the glory of a nobler philosophy and a more illustrious name.

"With these I applied myself for the full space of two years, to practise in the commonplaces and rules and other rudimentary elements, which are instilled into the minds of boys, and wherein the aforesaid doctors were most able and ready; so that methought I knew all these things as well as my nails and fingers. This at least I had learned, in the lightness of youth to account my knowledge of more worth than it was. I seemed to myself a young scholar, because I was quick in that which I heard. Then returning unto myself and measuring my powers, I advisedly resorted, by the good favour of my preceptors, to the Grammarian of Conches (William), and heard his teaching for the space of three years; the while teaching much; nor shall I ever regret that time. . . ."

John goes on to tell of his studies under Richard l'Évêque at Chartres, the German Hardwin, Master Theodoric, and Peter Helias. He continues:

"Since I received the children of noble persons to instruct, who furnished me with a living—for I lacked the help of friends and kinsfolk, but God assuaged my neediness—the

D

force of duty and the instance of my pupils moved me the oftener to recall what I had learned. Wherefore I made closer acquaintance with Master Adam (du Petit-Pont), a man of exceeding sharp wits, and, whatever others may think, of much learning, who applied himself above the rest to Aristotle; so that albeit I had him not to my teacher, he delivered himself openly enough; the which he was wont to do to none or to few others than his own scholars, for he was deemed to suffer from jealousy. . . .

"From hence I was withdrawn by the straitness of my private estate, the instance of my companions, and the counsel of my friends, that I should undertake the office of a teacher. I obeyed; and thus returning at the expiration of three years, I found Master Gilbert (de la Porrée) and heard him in logic and divinity; but too quickly was he removed. His successor was Robert Pullus, whom his life and knowledge alike recommended. Then I had Simon of Poissy, a trusty lecturer, but dull in disputation. But these two I had in theologics alone. Thus, engaged in diverse studies, near twelve years passed by me.

"And so it seemed pleasant for me to revisit my old companions on the Mount (in Paris), whom I had left and whom dialectic still detained, to confer with them touching old matters of debate; that we might by mutual comparison measure together our several progress. I found them as before, and where they were before; nor did they appear to have reached the goal in unravelling the old questions, nor had they added one jot of a proposition. The aims that once inspired them, inspired them still; they had progressed only in one point, they had unlearned moderation, they knew not modesty; in such wise that one might despair of their recovery. And thus experience taught me a manifest conclusion, that, whereas dialectic furthers other studies, so if it remain by itself it lies bloodless and barren, nor does it quicken the soul to yield fruit of philosophy, except the same conceive from elsewhere."

There were others, too, who beheld with a despairing dismay this mad rush of the scholars of Europe from the genial classics to a barren dialectic. Later on in the century, Peter of Blois pours out the vials of his wrath in a letter to a friend:

"You greatly commend your nephew, saying that never have you found a man of subtler vein; because forsooth, skimming over grammar, and skipping the reading of the classical authors, he had flown to the trickeries of the logicians, where not in the books themselves but from abstracts and note-books, he has learned dialectic. Knowledge of letters cannot rest on such, and the subtilty you praise may be pernicious. For Seneca says, nothing is more odious than subtilty when it is only subtilty. Some people, without the elements of education, would discuss point and line and superficies, fate, chance, and free-will, physics and matter and the void, the causes of things and the secrets of nature and the sources of the Nile! . . ."

Voices crying in the wilderness! The tide was in full flood; the schools of the infant Universities rang with the clamour of debate and disputation; the infant professions irremediably impaled themselves on the two horns of the syllogism, with results that still reverberate; and the course of civilization for centuries wandered in devious channels. The age of Aristotle and the Universities was at hand!

CHAPTER V

Genesis of the Universities

WHAT were these great institutions, the mediaeval Universities, the power and glory of their age, acknowledging no ancestors, yet siring an innumerable progeny? The intellectual ferment of the twelfth century was their seed-bed; the thirteenth century ushered them into full-blown splendour.

The very name "University" does not appear until the beginning of the thirteenth century. Yet that name tells us exactly what they were; how they came to evolve out of the chaotic welter and constant shifting of the student tribes and their almost equally peripatetic teachers. For "universitas" etymologically means "the whole." It was used in the Middle Ages long before the rise of what we have since come to associate with the name. Every trade guild of mechanics or artisans, every corporation of men associated together in a common enterprise, every municipality, every lodge with a mumbo-jumbo ritual or device for rendering Christian burial to its members, was a "universitas."

In the eyes of mediaeval man the Masons of today, the Knights of Pythias, the American Federation of Labor, the Corporation of London, the City of New York, the Rotarians, the Chamber of Commerce, the United States Steel Corporation, all would be entitled equally with Oxford and Cambridge, Yale and Harvard, to the sacred name of "University."

For that is what Paris and Bologna and Oxford and all their fellows were in the beginning. Trade unions, lodges for mutual help and comfort, and the security of decent burial in an alien and often hostile land. In Paris it was the masters, the teachers, who banded together for safety's sake; in Bologna it was the students themselves who organized. From such simple beginnings the great Universities arose.

For during the twelfth century thousands of eager scholars

42

were always leaving their homes and countries to travel abroad in search of knowledge. There were no particular sets of buildings where instruction might be had; there were no entrance examinations and set courses of study to be followed; no degrees beckoned at the end of the long path.

The cathedral schools were merely centred round the persons of the teachers who held forth within the confines of the cathedral walls under the benediction of the bishop. If anyone else wished to teach within these sacred limits he need only obtain the approval, later to become known as the "licence," of the Chancellor, or head teacher. The easiest and simplest way to obtain this approval was to grease the itching palm of the Chancellor, himself an ecclesiast. Simony was a frankly recognized institution in the mediaeval hierarchy of the Church, in spite of occasional thunderings from the Papal throne, which itself was too often tarred with the same brush. If the Chancellor possessed a conscience, he might require evidence that the applicant had some knowledge of the subject which he proposed to teach. Such evidence usually took the form of a testimonial from the master under whom the erstwhile student had sat.

Outside the cathedral, however, in the early days, no licence or authority was necessary to set up as a master or teacher, or to lure the unwary scholar to part with his money in return for wisdom from the oracle's lips. Abélard possessed no licence. The self-appointed master could set up school in his own home, in the public market-place, or in a house rented by him for that purpose; in short, wherever he could persuade pupils to come to him. Abélard had only to retire to a distant wilderness for scholars to swarm after him and thereby set up a school.

In Italy, there being practically no cathedral schools, not even this limited form of licence was required. Anyone who thought himself competent could set up as a professor in one of the many municipalities of that country.

But gradually, in Northern Europe, customs took shape and

became fixed. Men who wished to teach found it advantageous to obtain the Chancellor's licence. It was a mark, a *cachet*; it enabled them to solicit the students who thronged toward the cathedral centres. And the half-hearted inquiry by that worthy into the applicant's fitness was in some sort a recognition of the qualifications of his former master.

Gradually these licensees drew together. Most of them were strangers in a strange country. The foreigner was *persona non grata* almost as much as a Jew in Germany today. His country or province was powerless to protect him; he possessed no rights that the natives were bound to respect. His body was subject to the whim of lord or noble or xenophobic mob; his possessions were a standing temptation to those more powerful than he. The Chancellor, too, though his exactions in the way of petty bribes were not yet onerous, cast longing eyes on the teachers as an increasingly lucrative source of profit.

So the masters followed the example of all the trades of their day, and formed a guild, a trade union. Banded together they had numbers, strength; numerous and strong, they could protect their pupils from harm. They could resist oppression from whatever source; and like any other society of the kind, they could select their members. So it was in Paris. In Bologna the masters were chiefly natives, who required no such protection. There it was the students, who came from Germany, France, and England to study the Law for which Bologna was already famous. It was they who banded together into a "universitas" or union; several unions, to be exact; for the southern Italians were hostile to the outlanders from Northern Europe; or perhaps it was the other way about.

These, then, were the prototypes for the famous Master Universities and Student Universities peculiar to the Middle Ages. But the real name for what we think of as a "University," the institution itself, the locus of its being, so to speak, was a "Studium." The early centres—those like Paris, Bologna, Salerno, and Oxford, which sprang spontaneously into being without adventitious aid from Pope or Emperor—

were usually "Studia Generalia"; that is, places where students
were received from all parts of Europe. It was not until much
later that the two words became synonymous, and "University" came to cover them both. It was requisite for such a
"Studium Generale" to possess at least one of the higher
Faculties of Medicine, Law, or Theology, in addition to the
basic Arts Faculty; otherwise the school remained a purely
local "Studium."

What practical difference did this make? A good deal; the
fame of the Universities was more widespread; their eminence
acknowledged. A master admitted to teach in Paris, Bologna,
or Salerno was recognized as qualified to teach by all other
such institutions. He could pack up his things, if the whim
seized him, and migrate to another University, secure in the
knowledge that the Guild of Masters in the new centre would
admit him to their ranks without the tiresome necessity of
passing a new examination. This privilege was called *jus ubique
docendi*, the right to teach anywhere, and the few Masters'
Guilds who possessed this customary or usage right were
inordinately proud of it.

So far the Universities had evolved entirely on their own,
apart from a certain amount of rather passive supervision by
the Bishop and Chancellor of the cathedrals of the North, and
the municipalities of the South. But now other forces were to
take a hand. Pope and Emperor and King viewed these
astonishing growths with interest, each pondering how best to
turn these phenomena to his own advantage.

It was Frederick Barbarossa, King of Sicily and Naples, and
Emperor of the Germans, who took the initiative. In 1158, to
encourage students to congregate in his domains, he promulgated his famous *Habita*, the first general charter of privileges
for students anywhere.

"It is our desire," he decreed, "that the students and, above
all, the professors of divine and sacred laws, may be able to
establish themselves and dwell in entire security in the cities
where the study of letters is practised. It is fitting that we

should shelter them from all harm. Who would not have compassion on these men who exile themselves through love of learning, who expose themselves to a thousand dangers, and who, far from their kindred and their families, remain defenceless among persons who are sometimes of the vilest?"

After which somewhat rhetorical flourish he came down to brass tacks. No one was to inflict injury of any kind on a scholar, or to occasion any loss to him. Offenders against this law, no matter how highly placed, were condemned to make four-fold restitution of the distrained property, and lose their office. If a suit at law were brought against a scholar, the scholar had the choice of summoning his accuser to appear before his professors or the bishop of the city.

At one stroke the student class in Italy was raised from a state of outlawry to the most favoured position. They could snap their fingers at the local civil courts; the claim of a native accuser must be just indeed to obtain satisfaction from the defendant's own professors, dependent on that very scholar for their bread and butter, or from notoriously tolerant bishops.

Frederick Barbarossa was a shrewd ruler. He may or may not have been possessed of the ardent and altruistic love of learning to which he pretended, but he certainly realized the great practical advantages of encouraging schools in his domains. Firstly, they attracted thousands of foreigners, each a tangible source of revenue during the long years of study; secondly, these notable institutions were, so to speak, jewels in his crown; thirdly, they could be induced to express their gratitude for favours received by inculcating a spirit of loyalty to his person and the Empire. He may be said to have let the cat out of the bag when, in speaking of Bologna, he declared: "Their science enlightens the whole world and, thanks to it, subjects learn how to live in obedience to God, and to the emperors, who are the ministers of God."

Later on, his grandson, the great Frederick II, was to expand Barbarossa's idea by creating a University by special decree, the first of its kind in all Europe, if we except the somewhat abortive University of Palencia, founded locally some years before this by the King of Castile. Naples received its Charter in 1224, and Frederick attempted to give it a monopoly of teaching in his dominions, thereby drawing students away from Bologna, which was now a cog in the hostile Lombard League.

The Popes were not far behind. They were quick to realize the tremendous importance of the growing Universities. Perhaps they were not entirely happy over this passion for knowledge among the faithful; for inquiry leads to doubt, and doubt leads to scepticism — witness Berenger and Roscelin—but they were wise enough to see that the movement was too widespread, too strong, to be stopped in its tracks. So they did the next best thing; they quietly took over control, and prescribed the course which it should follow. By heaping benefits and favours on the struggling Universities, by protecting them against even kings and avaricious churchmen, they bound all grateful scholars to them with bonds of steel. There had been considerable alarm at the boldness and freedom of the earlier speculations, when the scholars were still foot-loose; the wisdom of the serpent foresaw that formal institutions with special powers and privileges would inevitably grow conservative, pillars of society and the Church, lending their weight and learning to the very dogmas which they were sworn to examine with an inquiring mind.

The Church, during the Dark Ages, had been forced to take control of education in the North. But there was no central authority. Each bishop was in unquestioned control of education in his own diocese. At first the bishop himself might be the teacher, or if he were lazy, or incompetent, or both, he could call in some wandering scholar and give him the job. At the same time, with the practical efficiency that makes the Middle Ages seem so modern, he would arrange for the hired master to act as his secretary, as keeper of the chapter seals, and as general factotum. His official title was Chancellor, or Scholasticus, and his ecclesiastical position was secured. As students gathered in increasing numbers, the Chancellor, himself, perhaps, grown fat and lazy, being now a person of importance, delegated the actual teaching to others, and became essentially a bureaucrat, a superintendent. And finally, in France, the myth grew up that he, as representative of the Church, had power over masters who desired to set up schools for profit even outside the cathedral walls. This was sheer usurpation of power, but the Church was shrewd enough to foster the belief, and finally to enforce it. The mediaeval idea that whatever was to be done, whatever was even to be thought, required authority from some superior power, would be astounding if we had not so many examples of the same insidious notion in our own day.

But, as we have said before, the opportunity for a little private graft was too tempting. If the master was to be paid by his pupils, why not charge him for the *licentia docendi*, the licence to teach? By the twelfth century, with the continual growth in the numbers of masters and pupils, the Chancellors were waxing wealthy. The poorer devils of masters, who could look forward only to a few starveling pupils, began to complain of the size of the fee. Others, whom the Chancellor refused to license for arbitrary or private reasons, joined in the general outcry. The clamour reached Rome.

Alexander III was Pope. He was a reformer, with unusual ideas about the prevailing sin of simony; and here was an opportunity of rebuking the haughty tribe of bishops, and incidentally, of centralizing control over education in Rome. In 1170-2 he issued a decree addressed to all the Chancellors of the schools of France, forbidding them, on pain of ecclesiastical penalties, to demand or collect any fee whatsoever in connection with the granting of a licence. Furthermore, they were not to refuse such licence to any able or learned man desiring to teach in the schools of the Church. In return for this derogation of powers, the Chancellor was

granted full supervision over all schools in the diocese, and
the right to judge of the fitness of the prospective teachers.
This latter was a most important privilege, and led in Paris
to the great struggle between the Chancellor and the Union
of Masters, which gave the final impetus needed to perfect
the University.

Even that struggle was deftly turned to account by the
Papacy. The Bulls issued by successive Popes, granting more
and more rights to the University, charters of privilege though
they were, made the Papacy the fountain-head, the controlling
influence. Once more, the power to grant implied the right
to withdraw.

The Popes went further. Taking a leaf out of the Emperor's
book, they began to found Universities of their own, where
none had existed before. It was gradually insinuated that a
new University could not be a "Studium Generale," with the
right of *jus ubique docendi* for its masters, unless it possessed
a Papal Bull of Foundation; or at least a charter from the
Emperor, who, theoretically, was likewise a universal power.
Again, this was sheer usurpation, and again the idea took
root. Local kings or municipalities might decide to have a
University, and might issue all the charters in the world, but
if they wished to obtain recognition for their University
outside their own domains, they must apply to Pope or
Emperor for a Founding Charter or Bull. And gradually
the Emperor was elbowed aside, leaving the Papacy in possession of the field. Even ancient and recognized institutions
like Paris and Bologna felt a little guilty at their nakedness;
they did not feel quite comfortable until they were decently
clothed in the armour of a Papal Bull.

Once the fashion was started, there was a veritable stampede
to found Universities. The Popes, generally speaking, founded
them to strengthen the Church, to eradicate heresy. Toulouse
was planted in the land of the savagely suppressed Albigensian
heresy, to stamp out the smouldering embers and safeguard
the future; Pope Pius II helped to establish the Universities

of Nantes and Bourges in the fifteenth century, to keep the local students from attending the University of Paris, when that institution had shown its gross ingratitude by supporting the Pragmatic Sanction.

For similar reasons the Kings of France showered favours on the University of Paris when they needed its support against the Papacy or the nation; while during the Hundred Years' War both French and English founded Universities in strategic centres to stir up feeling in their favour. Cities solicited them in order to establish lucrative sources of income; Florence as a means of repopulation after a particularly devastating plague.

By the end of the Middle Ages there were scores of Universities; some great centres of learning which dominated a whole age; others having some particular claim to fame; still others of purely local importance; and finally some that proved abortive or of ephemeral standing. It would be unprofitable to attempt a detailed account of each University, no matter how unimportant or negligible. But such Universities as Salerno, Paris, Bologna, Oxford, Montpellier, Toulouse, and Prague played leading parts in the history of thought and in the history of the Universities. It is with these that we propose to deal at some length, with occasional excursions into the by-ways of curious customs at other institutions.

CHAPTER VI

Salerno

SALERNO, on the south-western coast of Italy, was the site of the most ancient and most peculiar University in all Europe. As far back as the tenth century the town was famous for the number and skill of its physicians. The region abounded in mineral springs, and the lame and the halt and the blind foregathered there to bathe in its healing waters. Naturally enough, the physicians followed, eager to reap their harvest from such a concourse of the ailing.

How, when, or why a University arose from this mutually antagonistic horde of doctors is a mystery that may never be solved. Possibly it was to protect those already on the ground from an excess in congregation of quacks from the rest of Europe, as the fame of the health-resort spread; possibly the temptation to add to their income by teaching their mystery to budding Galens was too great to be resisted. At all events, by the eleventh century the Studium of Salerno was famous as a school of medicine throughout the length and breadth of Europe.

Its position was a particularly happy one. It stood at the crossroads of civilization; there Latin, Greek, Arab, and Jewish cultures met and mingled. The medical traditions of the Greeks and the Romans still lingered in what had been Magna Graecia, the most civilized section of the ancient world. Arabs and Jews came in from Sicily and Spain. There was still communication with Constantinople.

Galen and Hippocrates, the great Greek authorities, were studied in Latin translations; and the famous Jewish physicians, notably Isaac Judaeus, were known to the Salernians.

Salerno reached its zenith during the eleventh and twelfth centuries; it then began to decay. The reasons for the decline are simple. At the turn of the following century Arab medicine

51

began to invade Europe, bringing in its train new ideas, new herbs and formulae, strange compounds of alchemy and astrology; outrageous combinations of sound scientific knowledge and mumbling incantations.

This particular compound hit the fancy of mediaeval Europe, which swallowed it whole, the good and the bad. Other Universities, late-comers in the field, seized upon the new knowledge; Galen and Hippocrates, though not entirely discarded, were cast into the shade.

Salerno, out of sheer conservative resistance to anything novel, or perhaps in its blindness to the possibilities of the new medicine, refused to bow its head. Its obstinacy was fatal; students flocked to Montpellier, Padua, and Bologna instead. Diet and regimen might be sensible enough, but a patient could be more easily overawed by dark mutterings about the lunar influences, and nauseous draughts of strange ingredients. When one of Salerno's most learned doctors, Gilles of Corbeil, attempted to deliver a course of lectures at Montpellier, he was howled down by the students as a doddering old fogy.

Frederick II, in whose kingdom Salerno stood, came to the rescue in 1231. He forbade the teaching or practice of medicine anywhere within his kingdom of Sicily without his royal licence, which could be obtained only after examination by the masters of Salerno in conjunction with certain officials by him appointed. He also decreed a preliminary course in Arts and a minimum period of study. His rules were detailed and strict, affecting even apothecaries. One of these rules was very curious, and it throws a revealing light on the state of medical knowledge at the time. Druggists could sell their drugs only at a fixed price per ounce, regardless of the ingredients or the nature of the prescription.

But even this monopoly was unavailing. The students went elsewhere, though Salerno continued to vegetate down to the time of Napoleon, that ruthless destroyer of moribund institutions.

We have called Salerno a University; but if it was that, it was only just across the border-line. It was a Studium Generale, certainly, for students in the early days flocked thither from all Europe. It possessed a higher Faculty, the irreducible minimum, the Faculty of Medicine. It had no others. There were four great superior Faculties: Civil (Roman) Law, Canon (Church) Law, Medicine, and Theology. Very few Universities possessed all four; even Paris lacked a Faculty of Civil Law.

Whether or not Salerno possessed the basic inferior Faculty of Arts, we do not know. Even of its organization we know but little. It had a College of Doctors, the trade guild of the teachers in the Faculty of Medicine, and that is all we know.

Salerno was a peculiar and indeed unique institution. It stood apart from the rest of Europe, aloof and self-sufficient; though it was the most ancient of the schools, and its fame was widespread, it exercised no influence whatever on the growth and organization of the other European Universities.

There has come down to us a medical manuscript which is believed to have emanated from Salerno, and to have been written by its doctors as a practical guide for the use of Robert, Duke of Normandy, who had been cured of a fistulous wound there in 1096, and who left hurriedly for England to put in his claim for the then vacant throne. Its full title is the *Regimen Sanitatis Salernitanum*, or "Code of Health of the School of Salernum," and it is written in jingling doggerel verse.

Modern research has pretty well punctured its claim to be what it pretends to be; it is doubtless a patchwork of many writers, times, and schools. But to the Middle Ages it was a veritable medical Bible; its popularity was astonishing, and its authority second only to that of Hippocrates and Galen.

It is an extremely interesting production, containing plenty of sound advice, applicable even today, quaint quotable saws and proverbs, and also the most startling balderdash.

For example, what could be more sensible than this?

> "If thou to health and vigour wouldst attain . . .
> From heavy suppers and much wine abstain.
> Nor trivial count it, after pompous fare,
> To rise from table and to take the air.
> Shun idle, noonday slumber, nor delay
> The urgent calls of nature to obey. . . .
> Shouldst Doctors need? be these in Doctor's stead—
> Rest, cheerfulness, and table thinly-spread." [1]

Get up early, say the anonymous doctors, wash well your hands, face, teeth, and hair in cold water, move your bowels.

> "Cool not too soon the body when in heat."

"Fried meats do harm . . ." but boiled and roasted meats are approved; cheese, salt meats, goat-flesh, and hare provoke indigestion; new-laid eggs, rich broths, wine, wheat, and milk are praised for their strength-giving powers. And as for wines, the staid doctors become positively lyrical in their enumeration of the various types and what they are good for. Of water they are righteously contemptuous:

> "Who water drinks at meals hath mischief brewed;
> The stomach chilled voids undigested food."

But of wine—ah!

> "Let men drink wine, let beasts for fountains crave,
> But water-drinking *never* men enslave."

Of prunes, that mainstay of the boarding-house table:

> "Prunes cool the body and the bowels move—
> To all, in many ways, a blessing prove."

But figs, fie! They

> "Breed lice and lust in all who use the fruit,
> And yet Love's call, in turn, chill at its root."

Here is the plaint of the disgruntled physician in all ages:

> "When any doctor first attends a call,
> The patient would bestow the world and all;
> But once relieved and safely out of bed,
> The doctor's aid from memory has fled "—

---

[1] From the translation by John Ordronaux, *Regimen Sanitatis Salernitanum*, Philadelphia, 1871.

He should forestall such base ingratitude by asking for his fee at once:

> "Let doctors, then, of whatsoever school,
> Remember to observe this prudent rule:
> When tortured patients cry out, *Oh dear me!*
> Then let each say, *I'll thank you for my fee.*"

There is profound psychology in this:

> "Patients always pay those doctors best,
> Who make their calls in finest clothing dressed."

But there is another side to the picture:

Onions will cure baldness, if well rubbed in; leek is splendid for making barren women fruitful; the urine of a dog or the blood of a mouse will infallibly cure warts; pearls, or the stone found in a crab's head, will strengthen weak hearts; the juice of betony may be gathered only on the eve of St. John the Baptist; to prevent a woman from conceiving, all that is necessary is to bind her head with a red ribbon during the sexual act. A very pretty procedure and no doubt effective!

E

CHAPTER VII

Paris—A University of Masters

WHEN we try to visualize a University of the Middle Ages, it is not Salerno that the inner eye comes to rest upon, nor even Bologna, influential as she was, nor Oxford, the pride of England; it is Paris, the great overshadowing University on the banks of the Seine, whither all roads led; the intellectual centre of Europe, the *filia carissima* of the Kings of France; the darling and delight of the Popes of Christendom; the theological arbiter of the world; the very seat and repository of philosophy; the slavishly imitated progenitor of all northern Universities; the proud and haughty mistress, arrogant, sure of herself, acknowledging no overlord but the Pope, and restive even of his control; the streets of its Quartier filled with riotous, surging students, plangent with street cries, colourful with magnificent Rectors and dazzling processions; a city within a city, a State within a State, a nation within a nation, with its own laws, government, customs, privileges, and immunities.

No education was complete without a sojourn in Paris; the roster of its graduates was a complete list of all the great minds of Europe, of Popes and Kings and Princes spiritual and temporal. Its influence was enormous, its pride immeasurable. The twelfth century saw the beginnings, the thirteenth the full-blown glory, the fourteenth the eminence of its political and theological prestige; the fifteenth harvested the fruit of inner decay. Where else in the history of learning shall we discover a more splendid apparition?

The beginnings were modest enough. Prior to the middle of the eleventh century, Paris was a most inconspicuous centre of learning. Other schools far outshone the city on the Seine— Rheims, Chartres, Tours, Orléans, Fulda. Not until the end of the century did the scholars of Europe begin to congregate in Paris.

There were three Church schools: at the Abbey of Ste. Geneviève, at St. Victor's, and at the Cathedral of Notre Dame. Of these, only the Cathedral School was to play an important part in the genesis of the University; Ste. Geneviève was significant only as affording a haven for Abélard, and in the later struggle between Masters and Chancellor; while St. Victor, the home of mystical theologians, was completely outside the main current.

The early history of the Cathedral School of Paris is similar in general outline to that of all the cathedral schools of France. The rise of the Chancellor to a position of power over all teachers who wished to conduct a school has already been described. Toward the end of the twelfth century he was no longer permitted to charge fees for a licence, but he remained the arbitrary judge of the applicant's fitness.

Gradually the number of teachers increased. As soon as a pupil felt that he had learnt enough he conceived the ambition to impart his knowledge to others, and thereby to regain with interest the money expended in the painful pursuit of knowledge. Thus each pupil was a potential teacher, and naturally, after a while, the teachers began to get into one another's way. Pupils were fought over; there must have been price-cutting wars; there was certainly a great deal of propaganda and advertisement, and, of course, there was the common enemy, the Chancellor, only recently denied his opportunities of graft, but able in revenge to refuse the coveted licence. There are evidences that his relatives possessed mysterious tin boxes; that like a Tammany politician he could be "reached." And much as an English Prime Minister can subdue a recalcitrant House of Lords, he could license so many unqualified new teachers as to demoralize the whole profession.

Like sensible people, therefore, the masters already practising got together. There were plenty of precedents—the rapid growth of trade guilds was an outstanding phenomenon of the Middle Ages; association or organization for one purpose or another was quite the usual thing. There was no false nonsense about these clerics—every scholar promptly shaved his poll, and *ipso facto* became a member of that far-flung tribe—trade unionism was feasible, practicable, and the best means of safeguarding their rights. It was to be many centuries before teachers, the white-collared proletarians of a noble but slightly underpaid profession, once more forgot their dignities so far as to follow that mediaeval example.

With the coming of Abélard, Paris became at once a Mecca for scholars. His fame, and in lesser degree the fame of other masters of his time, brought thousands into the city. They swarmed in the dirty, narrow streets of the old town, to the amazement and consternation of the good burghers; they surged against the gates of Notre Dame; they crowded the little bridge, the Petit-Pont, with its gabled wooden houses; they sought quarters in every inn, hostelry, and private garret; they quarrelled and fought and jostled and sang.

The licensed Masters rubbed their hands and cashed in on the golden flood. So did the townsfolk, who converted stables and garrets into sleeping quarters, and put up the price of lodgings to exorbitant figures. The taverns promptly diluted their wine to avoid the chance of a shortage, and welcomed them in. The Chancellor managed to find pickings.

The organization of masters became less inchoate. Professional customs, unwritten laws, acquired all the binding force of statutes. No one should be granted the teaching licence unless he had in turn received instruction from a recognized licensed Master. Five to seven years of study was required. It was, of course, only a matter of courtesy to the old Master that he should be consulted by the Chancellor as to his pupil's qualifications. If he were not, the Masters had no legal remedy, but they had certain other very effective weapons against the new-comer. He was an outlaw, anathema; no regular professor would have anything to do with him, socially or professionally; he was denounced as a charlatan, students were warned against him, or lured away; the stubborn pupils were in turn refused admission to the guild when they were ready to teach; in short, life could be and was made pretty miserable for those who broke the rules.

Even in Abélard's time, something of this new feeling was already in the air. When Abélard himself, after studying theology under Anselm for less than the prescribed number of years, dared to lecture on the Bible without obtaining his master's permission, there was an uproar. It was scandalous, an unheard-of impertinence; more, it was an ecclesiastical offence; and the Council of Soissons afterwards considered it as a separate item in the charges against him.

So that it gradually became understood that it was not enough to obtain the Chancellor's licence; the aspirant must be approved by his teacher, and also by the whole Guild of Masters. A new ceremony was superimposed, the "Inception," the formal and ceremonial admission of the novice into the society of the teachers. Now he was a Master. Before that he was merely a Licentiate. This was the first evidence of a formal graduation, of an academic degree.

The monopoly of the teachers' organization was established some time during the latter part of the twelfth century. Yet they possessed no known written statutes until 1208; there was no official head until considerably later.

The first definite charter of privileges similar to that of Frederick Barbarossa in the South was granted to the Scholars of Paris by Philip Augustus, King of France, in the year 1200. It is a strange document, and the motive underlying it was even stranger.

The youths who flocked to Paris in the sacred pursuit of learning were inconveniently human. So, too, were their Masters—the Arts Masters, that is, for we do not wish to malign the grave and reverend Theologians or the hoary Professors of Canon Law. Students and teachers alike were susceptible to the joys of the tavern, the thrill of anticipating the turn of a pair of spotted cubes, the lure of a pretty face and ankle.

Resulting from the pursuit of these time-honoured accompaniments of learning, there were certain inevitable clashes with the plain citizenry of Paris. There were other causes of ill-will, such as the natural tendency of the bourgeoisie to charge the stranger within the gate all that the traffic would bear, and a certain resentment against all clerics, sacrilegious as that may seem.

There must have been plenty of minor incidents, riots, and skirmishes between the solidarity of scholars on the one side and the embittered townsfolk on the other, but the first serious conflagration, involving the most far-reaching consequences, occurred in the year 1200.

The servant of a German scholar went to an inn to purchase some wine, and became involved in a quarrel with the innkeeper over its quality. The innkeeper struck the servant, who incontinently ran home to report his woes. His master, the scholar, incensed at this presumption on the part of a townsman, gathered together some of his countrymen and fellow-students, and proceeded to thrash the surprised innkeeper to within an inch of his life. They then returned in triumph to their quarters, where they celebrated their victory, possibly in the victim's own wine. But the matter was not so easily settled. A wave of indignation swept through the city, fed by the remembrance of former and similar indignities. The Provost of Paris—the Chief of Police of his day—was appealed to. Like all good policemen, he burned to prove his mettle against the obstreperous students. He mustered a posse of armed citizens, and invaded the sacred quarters of the University. The scholars flew to arms, and the battle raged up and down the narrow streets. When it was over, five students were stretched out dead, including the scholar whose servant had started it all.

A mass meeting of the outraged students and their masters was held immediately. The schools echoed with cries for vengeance.

One for all, and all for one! Learning had been defiled! A delegation proceeded to wait upon the King. Grant us justice, they clamoured, or we scrape the mud of your city off our shoes for ever! It was the first time such a threat had been made. And it was effective! The King pondered gravely. He realized how easily it could be carried out. All that the scholars and masters had to do was to pack their knapsacks and journey to a more hospitable city. There was no fixed property to tie them down; they possessed no buildings, no endowments. They were, in truth, a peripatetic University. The results of such an exodus were obvious. The population of Paris would be almost halved; the loss of revenue would be deplorable; the world-wide fame of Paris as a centre of culture would be cancelled and the city would relapse into its former comparative obscurity.

Philip Augustus did not hesitate. He surrendered on all points. He decreed that the belligerent Provost be sentenced to perpetual imprisonment, with the proviso that if he wished to submit to the mediaeval ordeal of water or fire, he might do so. If convicted by the ordeal, he was to be hanged; if acquitted, banished for ever from Paris. His accomplices— those of them who had been captured—were to receive the same fate. Those scoundrels who had fled the King's (and scholars') just wrath were to have their dwellings torn down so as to leave no evidence of their existence. This part of the sentence the scholars themselves proceeded to execute, to the accompaniment of much cheering and dancing in the streets. For the first part, the Provost solved all difficulties by obligingly breaking his neck in a futile attempt to escape from prison.

Such personal vengeance, of course, was exceedingly satisfying to the enraged scholars, but much more important to the budding University were certain other provisions, on which the far-seeing masters were shrewd enough to insist for their future protection against similar outrages.

Henceforth, the King decreed, any scholar who chanced to

be arrested by a royal officer must forthwith be handed over to a proper ecclesiastical authority. This because the scholars were clerics, and not subject to secular penalties. The citizens of Paris, through their representatives, were required to swear to respect and maintain the privileges of the scholars; so, too, was the Provost of Paris on assuming office. This in the presence of the Masters in church assembled. No prisoner who had assaulted a scholar could thereafter claim the privilege of justification by ordeal or trial by battle. Nor could the goods of scholars be seized by the secular arm of the law in any civil action.

A most extraordinary bestowal of privileges, deriving from a most untoward cause. A casual blow to a menial, who no doubt deserved it, to have such far-reaching consequences! But then—a shot at Sarajevo started a World War; the killing of a missionary may add a dominion to an Empire. Pretexts for long-contemplated action always offer themselves in the end. Yet it must be noted that there was still no official recognition of a University as such. The charter was granted "to the Masters and Scholars of Paris." Nevertheless, it was a great advance, and was soon to be followed by a greater. The Parisian scholars had tasted power and, above all, had realized what a weapon they possessed in the threat of a Dispersion.

Within the next few years organization progressed rapidly. By 1210 there were written statutes in existence. The Masters had constituted themselves into a formal "Universitas," a trade guild, with guild forms and guild practices. The dress of the subscribing Masters was carefully regulated; observance was compelled of "the accustomed order in lectures and disputations," and "attendance at the funerals of deceased masters" was required of all their colleagues. Innocent III, in furtherance of a deliberate policy, granted authority to the Guild of Masters to elect a Proctor to represent them as a corporate body at the Papal Court. This was an important step forward; it made the University a corporate unit, with the essential right of suing as such, and incidentally, of being sued.

Having defeated the townsfolk and the powerful Provost of Paris, and extorted concessions from King and Pope, the Masters, many of whom were mere beardless youths, turned their attention to their natural enemy, the Chancellor of the Cathedral of Notre Dame. It irked their independent spirits that this outsider, this mere underling of a Bishop, should have autocratic control over them. It was the fly in their ointment. Otherwise they were a democracy, a pure, unadulterated, self-governing democracy, in an age of feudal autocracy. The struggle was to be long and unceasing.

The Chancellor was the only official who could confer the coveted licence to teach; it was an arbitrary right, to be granted at his discretion. He could revoke the licence, or deprive a scholar of his "scholarity," for cause. He was an ecclesiastical judge as well, and had criminal jurisdiction over scholars. He could enforce his decrees by the ecclesiastical penalties, involving the supreme one of excommunication, and he had a prison in which to jail recalcitrant offenders. He even claimed the right to legislate and pass ordinances for the government of the schools.

No wonder the Masters rebelled! But what could they do? For one thing, they could and did refuse to recognize any Master licensed by the Chancellor of whom they did not approve. He could not join their association; he was outside the pale. It did not take the budding teacher long to recognize how important it was to be admitted, or "incepted" into the Society of Masters; just as important, in fact, as the receipt of the Licence. Accordingly, every candidate was careful to fulfil the University's conditions, illegal though they were, and to apply for admission at the earliest opportunity.

But still the Chancellor held the whip, and he cracked it continually. He had delusions of grandeur, he saw himself the arbiter of the intellectual destinies of Paris, and therefore of all

Northern Europe. He demanded that each Licensee, as a pre-
requisite, should take an oath of obedience to himself. Instantly
the schools were in a ferment. The modern mind cannot
envisage the tremendous sanctity of an oath to the mediaeval
man. Our courts of law are daily the scenes of blithe and casual
perjuries; an oath is something to be taken and forgotten
whenever convenient. It was not so in the Middle Ages. An
oath was a tremendous swearing in the name of God. Its
breach was literally a damning of one's immortal soul. It
placed the perjurer outside the consolations of the Church; it
led to inevitable excommunication. Only the Pope could
absolve from the binding force of an oath. The Chancellor, if
he had his way, would be in a very strong position.

The Masters took up the gage of battle. They appealed to
Rome. Their agents at the Papal Court argued the matter
publicly, and privately they exercised more subtle lobbying
tactics. The Pope listened graciously, and in 1212 forbade the
exaction of such oaths. He did not care much for the Bishop of
Paris and his henchman; they had too much power as it was.
More, he insisted on strict compliance with the general rule
that no fees whatsoever be required for the Licence; and that
the Chancellor grant it to *all* candidates who were recommended by a majority vote of the Masters in any of the
Superior Faculties, or in Arts by a committee of six, three to
be chosen by that Faculty, and three by the Chancellor
himself.

The Chancellor had also proved himself a petty tyrant. He
had imprisoned scholars for the most trifling offences, and had
made it a practice to exact pecuniary fines by way of ecclesiastical penances, which he forthwith pocketed. Hereafter there
was to be no imprisonment pending trial for the lesser crimes;
and an imposed penance was to be just that—a spiritual
cleansing, and not a matter of money payment. The right of
the University to govern itself and administer oaths of obedience to its self-imposed laws was recognized "on occasion of
the murder or mutilation of a scholar or of a grievous injury

to a scholar, if justice is refused, for taxing the rents of Hospitia, concerning dress, concerning burial, concerning lectures or disputations," provided "that the Studium be not thereby dissolved or destroyed."

The University had attained its majority. It had won a sweeping victory; it had achieved autonomy. Now and in the future it had only to appeal to the Pope for redress of wrongs, real or fancied, and the favour was almost invariably granted. Only later, when the even more pampered Mendicant Orders were involved, did the Papacy turn against the University. By such means did Rome attempt to bind the best minds of the day, the articulate voices of the age, to its devious purposes.

But the Bishop of Paris had still another string to his bow. Pope or no Pope, he did not intend to permit these upstart Masters to escape from his domination. He exhumed an ancient statute against "conspiracies." To his jaundiced eye the whole Society of the University was but a vast unlawful conspiracy by lowly clerics against their superiors; to wit, the Bishop, the Chancellor, and the Chapter of Notre Dame. He thundered wholesale excommunication against the entire body of Masters. The battle was joined again, and this time it was a fight to a finish. It was fundamental, imperilling the very existence of the University. Once again the Papacy came to the rescue. The Bull of 1219 forbade the wholesale excommunication of the University without the express permission of the Papal See. The Chancellor's right to imprison was abolished.

The fight was over and won, except for one more skirmish, and here, for once, the Pope took sides against his protégé. The Masters had made themselves a great seal. A seal in the Middle Ages was very important. To this day some relics of that importance linger in the law. An instrument under seal possesses esoteric qualities not visible to the lay mind. With a seal a society has a legal existence; without, it is formless, inchoate. With a seal the University could proceed to borrow money and incur obligations; and money was a commodity of which the notoriously poor and reckless Masters were always in dire need.

Notre Dame, ever alive to an opportunity to strangle the upstart, complained to the Papal Legate in Paris, Romano, Cardinal of S. Angelo. He seized the seal, and in 1225 he solemnly broke it into little pieces, warning the Masters not to make another.

A furious mob of students, led and instigated by their Masters, stormed the obnoxious Legate's house. Swords, daggers, and cudgels were much in evidence, and there was no question of the scholars' readiness to use them. The doors were battered in, and only the prompt arrival of the King's soldiery saved the terrified inmate from being torn to pieces. Such was the ensuing hubbub that the Cardinal, Prince of the Church and armed with plenary powers, was compelled to flee from Paris in hot haste.

It is a testimony to the power of this new University that at the ensuing Council of Bourges some eighty Masters appeared and received unqualified absolution for their participation in this atrocious assault, the most heinous offence in all the vast category of ecclesiastical crimes.

And it is a further testimony that in 1246 the right to employ a seal was duly granted the University. Not that the resourceful Masters had waited until then. They had evaded the restriction for years by utilizing the new-born Nations, a curious form of organization which will be described later. Each Nation, not coming under the Prohibition, and subject to no supervision, made its separate seal. The use of the four seals of the four Nations signified the bond of the entire University.

Thenceforth the Chancellor was little more than an abstraction. His domination was broken for ever. True, he still granted the Licence to teach, but he had no power to refuse whenever the respective Faculties of the University recommended its bestowal.

Having conquered one enemy, the exuberant University

looked about it for more trouble, and promptly found it;
this time with the Royal Court as antagonist. It has been
aptly said that the mediaeval Universities thrived on their
misfortunes. The first charter of privileges was granted by
Philip Augustus after the death of five students; the tyranny
of Bishop and Chancellor brought a surfeit of Papal Bulls,
and another brawl in 1229 led to far-reaching results. Similar
consequences from similar drunken brawls or murders
followed in almost every University in Europe; for example,
there was a notable affray in Oxford that ended in the complete
subservience of the Town to the University *in perpetuum*.

But to return to the Great Dispersion of Paris. In 1229,
according to the contemporary chronicler, Mathew of Paris,
certain clerks, drunken with good wine, quarrelled with an
innkeeper in one of the suburbs of Paris over the price of
their potations. The argument followed the usual course and
ended in blows. The villagers, hating all clerks with a ferocity
incongruous with our ideas of the religious subserviency of
the Middle Ages, rushed to the defence of their neighbour.
The clerics were soundly beaten.

Thirsting for revenge, the scholars returned the next day
from the city, accompanied by pugnacious comrades, and
armed with swords and clubs. They wrecked the offending
tavern with methodical efficiency; then, still not satisfied,
they invaded the streets of the village and proceeded to beat
up every man and woman they met.

The village Prior complained to the Bishop of Paris and
to the Papal Legate. These worthies eagerly seized upon the
occasion. The Bishop had his own axe to grind, and the
Legate was that same individual who had narrowly escaped
mayhem at the hands of the students some years before.
The wounds to his pride had never healed. The two prelates
hurried to the Queen Mother, Blanche of Castile, then in
control of the government, and demanded redress.

"With the impulsiveness of a woman and the haste of an
agitated mind," the Queen ordered the Provost and his guard

to arm and punish the perpetrators of the outrage. Again, note the irony of fate. For the Provost of Paris certainly had no love for the arrogant University. A predecessor had died in jail as a result of its machinations; he himself had had to eat humble pie and swear obedience to its Statutes. He therefore took an unholy joy in obeying the Queen's command. The townsfolk and guards, resenting the insults and blows received from the insolent scholars, and with memories of seductions and rapes and murders, fell in with alacrity.

They came upon an unarmed group of clerks, engaged in innocent sports outside the city walls, who, it seems, were entirely innocent of the original outrage. But that meant nothing to the zealous Provost. The startled scholars found themselves suddenly attacked. When the mêlée was over, several had been killed outright, others had been drowned in the Seine, and many were sorely wounded. That night all Paris rejoiced; the Provost strutted; there were snickerings in the holy precincts of the cathedral; and the Cardinal Delegate's *amour propre* had been salved.

For a moment it must have seemed as if the University had not a friend in the world. Even the monarchy, in the year 1200 its staunch defender, had now turned against it. It seemed as though the University were doomed to extinction; the enemies it had made were many and powerful.

Then it was that the young Masters, and the still more youthful students, showed the mettle that was in them. The University promptly suspended all lectures and classes, and went *en masse* to the Queen, Bishop, and Legate, demanding satisfaction. It was met with sneers and mockery.

The University marched back to its quarters, and a momentous decision was reached. Unless, read the solemn document, within one month "satisfactory reparation is made to the whole body of masters and students for the atrocious injuries suffered by them . . . no one shall be permitted to remain in the city or diocese of Paris to study, either for the purpose of teaching or being taught." And such prohibition was to remain in effect for a full six years.

Promptly on the appointed date, the array of hostile powers still adamant, the Masters and Scholars made good their word. The thousands of clerks packed their belongings and swarmed out of the interdicted city, to the accompaniment of some jeers but more qualms on the part of those prudent citizens whose purses were like to suffer by their departure. The scholars scattered over the face of Europe. Some returned to their far-off homes, to renounce learning for ever and to dream of the fleshpots of Paris; others migrated to England, and the infant Universities of Oxford and Cambridge; Toulouse, Orléans, Bologna, all felt the life-giving influx of the celebrated Masters of Paris. It was Angers, however, as nearer and more convenient, that received the greatest number. Possibly its claim to University status dates from this migration. Meanwhile Paris, the proud, the pre-eminent, lay shattered, mourning her lost glories.

The repercussions of the migration were vast and immediate. It is doubtful if the outraged University was fully aware of all the implications of its act. Henry III of England cast a longing eye in its direction, and sent a letter post-haste to the scattering scholars. It is a masterpiece in its way, and deserves to be quoted in full:

"The King, to the Masters and the Body of Students at Paris, Greeting,

"We piously hope for the betterment of your condition, and that it will be changed to one of deserved freedom, for you have suffered with fitting humility the trials and tribulations that you have been forced to endure under the iniquitous law of Paris, and through it all you have shown due deference to God and the Holy Church. Hence, we announce to you all, that if it should please you to transfer yourselves to our kingdom of England and remain in it for the purpose of study, we assign to you whatever boroughs, cities, or villages you may select. Further, we will see to it that you shall enjoy every possible liberty and assurance of peace that is pleasing to God and such as would completely satisfy you."

The young King of France, Louis IX, chafing at his mother's hasty act, confirmed the old privileges of the University, and promised rigorous punishment of the culprits, if only it would return. It was too late; the scattered Masters were no longer to be placated with half-measures.

The Pope took a hand. Letter followed vehement letter. He wrote to the Bishop of Paris, berating him in most unclerical language, going so far as to say: "We are so confounded by your acts that we are forced to declare, although unwillingly, 'We regret that we made this man.' . . . Not only have you made no attempt to act as a mediator in the affair, but it is said that you have actually given such counsel and advice as would prevent the proposals made by either side from being accepted." He speaks of having ordered two outside bishops and one archdeacon to act as mediators, and exhorts the Bishop of Paris to bestir himself and see to it that suitable satisfaction be offered to the aggrieved masters and students. "Thus you may atone for the stain of your former offence or negligence. . . ."

The Pope wrote also to the mediators whom he had appointed, urging them to act without delay, and to Louis, King of France, and Blanche, his mother, requiring them to accept the mediators' advice and follow it faithfully. "Lest," he closes significantly, "if you do otherwise, which we do not believe will be the case, we should see wisdom and benignity rejected, without which the unity of power is scarcely able to exist, and we, who are not able to permit this kingdom (of France), which has thus far been blessed by Heaven, to be dishonoured in any such manner, would be forced to make other arrangements in the matter."

Formidable language to a reigning sovereign! Yet this same arrogant pontiff, when writing to the Masters and Students of Paris and Angers, adopts a mild and propitiatory tone. In the famous Bull of 1231, almost two years after the event, known to history as the Bull *Parens Scientiarum*, he grants the prodigals the most comprehensive privileges. This is the final charter of liberties, the capping-stone to unprecedented powers. The demands of the Masters, now far beyond those which arose out of the original quarrel, are met almost in full.

The first victim is the Chancellor. It is decreed that the next Chancellor of Paris shall take oath to confer no licence to teach unless deserved, and admit no unworthy persons when the approval of the Nations and the Masters is lacking. The Bull grants the University full power to make regulations as to the manner and hours of lectures, the style of dress, the burial of their dead, the taxation of hospices (meaning the right of the University to fix what it deemed reasonable rents for the lodgings of its students in the houses of private citizens of Paris). Students are not to be imprisoned except for cause, and then only in the bishop's prison; and most important of all, it recognizes the unqualified right of an aggrieved University to cease and suspend lectures, and go on strike until its demands are met. The Supreme Court of the United States has restricted the powerful weapon of the strike far more narrowly than did this old mediaeval dispensation. Lest it be deemed that this grant was meaningless, consider that practically every preacher, every prelate, every member of the higher clergy in Paris was a former University student, and as such, was bound by his solemn oath to obey its commands. Hence, in a *cessatio*, the pulpits of Paris became deserted; all priestly activities ceased; and the burghers were left without the aids and consolations of the Church.

In the matter of the rentals of lodgings to students, always a sore point between citizen-landlord and student-tenant, Gregory IX wrote a final letter to the King: "Inasmuch as many (students) are compelled to take hospices (lodgings) that are much too dear, grant to them further, without hesitation, that the regulation of hospices shall be placed in the hands of two masters and two citizens, who shall faithfully

F

take oath and shall be chosen for this purpose with the consent of the masters, or, if the citizens are not interested in the matter, it shall be done by two masters as has formerly been the custom."

For two long years the Dispersion continued, while Bishops, Popes, and Kings took a hand. Letters were exchanged, threats were employed, Bulls issued in unending profusion; the Court of France took alarm at the loss of revenue and prestige, as a result of which Paris sank nearly to the level of a provincial town, and gave in on almost all points. The original controversy was overlaid with new demands, and after two years' absence the Masters and their pupils began to trickle back and to resume their studies. Small wonder that their pride and arrogance knew no bounds; the University was now an independent republic, swollen with privileges, and with the formidable weapon of the *cessatio* at its disposal; often to be used or threatened in the future, sometimes for the most trivial of reasons.

In 1304 the Provost of Paris hanged two students. The University promptly decreed a *cessatio* until the offending official was compelled to remove the stinking corpses from the gibbet where they had swung for two months, kiss them fairly on the mouth, and bury them with his own hands in hallowed ground.

In 1453 a riot involving the archers of the King led to a *cessatio*, which came to an end only when the Parlement ordered eight of the guilty archers to make amends by going before the University authorities, clad only in their shirts and carrying torches, to sue for pardon on their bended knees.

This terrible weapon was used chiefly in conflicts with royalty. Lesser officials dared not offend the powerful University. Nearly every high official in Paris, or for that matter, in Europe, was a graduate of the institution, and by reason of his oath, subject to its commands. There is the famous case of Hugues de Besançon, Bishop of Paris, who in the course of his ordinary ecclesiastical duties fined a student who was admittedly guilty of rape. The University objected vehemently, and because as a youth the Bishop had studied in the Faculty of Canon Law, and had taken the usual oath to defend the University privileges, it took measures against him.

The walls of his cathedral were placarded with broadsheets proclaiming him a perjurer and forsworn, and all those bound by the University ties were warned to have nothing to do with him. The Bishop, powerless to resent the insult, and finding himself at once the laughing-stock and shunned of Paris, was finally compelled to travel to the Papal Court at Avignon to obtain absolution from his oath in so far as it interfered with his episcopal duties.

Finally, both King and Pope became weary of these constant strikes, which were often declared on the most trivial pretexts. In 1432 Pius II prohibited further cessations, without any appreciable result. Then Louis XII, feeling secure in the strong, autocratic kingdom which his predecessor had fashioned, played his hand. He had issued orders correcting certain University abuses; that still arrogant body placarded the city, announcing a strike; whereupon the King took decisive action. At the head of his troops, armed and accoutred for battle, he marched into the sacred precincts of the University. The offending placards were torn down, and the Masters, by now thoroughly cowed, surrendered. Thereafter there were no more strikes, or threats of strikes. The rising star of the French autocracy had overshadowed the arrogance of its beloved daughter. The Middle Ages were over.

CHAPTER VIII

The "Nations"

VERY early in the history of the University there arose certain
peculiar organizations known as the "Nations." Of their
origin and early development almost nothing is known; even
their constitution was the subject of dispute until recently.
Early authorities held that both masters and students were
members; it is now pretty definitely proven that the Nations
were clubs of masters only, though the students of similar
origin were doubtless brought under their protection.

There were four of these Nations—the French Nation,
largest in point of numbers, and comprising scholars from
Paris, Sens, Rheims, Tours, and Bourges, together with an
unaccountable complement of men from Spain, Italy, Portugal,
and the Orient. Next came the Nation of the Picards, with its
five provinces, including the Netherlands. Then the Norman
Nation, comparatively homogeneous. Finally there was the
English, later to be known as the German Nation. Its lack of
numbers was compensated for by its disproportionate influence
in the affairs of the University. It really comprised all scholars
foreign to France and hailing from Northern and Eastern
Europe. There were English, Scotch, Irish, Germans, Poles,
Hungarians, Scandinavians, and others in its polyglot ranks.

What were the Nations? Clubs, societies for mutual help,
havens of refuge for foreign students in the early days when
the University was not a definite organization, when scholars
were aliens in an alien land.

"We are here," said the masters and students of Paris in
1231, "as foreigners, without the support of relatives or friends,
exposed each day to atrocious insults which touch even our
persons."

"We believe," declared Philip the Fair as late as 1312, "that
it is proper to hold in great respect the labours, the vigils, the

drudgery, the deprivations, the pains and perils encountered by the students in order to acquire the precious pearl of science, and that it is just to consider how that they left their friends, their relatives, and their country, how that they abandoned their goods and their fortunes. . . ."

What more natural to suppose than that these aliens in a hostile city should consort with their own kind for comfort and protection, Scotch seeking Scotch, Norman foregathering with Norman? By 1219 these loosely-knit groups were to coalesce into four stronger, larger groups, called Nations. For years they were to constitute the very heart of the University, both socially and politically.

The Nations were composed of the Arts Masters only—the youngest teachers in Paris, and the most numerous. Immediately on graduation and inception into the Guild of Masters, they were required to remain and teach for the ensuing two academic years. In most instances these Regent, or teaching Masters, continued their studies in one of the higher Faculties. But their membership in the Nation expired as soon as they received the Doctorate of the superior Faculty.

Each Nation had its own officers, its own customs, its own feast days and private patron saints. The English Nation, for example, worshipped in the church of St. Cosme et St. Damien, where its archives were kept. Its patron saint was Edmund, King of England, but when, during the Hundred Years' War, anti-English sentiment grew strong among the more patriotic Frenchmen, and the name was discreetly changed to that of the German Nation, Charlemagne was duly elected as its patron.

The meetings of the Nations were held in secret, with due pomp and ceremony. Their chief officer was the Proctor, who was the official spokesman for his fellows of the Nation; then came the Receptor, the treasurer; and a number of outside Beadles, who were general assistants, messengers, and heralds.

The earliest Faculty of the University, the Arts Faculty, was practically a roster of the four Nations. They *were* the University. But gradually the other Faculties took shape and form. Medicine, Canon Law, Civil Law, which was almost immediately scotched by the Papacy; and supreme on the heights, Theology. The youthful Masters of Arts, as they graduated from these higher Faculties, perforce quitted the Nations, but they were still bound by their oath.

The chief business of the Nation was to take care of its members in life and in death. Meetings were held regularly, at which local matters were discussed, including outrages upon the person or dignity of its members, and also University business for which their vote was necessary; but above all, finances. For money was the essence of the organization to these youthful, exuberant masters.

Money was obtained largely from the fees collected from candidates who received their degrees through the Nation. There was no fixed charge; the fee was levied on the sensible basis of what the student could afford to pay. The unit was the amount which the student required for his weekly living expenses, called a *burse*, and the fee was so many *burses*. The Nation was not hard-hearted; the poor student whose *burse* was less than sixteen *denarii* per week, was magnanimously admitted gratis. His promise to pay when he became rich, if ever, was considered sufficient. Fees were collected also from newly elected officers, a general tendency in those days that some-times made candidates for honours somewhat less than anxious about their election. Then there were fines inflicted on members who failed to attend the numerous masses and vespers of the Nation, or those who infringed the statutes; the initiation fees of members, and receipts from holdings of real estate, though these were usually more of a liability than an asset. In other words, these academic scholars were most ingenious in the ways and means of raising money.

But it must not be thought that the Nations ever became wealthy corporations. Far from it; throughout their existence the one cry was the lack of funds. For money to the Masters of Art meant but one thing: the wherewithal to treat themselves to a banquet or a drinking-bout. Let a candidate be initiated, or an officer elected, who was able to pay immediately, and the band of learned teachers tumbled over themselves to get to the nearest tavern, where the capons were soon turning merrily on the spit, and the wine flowed down capacious gullets until the Nation's treasury was once more depleted. The learned clerks were a hard-eating, hard-drinking lot, without a thought or care for the morrow.

In later years each Nation leased or owned outright its own school buildings, where its masters lectured. The *Rue du Fouarre* (Straw Street) was the particular kingdom of the Arts Faculty. This narrow turbulent street, so called because of the straw that littered the floors of the schoolrooms in which the scholars sat cross-legged, was the most famous of mediaeval streets. Dante mentions it with longing in the *Paradiso*; so does Rabelais, and many another. The dilapidated, crowded houses were always giving the Nations trouble; they were draughty, cold, ill-ventilated, leaky, always in need of repairs, and there was never any money to pay for them.

During the fourteenth century there was a scarcity of schools, and naturally the senior masters obtained first choice of the more desirable quarters. This led sometimes to bitter quarrels between masters who claimed equal eminence. Not all were as sensible as the two masters who settled the dispute by tossing a coin. The juniors, of course, took the leavings; and sometimes they were not enough to go around. One master had to set up his school at the back of a tavern, where he taught his pupils the mysteries of Dialectic to the accompaniment of the clink of tankards. Another established himself on the premises of a barber, where he had not even a chair with which to support his dignity. There is some evidence that even the houses of ill-fame were utilized by masters in search of accommodation.

There were quarrels, of course, within the ranks of each Nation, but toward the outside world, and notably toward a rival Nation, it presented a united front. There were bickerings and feuds, vituperation and more tangible cudgellings that sometimes ended in bloody riots. In 1281 there was open warfare between the English and the Picards. The beef-eating English stormed the houses of their slighter comrades, burnt them to the ground, and forced the Picard masters to flee for their lives.

Jacques de Vitry, the famous reformer-preacher of Paris, thundered:

"They (the scholars) wrangled and disputed not merely about the various sects or subjects of debate; but the differences between the countries also caused dissensions, hatreds, and virulent animosities, and they impudently uttered all kinds of affronts and insults against one another. They affirmed that the English were drunkards and had tails; that the sons of France were proud, effeminate, and carefully adorned like women. They said that the Germans were furious and obscene at their feasts; the Normans, vain and boastful; the Poitevins, traitors and adventurers. The Burgundians they considered vulgar and stupid. The Bretons were reputed to be fickle and changeable, and were often reproached for the death of Arthur. The Lombards were said to be avaricious, vicious, and cowardly; the Romans, seditious, turbulent, and slanderous; the Sicilians, tyrannical and cruel; the inhabitants of Brabant, men of blood, incendiaries, brigands, and ravishers; the Flemish, fickle, prodigal, gluttonous, yielding as butter, and slothful. After such insults, from words they often came to blows."

Nationalistic rancour and hatred of the foreigner are not modern inventions, nor are men of education necessarily immune to unreasoning prejudice.

It was against the French Nation, however, that most of the animosity was directed by the others. Each Nation, as has already been shown, had its own seal, and the prohibition against a common University seal was evaded by the use of the four seals of the Nations. Thus they came to represent the University, and the voice of the Nations was the voice of the University. But each Nation voted as a unit, and a vote, to be effective, had to be unanimous. The French

Nation, which at times outnumbered all the others put together, resented an arrangement which left foreigners in control. There were constant fights, and on more than one occasion the Faculty of Arts split into two bodies, the French electing their own Rector for the University, and the other three Nations another.

The other Faculties of the University—Medicine, Canon Law, and Theology—though graduate bodies, and superior to the lowly Arts, had yet comparatively little to say in the government of the University. There were good historical reasons for this anomaly. The Arts Faculty was the first to organize itself; the Nations composing it were compact bodies with definite aims before the higher Faculties were anything but inchoate groups of individual Doctors. Then, too, the youthful Masters of Arts, strong in numbers and turbulent in spirit, were more prone to be involved in the brawls and affrays that led to the granting of the great charters of privilege to the new-born University. To the victors belong the spoils!

At some time during the first half of the thirteenth century the Nations of the Arts Faculty decided upon a common head, or Rector. He was elected from their own body by the Nations, voting as units. His term of office was extremely brief—from four to six weeks until about 1280, when it was lengthened to a period of three months.

At first he represented the Arts Faculty only, but soon he was employed in the collection of money, conduct of litigation, and execution of the decrees of the University as a whole. The other three Faculties, each headed by a Dean, were no doubt glad to unload these onerous duties onto the shoulders of the youthful Rector of the inferior Arts, not realizing the inevitable result. Before long he became the actual, if not the titular head of the entire University, and the grave and reverend Theologians, Canon Lawyers, and Doctors of Medicine bowed to his control. They could not help themselves; they were passing through the turbulent period of riots, secessions, conflicts with Chancellor, Bishop, Provost, townsfolk, and royalty. They needed the numbers, the good right arms and cudgels, the leather lungs of the Masters of Arts and their pupils. So they had to pay the piper.

By the end of the thirteenth century the Rector wielded the actual power of the University; by the middle of the fourteenth century even the title was his. The Nations had devised an ingenious system for ensuring the supremacy of their Rector. It involved the use of the oath, the binding force of which was to be employed again and again. At first the fledgling Bachelor of Arts was required to take an oath binding him to obedience to the Rector "as long as he should profess the Faculty of Arts." This was altered during the thirteenth century to read: "to whatever state you shall come." Since most of the Doctors of the superior Faculties had come up through the Parisian Arts Course, the oath bound them throughout life, on pain of being held perjured, false, rebels, and rotten limbs. The young man of twenty-two to twenty-five, clothed in the temporary majesty of his office, demanded and obtained unquestioning obedience.

The Rector of Paris was in truth a magnificent and splendid personage. He was addressed with formal deference as "Messire," "l'Amplissime," "Amplissime Rector." He yielded to no man in precedence; he clad himself in ermine and purple; he sat on Royal Councils. In the great processions that the University and the townsfolk of Paris loved so well, he walked side by side with the Bishop of Paris, ahead of Archbishops and even Cardinals, ahead of the lords of Parlement, and even the lords of royal blood. The Dean of Theology, though an Archbishop and a Papal Legate, once dared to sit in the Rector's chair of state at St. Germain-des-Prés; the indignant Arts men dragged him off by the ears. Pomp and circumstance attended him everywhere. A brief but gorgeous career, like that of a butterfly sipping nectar on a warm summer's day. One suspects, after examining his fluttering glory, that his power expended itself mainly in magnificence.

By contrast, the Deans of the three superior Faculties were but birds of sober plumage, as were the Proctors who headed the separate Nations.

In Abélard's time the Arts—comprising Logic and Philosophy on the one hand, and Theology on the other— were the great and absorbing studies. Theology, most arduous and subtle of sciences, beloved of Popes, was the glory of Paris. No other University approached Paris in the eminence of her theologians; their lightest word commanded instant respect throughout Europe. Paris led, and Rome followed.

Pope John XXII once ventured an opinion that the Saints did *not* enter immediately into a full vision of the Trinity. It was his contention that they, like ordinary mortals, were compelled to wait for the Day of Judgment. A most knotty question, in sooth, and it excited so much argument that in 1332 Philip of France determined to put an end to the uproar. Accordingly he demanded of the Theological Faculty of Paris that they should settle the matter forthwith. The thirty learned Doctors examined the question *de novo* and with painstaking care, and delivered themselves of a round condemnation of such an unorthodox opinion on the part of a Pope. The King dispatched a copy of the report to the Pope at Avignon, and peremptorily requested His Holiness to retract his error, and forthwith punish all others who professed similar heresies. The Doctors of Paris, the King said sharply, knew what was to be believed in matters of faith much better than the lawyers and lackeys who surrounded His Holiness. The Pope was almost abject in his reply. He apologized for venturing an opinion on a point in theology when he himself was not a Doctor of Theology, and hastily disclaimed any position but that of a neutral in the moot question.

As a matter of fact, very few other Universities possessed even the rudiments of a Theological Faculty. The Popes discouraged them, in an attempt to give Paris an absolute monopoly. They possibly felt that while it was essential to have a body of learned Doctors to determine doctrinal matters for the Catholic Church, yet Theology held explosive possibilities. Permit too many men to set themselves up as experts in matters of faith, let them be scattered over many lands and in diverse surroundings, and inevitably there would be trouble; trouble for themselves and for the Church they were sworn to uphold. Too many cooks have spoiled more than one broth. It is but one more example of the worldly wisdom and subtlety of the Papacy that it chose to concentrate this study in one centre, where it could be readily observed and protected from contamination, and where the few experts could be so dazzled with prestige and flatteries and the prospect of fat benefices that nothing radical or heretical could possibly emanate from them.

Medicine established itself as a Faculty some time in the last quarter of the twelfth century, but it never aspired beyond mediocrity. Salerno, and later Montpellier, far surpassed it in prestige.

The study of Canon Law began in Paris at about the same time, and became almost at once a lucrative Faculty. This study of the laws governing the Church and its multifold affairs proved a lure to many a student. There was money in it for the clever, ambitious young lawyer, and many preferments within the gift of the Church. Few young men would face the long, arduous years of toil required of Theology as against the comparatively quick and easy path of the Canon Law.

Civil Law, if it ever was a Faculty in Paris, was extinguished by Honorius III in 1219, who categorically forbade its further study. The ancient Roman Law, universally applied to commerce, trade, and the affairs of towns and nations in the Middle Ages, was even more a source of secure income than the Law of the Church. Lawyers were in great demand, and the Papacy viewed with grave alarm the deserted schools of

Theology. Even parish priests, regulars, and beneficed clerks deserted their stations to study the fashionable profession.

"We forbid," decreed Honorius III, "under pain of excommunication, whether in Paris or the neighbouring towns and cities, any person to employ himself in teaching or learning civil law. We have learned with sorrow that, abandoning the study of philosophy, to say nothing of that of theology, the majority of the clergy hasten to the lectures on secular law; and that in the majority of States no one is chosen by the bishops to occupy positions of dignity and honour, or ecclesiastical prebends, unless he is either a professor of civil law or an advocate."

It was not too great a deprivation for budding attorneys; there were plenty of Universities that specialized in the study of torts and contracts; especially Bologna, the greatest of them all.

CHAPTER IX

Conflict with the Mendicant Orders

THE University of Paris had by now become a great institution; it had met and defeated Bishop and Chancellor, Town and King. The Pope had steadily proved its friend, backing it to the utmost, no matter how outrageous its demands. But now there appeared a new enemy, unobtrusively and insidiously at first; one that the arrogant Masters of Paris felt could be crushed in a moment if they so desired. But to their great surprise, when the time came for a contest, the meek and lowly enemy showed unmistakable vigour, and to their dismay, the Papacy, that long faithful friend, turned traitor and defended the privileges of the intruder as vehemently as ever it had those of the University. A new favourite had been found.

The history of the Mendicant Orders, or Begging Friars, and their relation to the University, lends point to the belief that the tender solicitude of the Popes for their beloved daughter, the University of Paris, was not inspired by regard for learning and knowledge, as has often been pretended, but was rather part and parcel of a subtle policy for the enhancement of the glory of the Papacy, and incidentally, of the Church.

The mediaeval Church, by the latter part of the twelfth and the beginning of the thirteenth century, had become a tremendous institution. It was no longer merely a religious corporation; it was a political and international State; it dictated to kings and nobles alike; it was itself the largest owner of land, the greatest feudal lord of the time; the professional classes of lawyers, doctors, teachers, and judges were almost completely under its control; those sworn to its obedience were numbered by hundreds of thousands; it paid no taxes, yet it mulcted all Christendom of almost fabulous revenues; its fellowship was exempt from military service and national obligations; if clerics committed crimes, they could be judged only in the tribunals of their own order.

Thus there arose within the boundaries of each State a vast number of ecclesiastics, acknowledging no overlord but the super-State of the Church, viewing the peasant laity as an inferior order of creatures and merely the material source of their physical comfort, bowing to the powerful lords and feudal nobility only because there were definite advantages to be derived from them. Is it any wonder that this horde of tonsured clerics forgot their historic and primitive functions as shepherds of their flocks, as healers of the souls of the people entrusted to their care? Is it any wonder that the lower clergy particularly, themselves of peasant origin, grew to be lazy and slothful, corrupt in the worst sense of the word, ignorant of learning, unable to understand even the few Latin prayers which they mumbled in barbarous accents, celibate in theory, yet living in open and unabashed con- cubinage; no virgin or personable married dame immune from their roving eyes, heedful only of their bellies and their vicious appetites? It is true that one cannot indict a class; there were notable exceptions; the higher clergy were as a rule more urbane and civilized, their appetites more discreet; a good proportion were University graduates, and possessed of the teacher's licence; they erred rather on the side of worldly and political ambition.

But the peasant and the small-town burgher came into contact with the lower orders only. William of Puylaureus writes bitterly: "They (the parish curés) were classed with the Jews. Nobles who had the patronage of parochial churches took good care not to nominate their own relatives to the livings; they gave them to the sons of their peasants, or their serfs, for whom they naturally had no respect."

The Council of Avignon of 1209 took cognizance of this deplorable state of affairs. It used vigorous language. "Priests do not differ from laymen either in appearance or in conduct. . . . They are for ever plunging into the most shameful debauchery."

The laity, the common people who footed the bill, were becoming restive. They muttered and grumbled. It was becoming impossible to feel any respect for clerics as individuals. Satires and Goliardic gibes multiplied. Sects and heresies took root in disaffected soil, culminating later, in the South of France, in the great Waldensian and Albigensian movements.

The Papacy recognized the dangers of the situation. Council after Council, Pope after Pope, inveighed against the sloth and corruption of the lower clergy. The Universities had immeasurably raised the standards of the higher ranks of the hierarchy, but the substratum was untouched.

The new movement of the Friars was therefore seized upon as a present from God. St. Dominic and St. Francis, as dissimilar as two men could possibly be, nevertheless founded two Orders that tended toward the same effects. There had been monks before, thousands upon thousands of them, bound chiefly by the Benedictine and Cluniac Rules, but they were withdrawers from the world and their fellow-men; they were interested solely in their own selfish salvation; the rest of mankind could go to the devil for all they cared.

Dominic, an ambitious, orthodox zealot, regarding the Benedictine monk in his cave-like retreat and the ignorant, pleasure-loving priest with equal abhorrence and contempt, conceived the idea of a new order of monks. A body of fanatically devoted men, stripped of all worldly possessions, vowed to poverty as to a blessed mistress, barefoot, clad only in rough, black, corded gown, begging their meals from door to door, learned in theology and the subtle dogmas of the Church, militant, preaching, exhorting, converting, proselytizing, bringing the terrors of hell and the raptures of heaven home to the very Christians whom the priests had neglected so long; here was a terrible weapon in the hands of the Church.

The movement took hold almost at once. The Popes were wise enough to foster and encourage the spirit of martyrdom; and soon Europe was overrun with begging Friars, bringing the gospel to all men. Very early Dominic realized what the Jesuits were to teach much later: that no one wielded more influence than those who exercised control over education. Accordingly he encouraged, and indeed insisted upon, the highest theological training for his preachers. They were to be men of learning, well able to cope with heretical doctrines and show them up in their true, damnable light. It was obvious, therefore, that he should cast longing eyes upon the Universities. He set up headquarters for the Order in almost every University centre: in Italy, Bologna was chosen; in France, Paris; in England, Oxford. The Masters of the Order, its most learned Doctors, preached to the students, seeking to entice the scholars of Europe into the fold, rejoicing when they could report the capture of a "famous Master" or "worthy Bachelor."

Francis, that meekest and most lovable of saints, started from different premises. His loving-kindness embraced not merely man, but also the beasts and birds and flowers of the field. All were God's little children, and worthy of his efforts. He longed to bring all these children into the kingdom of heaven, by insisting not upon the fires of hell, but upon the joys of peace and charity and poverty. He was not interested in dogma or learning; it was the lowly, the ignorant, that appealed to his emotional sympathies. Accordingly the first members of his Order, grey-gowned and barefoot, went into the slums and hovels and houses of prostitution, and ignored the haughty Universities. But as time went on, later Generals, more worldly-wise than their Founder, and watching with envious eyes the advance of the Dominicans, began to emulate the rival Order. They, too, established branches in the University towns, and sought recruits among the masters and students. By 1230 both were securely established in Paris. Later Mendicant Orders followed closely in their footsteps; the Carmelites, the Austin Friars, and others; but they never achieved the prominence of their progenitors.

It was not long before the Mendicants, notably the Dominicans and Franciscans, conceived the ambition of obtaining control of the Theological Faculty of Paris, and of utilizing it for their own propagandist purposes.

At first the University was not particularly hostile; it did not even recognize the peril within the gates. The early Friars studied in the secular schools under the secular Doctors, and were meek and self-effacing enough. The Great Dispersion of 1229 altered matters considerably. The Friars were not particularly interested in the principles involved, nor did they wish to antagonize the Court, in which they were just beginning to obtain a foothold. Accordingly they remained behind while the secular masters and students ate the bread of exile, and opened their own schools of theology. Roland of Cremona, an Italian Dominican, was the first teacher.

When the University returned to Paris, the Friars who had remained, and the schools which they had opened, were regarded with some resentment. But there, as yet, was no open breach. Then the Friars brought off an effective coup. In the year 1250 they procured a papal Bull enjoining the Chancellor of Notre Dame to confer the Theological Licence upon their candidates on the strength of their own examinations, and without having to consult with the secular Doctors of the Paris Faculty in Theology. This was a stab in the back for the University. At one swoop the long years of struggle to obtain control over the admission of its own Masters were rendered fruitless—at least, as regarded Theology. The University had no control over the Friars' schools; it could set no requirements for the degree. The Theological Faculty was soon filled with Mendicant Doctors who had not been admitted into their ranks, and who had taken no oath of obedience to the University or to its Statutes.

The University struck back almost at once. In 1252 the

Faculty of Theology passed its first known written Statute. It decreed that "no religious not having a college in Paris" be admitted to the Society of Masters; that each existing religious college be restricted to one Master and one School; that no bachelor be promoted to a chair unless he had already lectured in a school of an actual regent Master. Any Master refusing consent thereto was to be ejected from the Society of Masters.

There the matter rested for a few months, the antagonists watching each other warily, like boxers waiting for the first false move. It came soon enough. Another of the numerous University affrays was in the making, and again the learned scholars seized upon the occasion to press for an extension of privileges.

Late in the year 1252 a student was killed in a street brawl by the Provost's men. Others were wounded and imprisoned in the Provost's prison, in defiance of all scholastic privileges. The University promptly rose to the insult. It decreed an immediate Cessation. All obeyed, except two Friar Doctors, one a Dominican and the other a Franciscan. Since their oath exacted obedience on penalty of spiritual thunders, they appealed to Rome to relieve them of the oath or to annul the Cessation. As a result the Cessation was a failure, and the University went back to lectures somewhat crestfallen. But the righteous indignation of the Masters at the strike-breakers was extreme; they swore a great oath to insist on justice. The two dissenters refused to swear, and this time they were joined by still another Friar Doctor. The University Congregation pounced joyfully upon this last defiance, and expelled the three from its Society, warning all pupils against attending their lectures.

As a result of much backing and filling, justice, as the scholars conceived it, was finally granted them. Two of the Provost's men were convicted of the outrage, and in true mediaeval fashion were dragged through the streets at the heels of galloping horses, and finally hanged. This did not improve the position of the Friars. Their expulsion was not revoked.

The University went further. In a Congregation of all the Faculties a Statute was passed that no one be admitted to the fellowship of the University unless he first took an oath to obey all the Statutes and observe a Cessation when ordered. Of course, all the secular Masters, who had graduated in Arts, had already taken such an oath, but the Friars, who never attended the Arts Faculty, being interested only in Theology, had escaped it.

In 1253 the Friars were once more expelled and declared excommunicate by the University. All this while they had been busy in Rome. For once the University agents found the Pope obdurate. The Mendicants had been busily at work. A Bull was procured peremptorily demanding that the University should readmit the Friars. The order was given to the Chapter of Notre Dame, the implacable enemy of the University, for execution. Before the bewildered Masters could rub their eyes, they found themselves suspended from all offices and privileges by the gloating Chapter. Once more the scholars of Paris found themselves beset by enemies, and this time the Pope was ranged on the other side.

They shook their heads doggedly, and breathed open defiance, Bulls, suspensions, excommunications notwithstanding. The Friars were banned, and they were to remain so. The beleaguered University turned to the King for help, only to find new enemies. The Court had come wholly under the influence of the Friars; the King's confessor himself was one of them. There was no help to be had in that direction.

And now the new Pope, Alexander IV, himself under the influence of the ambitious Mendicants, and feeling that their conservatism was a safer prop to the Papacy than the hitherto favoured University, turned a complete somersault. In 1255 he issued the Bull *Quasi lignum vitae*. He decided practically every disputed point in favour of the Mendicants; the expulsion of the Friar Doctors was annulled, and the Chancellor was directed to grant Theological Licences to as many Friars as he saw fit. Only one point, seemingly, was in favour of the University. The Friar Doctors were to obey a duly ordered Cessation; but there was a catch here. It was to be valid only if decreed by a vote of two-thirds of the Masters in each Faculty. Inasmuch as by this time the Mendicant Doctors held more than a third of the chairs in Theology, they could at their pleasure stop all strikes on the part of the entire University.

The Masters of the University breathed open defiance. They refused to readmit the expelled Dominicans, whereupon they were excommunicated *en masse*. This was a terrible punishment. It meant that the thousands of scholars of Paris were beyond the pale of the Church; Ishmaelites, damned to all eternity. But the rebels took counsel, and devised an ingenious plan. As individuals, the masters and students sent a letter to the Pope, declaring in formal terms that the University was dissolved, and that they—again as individuals—voluntarily renounced all the Papal and corporate privileges and immunities it had taken them so many laborious years to secure. The great University of Paris was no more!

But—and this was the crux—the Nations, the organized groups of Masters, had nothing to do with the dissolution. They considered themselves as privileged to continue in their vocation. The University as a corporation of the whole teaching body was gone, but they remained. They claimed the right to hold schools in their own houses, and to exclude unwelcome intruders, just as any private society might do.

And if the individual Master forbade his pupils to approach a Mendicant convent for any purpose, to confess to a Mendicant, to give him alms, to attend his sermons—well, that was a private matter. But God help the pupil who disobeyed!

Mere "boycotting" was not enough for the hot-blooded Masters. They proceeded to violence. It was as much as a Mendicant's life was worth to appear upon the streets. A cry was raised, and as if by magic the masters and students poured out upon the luckless Friar. He was abused, set upon, and beaten; the contents of chamber-pots were emptied upon him from upper windows; stones and clods of earth whizzed around his devoted head. The convents of the Mendicants had to be guarded night and day by the royal troops in order to save them from being stormed and sacked.

The Mendicants had won a victory, it was true, but it began to look like a Pyrrhic victory. The Pope raged at the treatment accorded his favourites, and issued Bull after Bull to enforce better terms, but their execution had to be entrusted to the secular priests. And the vast majority of the secular clergy secretly sympathized with the embattled University. In the first place, a good number of them were University graduates, bound by ties of affection and formal oaths. In the second place, the seculars resented the sudden rise to power of the obstreperous Mendicants. These barefoot fanatics, vowed to poverty, were winning the people away from them as they had already won the favour of the Pope; they threatened their easy lives; and further, the seculars felt for them the contempt that all civilized people must feel for the fanatic, the zealot, the single-tracked mind. The University, too, had adroitly linked its conflict with the general secular struggle against the Regular encroachments. Bishops and clergy in all parts of Europe raised their voices in protest.

The laureate of the King of France himself attacked the Dominicans. "They preach to us that it is sinful to be angry and sinful to be envious, whilst they themselves carry on war for a chair in the University. They must, they will, obtain it. . . . The Jacobins are persons of such weight that they can do everything in Paris and in Rome."

The storm rose to such dimensions that had Innocent IV lived, the University might eventually have triumphed. But he died suddenly, in answer, said the triumphant Dominicans, to their prayers. Alexander IV, his successor, as has already been noted, was a henchman of the Mendicants, and a bitter and unyielding foe of the University.

Gradually the opposition broke down, owing, more than to anything else, to the patronage at the command of the Pope. The striking Masters could set up a schismatical University, but they found themselves left out in the cold when it came to the distribution of benefices and comfortable livings. That hurt where it always hurts the most; in the pocket. Reluctantly but inevitably the Masters slunk back to the official University, pocketing their pride, obtaining absolution for their sins, and putting themselves once more in line for ecclesiastical favours. The strike was over, and the Mendicants were victorious; the first to triumph over the scholars of Paris. Yet they did not escape wholly unscathed; their exclusion, both social and professional, while wholly unofficial, was nevertheless quite effective. They were made to feel their ostracism.

When Urban IV became Pope in 1261, there was once more a pontiff who had a warm spot in his heart for the disgruntled University. The thunderous Bulls were allowed to lapse into desuetude. The Faculties of Arts and Medicine continued successfully to refuse admission to the Mendicants; in practice, the Friar Doctors lectured only to their own brethren; no seculars attended. And when in 1318 the University once more demanded the oath of obedience from the Friars, they quietly submitted. The Homeric conflict of two generations before was forgotten.

But there was one most important consequence. The scholars had long memories. They remembered, and resented bitterly, what they considered their betrayal by the Pope. Up till that time the Papacy could regard the University as its staunchest defender, the very citadel of orthodoxy and loyalty. But when the Pope turned to the Mendicants he lost the University. The fact that their privileges were eventually restored did not matter. The memory rankled, and the scholars were good haters. The Popes had unwittingly reared up a hostile element, and they were to rue it. The University became increasingly nationalistic, and when the great controversy of the French National Church against the supremacy of the Papacy arose, it was the University that became the great champion of the Gallican principle.

The conflict had another important result. The College of the Sorbonne was founded primarily to provide secular Theologians to offset the Regulars, and while not the first college in point of time, it did more than any other to determine the collegiate structure that was to influence the future development of Paris, and in an even greater degree, of Oxford and Cambridge.

CHAPTER X

Aristotle Enthroned

AT the end of the twelfth century the "new" Logic of Aristotle had taken the youthful University of Paris by storm. The classics, the study of humane letters, beloved of John of Salisbury, were swept away by the passion for Logic, for disputation.

Stephen of Tournai might cry angrily that "babblers of flesh and bone irreverently discuss spiritual things, the essence of God, the incarnation of the Word! At the crossroads one hears these subtle logicians divide the indivisible Trinity! There are as many errors as there are teachers, as many scandals as there are hearers, as many blasphemies as there are public places. . . . It is not fitting that things Divine be thus demeaned and made vulgar playthings. It is not meet that almost anybody may be heard shouting at the street corner: 'Here is Christ, He dwells with me!'"

His scorn of the youthful Masters of Arts was overwhelming: "These well-primped adolescents have the impudence to occupy masters' chairs; they have no down upon their chins, yet behold them in the positions of mature men. They write manuals too; *summas*, poorly digested compilations, flavoured but not made tasteful by the salt of philosophy."

Yet all the wailings, all the anguished cries, were unavailing. The beardless youths continued to divide the indivisible, and Dialectic and Aristotle were simultaneously enthroned, never to lose their supremacy until the Renaissance swept them both into the discard.

By the beginning of the thirteenth century, more of Aristotle arrived in Western Europe. It had been a long and devious journey for the old Greek, and by the time he was safe in port he was so overlaid with accumulated grime and patches as to be hardly recognizable. But the scholars of Paris and elsewhere welcomed him with open arms, grime, patches, and all. This was Aristotle the scientist, the metaphysician, the philosopher, hitherto unknown, almost unsuspected. At one bound he became "The Philosopher," an authority equal in eminence almost with the Bible itself.

How did his wisdom reach the West? It sounds almost like a bad jingly jest. Mainly in the form of Latin translations of Spanish translations of Hebrew translations of Arabic translations of Syriac translations from the original Greek! And overlaying even the garbled, mangled text, were the commentaries of the Arabs and the Jews, vast, learned, overwhelming. What an astounding metamorphosis for the Peripatetic!— and how eagerly the scholars lapped up the whole indigestible mess!

At a time when Latin Europe was a welter of barbarism, the Mahommedans in the East were producing a civilization comparable in cultural values to that of the Roman Empire. In 750 the Abassids at Baghdad studied and appreciated Aristotle in translations which the Syriac Christians had made. Arabic versions passed through Africa and across the Straits of Gibraltar into Mahommedan Spain, where a new Renaissance of Arab learning was taking place. The schools of Cordoba vied in glory with the most famous schools of antiquity. Philosophy took root and flourished. The Jews, tolerated and accepted for once in their history of age-long persecution, swelled the stream of Moorish culture with their intellectual acuteness and their passion for knowledge.

Arab and Jew ruminated on the Aristotelian metaphysics, flavoured it with their own philosophical and racial idioms, and brought forth their commentaries and interpretations. There was the mighty Averroës, who was to become second only to Aristotle in his influence on Western Europe; Avicenna, the metaphysician and writer on medicine; Al-Ghazali of Nishapur and Baghdad, the greatest theologian of Islam; Saadia Ben Joseph, the first great Jewish philosopher since Philo of Alexandria; and the greatest Jew of all, Maimonides.

It was Bishop Raymond of Toledo, fired by the intellectual light that played across the border of Moorish Spain, who established a veritable school of translation. Unfortunately his Latin translators knew no Arabic. He had therefore to employ Jews, who knew Arabic but little Latin, and some of them only the Spanish vernacular. The translations, consequently, were almost incredibly bad. Years later, Roger Bacon was to inveigh against such wretched balderdash, and to insist that scholars should study Greek in order to obtain the unadulterated Aristotle.

Aristotle, as Bertrand Russell has pertinently remarked, should be regarded as one of the chiefest misfortunes of the human race. He was a great man, one of the greatest that ever lived. He it was who first attempted an orderly synthesis of all knowledge; and his practical, sensible reasoning and philosophy were immeasurably superior to the misty idealism of his great rival, Plato. His system of ethics was eminently Greek in its sanity; his observation of natural phenomena was catholic and indefatigable.

Yet his influence was pernicious; he did more than any other man in the history of the world to retard the progress of civilization. His authority stayed the progress of all independent thought, all original research. There was submitted to the newly awakened intellect of Europe a complete, formalized system of logic, philosophy, ethics, and science, omitting no form of knowledge, hallowed by an immortal name, dogmatic on every point. Is it any wonder that the Middle Ages, accustomed for long generations to bow in superstitious reverence before the very name of authority, should have transferred part of their allegiance to Aristotle? This pagan philosopher, this infidel with his anti-Christian doctrines of the eternity of matter, the unity of the "active" intellect, and the denial of personal immortality, became at one bound a veritable Pope, whose theses it was heretical to dispute.

"To show that Aristotle was on your side practically amounted to winning the game."

All the energies that had gone to make the renaissance of learning of the eleventh and twelfth centuries were devoted to the task of endlessly studying, expounding, interpreting, debating, and twisting what one man had once said, and what countless commentators believed he had said. Men no longer had time for literature, or the acquisition of culture, or the direct observation of the natural world; had not Aristotle observed it once and for all?

This irruption into Western Europe of the works of Aristotle, together with the countless Arab and Jewish commentaries, evoked, by its impact with the old Augustinian and Platonic doctrines, a conglomeration of diverse influences and eddying currents of thought such as almost defies analysis. There was the traditional Augustinian and Platonic doctrine of divine illumination by intuitive knowledge; there was the practical Aristotelian empiricism; there were the sceptical and agnostic Moors, Averrhoës and Avicenna, with their theses that no science could prove the existence of its own object; and there was the Jew Maimonides, with his commingling of ancient Hebraic thought and the newer Greek influences.

It was inevitable that these dissimilar elements would sooner or later engender a mortal conflict, and it was in Paris, the intellectual catalyst of Europe, that the explosion took place. The young students hastened through a few rules of grammar, learnt as much Latin as was necessary to make themselves understood, picked up the harsh, hair-splitting, technical jargon of the schools, and plunged into the smoke and dust of the arena.

Hearken once more to that old groaner, Stephen of Tournai:

"Beardless youths sit in the chairs of the old professors, and they who are scarcely pupils are anxious to be called masters. . . . Neglecting the rules of the arts, and discarding the books of good authority, with their sophistications they catch the flies of senseless verbiage as in the webs of spiders."

It must not be imagined that the Church was placidly looking on while this mixture was seething and boiling. There was too much intellectual dynamite involved. Generations earlier, it had been the Scholastic Dialectic of Abélard that had come to trouble her peace, and that menace had been met by ingenious absorption and adoption of the alien technique, until now it strengthened the very fabric of what it had seemed to tear down. Now there appeared a greater, more formidable enemy, a veritable new god. He came preaching strange un-Christian doctrines, accompanied by infidels, agnostics, and heretics.

There were some bolder spirits among the Schoolmen, restive under the formalized thinking prescribed for them by the Church, who seized upon these heretical elements. As a result there was an outburst of speculation and free thought that shocked and alarmed the Church.

The authorities acted with promptitude. Various heresies, innocent enough to modern ears, were anathematized; their adherents were excommunicated and compelled to retract, their works were condemned to the flames, and their bodies as well. The Church was on the warpath, and fire and flame appeared to the mediaeval theologian an effective means of proving one's opponent wrong. The Inquisition was born, that dread engine of repression. Paris echoed with the cries of the schools and the crackling of *autos-da-fé*.

The Provincial Council in 1210 forbade the teaching of the new Aristotle in Paris on pain of excommunication. Five years later the study of the *Organon* was permitted, but the *Metaphysics* was still forbidden. Anything of Averrhoës, the infidel, was of course damnably tainted. Yet the heretical doctrines circulated surreptitiously. Amalric of Chartres continued to teach the reprehensible Averrhoës in what he thought was a perfect disguise, and was burnt for it. Siger of Brabant did the same with greater subtlety, and barely escaped with his life.

In 1215, the Statutes drawn up for the Masters of Paris by the Papal Legate, Robert de Courçon, forbade the reading of the physical and metaphysical works of Aristotle, and an oath that he would not read the works of certain heretics was imposed on the candidate in Arts!

The Pope, while granting the University additional privileges, found time to repeat the old prohibitions.

"These books of natural philosophy . . ." he says, "shall not be used in Paris until they have been examined and purged of every suggestion of error. The masters and students of theology should strive to occupy themselves in a laudable manner in the field which they profess, and should not try to be philosophers, but should rather seek to become learned about God."

This afforded the necessary loophole, as was intended. For the Church, seeing by this time that Aristotle could not be suppressed, adroitly tried to disarm him and all concomitant heresies. It was the old trick that had proved its effectiveness time and time again. In early pagan days, the new religion readily absorbed certain pagan practices and rites, so that the change-over to Christianity should not be too violent. When Abélard's method seemed dangerous, it was twisted into a bulwark of defence. So, too, with Aristotle. The fight for the appointment of Dominicans and Franciscans as Professors of Theology in Paris was part and parcel of the scheme. These orthodox fanatics could be trusted to crush the rising rationalism. They did more even than the Church had dreamed.

Availing themselves of the implied permission of the Bull, they laboured to reconcile Aristotle and the Christian dogma. By so doing they could crush once and for all the new movement that had its inception in the works of the Greek philosopher, while his enormous prestige among all men of learning would serve to strengthen the pillars of the Church.

This tremendous intellectual achievement was the work of

two Dominican Friars, Albertus Magnus (1193-1280) and St. Thomas Aquinas (1225-1274).

By the middle of the thirteenth century the Mendicant Friars had acquired a preponderant influence over the course of scholastic philosophy. In Paris it was the Dominicans who exercised control; at Oxford the Franciscans. Not that there was not considerable opposition to such new-fangled ideas among the fundamentalists of both Orders. Learning is of the Devil, they cried; let us pray to God and abjure the pride of intellect. Even among the Dominicans a special dispensation was required for study; but the brilliant success achieved by Albert and Thomas awakened the two Orders to the potency of the weapon which was placed in their hands. Thereafter they were only too willing to encourage learned theologians (of the right shade of orthodoxy) within their ranks.

Albertus Magnus, Albert the Great, was a Saxon, who had travelled much and observed more. In an age when no one thought of observing a natural phenomenon, but rather read Aristotle to see what he had to say about it, Albert was famous for his scientific achievements. He was a unique figure in the thirteenth century; he observed innumerable phenomena and collected a vast storehouse of materials; he studied the orbit of a comet and the nature of metals; he delved deep into alchemy, and opened new paths for others to explore. Even Roger Bacon, who disliked him intensely, attested to his scientific knowledge. He was familiar with geography, astronomy, mineralogy, alchemy, zoology, and botany—an impressive array; he helped to create the new and startling discipline of the experimental method; he proclaimed the merits of experiment and induction.

But it was not as a natural scientist that the Dominicans, whose Order he joined early, cherished him. There is no doubt that they looked askance at these perilous divagations, as did the Franciscans later at those of Roger Bacon. But they forgave these peculiarities with a shrug, because of the immense service which Albert had rendered the cause of orthodoxy in general and the Dominicans in particular by his happy idea of reconciling Aristotle and the Church dogmas, in obedience to the hint contained in the Papal Bull. His aim was to make Aristotle, the Greek, "intelligible to the Latins." Accordingly he paraphrased the whole of Aristotle's treatises into the peculiar scholastic jargon which was intelligible to the schools; subjecting them to a doctrinal purification so as to render them harmless to budding intellects, and correcting his author wherever he deemed it necessary in the interests of the Church and of Scholasticism.

It was Thomas Aquinas, however, afterwards to be sainted for his services, who performed the impossible. This Italian, who had received his early education at Monte Cassino and the University of Naples, became a Dominican in Italy, and promptly went to Paris to attend the lectures of Albert the Great, then at the height of his fame. He followed him to Cologne, whence he was recalled to Paris by the Order to assume one of the two Dominican Chairs at the University.

In Thomas, scholastic philosophy reached its pinnacle. Not even Abélard exercised anything like the influence of Thomas Aquinas; the whole of the ensuing Middle Ages took its tone and colour from his intellect; the foundations which he laid are to this day the basis of Catholic dogma; and the latest of the twentieth-century encyclicals of the Church, openly or by implication, adhere to the Thomist doctrines.

He took the *bête noire*, Aristotle, on the one hand, and the body of Christian theology, on the other, examining them by the methods of logic and syllogistic reasoning with such consummate subtlety and intellectual grasp of essentials that the conflicting authorities emerged fused into unity, the irreconcilables reconciled. It was a complete Catholic system in which Aristotle and the holy Fathers found themselves amalgamated. Henceforth they were both deities to whom it was necessary to bow down and worship, and the combination to the mediaeval mind was irresistible.

He drew the line carefully between those dogmas which come from immediate experience, and which are therefore subject to the processes of reason, and those revealed mysteries of the Christian faith which, being divine in origin, could not be questioned, yet on which reason could be employed to examine the credentials of the authorities who had proclaimed the revelations. A nice distinction, and a deft one. Reason, he argued, could not possibly destroy faith; it must of necessity strengthen that essential quality in man. Revelation, the divine source, was to be accepted on the proven authorities of the Scriptures and the Church Fathers; Aristotle was to be considered the chief authority for "natural" truth or reason. These two categories of truth cannot be incompatible since they both originate ultimately in God's truth. When he had finished, Aristotle was a true Christian, and a member of the Catholic Church to boot!

It was a marvellous achievement, and after the first rubbing of eyes and the mutterings of certain envious individuals, some from within his own Order, but mostly in the ranks of the great Franciscan rival, it came to be generally accepted. Catholicism was fixed for all future time. More than that, the Scholastic philosophy, which had still been somewhat suspect, came into grace, and lost heavily thereby. One might even date the decline of Scholasticism as an intellectual force from the too ready acceptance of the Thomist philosophy. Reason was to be for ever debarred from questioning the revealed truths, as it had once been employed by Berenger and Roscelin, and Aristotle was the father of all other forms of truth. The limits were too narrow, and philosophy frittered itself away in timid subtleties.

It must not be supposed, however, that Thomas was accepted without a struggle. The Franciscans, who had heretofore been at peace with their more orthodox and aggressive

H

brethren, the Dominicans, opposed the new doctrines. The Dominicans pressed Thomas to their collective bosoms, and insinuated that their brothers in Christ were animated by the meanest form of jealousy. After all, what could one expect of ignorant preachers who adopted the methods of blaring Salvationists? Thereupon the war was joined with a vengeance, to the glee of those seculars who had no use for either Order, and sarcastically compared them to Jacob and Esau quarrelling in the very womb of their mother.

It was this external conflict that brought the Dominican dissenters into line, on the familiar principle of Order-patriotism, with the result that in 1278 the Thomist doctrine was adopted *in toto* by official decree. The Franciscans, however, had sufficient influence in Paris to include a condemnation of certain Thomist doctrines in a maze of Averrhoist errors. But they were opposing an irresistible tide; by the end of the century Thomism was everywhere triumphant except at Oxford, where the Franciscans were dominant.

Averrhoism, the doctrine of a single intelligent soul for all humanity, which, as a consequence, negated personal immortality, and included moral determinism, was disposed of at the same time. It had flourished greatly in Paris for a while, though repeatedly condemned. There is no question that these doctrines were anti-Christian, yet their proponents took a leaf out of the book of the regular theologians. In the face of all evidence, they loudly asserted their orthodoxy, and proved it by the most ingenious argument that had ever originated in the fertile mind of man. "That which is true in philosophy," they said, "may be false in theology, and vice versa." A most convenient doctrine, that might lead to surprising results if applied in other fields; but the Church was not impressed. It proceeded vigorously to efface all outward evidences of the pernicious heresy, and in so doing it managed to suppress the last vestiges of independent thinking.

What is most surprising in this whole hullabaloo about the

forbidden books of Aristotle, until he was washed clean and
made into a Christian gentleman, is that the prohibition
applied only to Paris. It sounds a little as though the Popes
had felt that the scholars of Paris were intellectually too delicate to withstand such strong meat, but that in other Universities they were of more robust constitution. John of Garland,
in inviting students to the newly formed University of
Toulouse, expressly founded by the Pope to extirpate heresy,
stressed the point that there the fortunate students could hear
openly the forbidden works of Aristotle.

What this really meant, of course, was that to the Church,
Paris was the centre and only fount of Theology. Pollute the
source, and the contagion would spread over all Europe;
whereas to non-theological students in institutions on the
periphery of learning the heresies would be incidental and
immaterial. The same tender solicitude for Paris, and Paris
only, as a centre of Theology, is seen in the banning there of
the study of Civil Law, on the ground that it would tempt
the Theologians away from their proper tasks.

CHAPTER XI

Paris and the Great Schism

IN the first century of the University's existence it was the Pope, and the Pope alone, who claimed to have any authority over that proud and turbulent institution; and as we have seen, that authority was suffered only because it was almost uniformly favourable. But in the controversy with the Mendicant Friars the Doctors of the University realized with a shock that the Papacy had adopted a new favourite. The old loyalties, the old gratitudes, died a sudden death, and thereafter the University was to give many and notable proofs of its bellicosity and rancour.

Philip IV of France, during a long-drawn-out war with England, found his treasury exhausted, and the usual sources of revenue were insufficient to enable him to carry on. Not unnaturally, he cast a speculative eye upon the vast untapped riches of the Church. Now it was an unvarying rule, laid down by the Church itself, that ecclesiasts and ecclesiastical property were wholly immune from secular taxation. Yet Philip decided to risk the plunge. He demanded an extraordinary subsidy from the French clergy for the provision of further sinews of war. To his surprise, most of them complied without hesitation. This may have been due to patriotic motives; it may have been due to something else. But the Cistercian monks, having technically withdrawn from the world, had no patriotism; and never having worked for their riches, were all the more strongly attached thereto. They, therefore, promptly appealed to Rome against such sacrilege.

Boniface VIII took up the gage of battle, and in 1296 issued his Bull, *Clericis laicos*, which forbade all princes and rulers of the earth to tax his beloved clergy in any wise on pain of excommunication and interdict. Philip retorted by forbidding foreigners to enter France (which kept out the

Papal legates and the Papal fiscal agents), and forbade the export of money or jewels or precious metal (thereby cutting off the very substantial revenue that had flowed regularly to the Papal coffers from the kingdom of France). This was a manœuvre well calculated to anger the pontiff mightily.

He summoned the French bishops to council in Rome, in order to compel the King to yield. Philip countered by summoning the States-General. He was by way of being frightened at his own audacity, and wished to sound public opinion, to see how far the country would back him. The States-General rendered its opinion through the nobles in ringing terms: "Neither we, nor the Universities, nor the people of the realm of France, recognize or require any other authority in this issue save that of the King of France, our ruler."

Note that the University delegates, a powerful unit in the convention, concurred. The Papal chickens were coming home to roost!

In the same year, 1302, the Council of Bishops convened at Rome. Only a few French bishops dared to brave the King's wrath and attend. But the rump council, under the thumb of the Pope, proceeded with its dirty work. The famous or infamous Bull, *Unam Sanctam*, was broadcast to an astounded Europe. "We declare, assert, and affirm," it ran, "that submission on the part of everyone to the bishop of Rome is altogether necessary for salvation."

There is no doubt that Boniface had delusions of grandeur in asserting such a preposterous claim. Innocent III, a far greater and ambitious Pope, no matter what he may have secretly felt, knew better than to issue such a pronouncement. The arrogance of the Papal pretensions left Europe breathless; it caused thoughtful men everywhere to examine a little more closely the Papal claims to *any* pre-eminence whatsoever.

The King, seemingly unimpressed, seized the offending bishops' property; whereupon he was excommunicated. The Universities, as clerical bodies, should have severed all relations, temporal and spiritual, with the outlawed King.

They did nothing of the kind. On the contrary, William de Nogaret, Professor of Law in the University of Toulouse, the Pope's own pet institution, in an assembly of the nobles, submitted a thesis to the King in which he accused Boniface of heresy, simony, immorality, and other horrendous crimes, claimed that his election had been tainted with illegality, and petitioned that the States-General be again summoned as a preliminary to a Council of the Church of France for the express purpose of deposing the Pope. The King fell in with the idea—it may have been his in the first place—and the States-General convened. The University deputies ranged solidly behind the King. They were patriots now, royalists. A long list of indictments was read against the Pope and passed with hardly a dissenting voice. The King sent them broadcast to every body of influence in the country, which necessarily included all the Universities.

Boniface retorted by depriving the ingrate Universities of their right to confer degrees or to have professors appointed; and with a spacious gesture, he deposed the King of France. Unfortunately, while he was thus disposing of the fortunes of a foreign power, he found that he had little or no power in his local Rome. Nogaret and Colonna arrested the Pope; the people of Anagni set him free; Orsini confined him in the Vatican; and there he died.

His successor lasted for eight months only; then he, too, conveniently died. Clement V, who had been Archbishop of Bordeaux, fearing for his life and preferring safer quarters, moved the Holy See bag and baggage to Avignon, where for the next sixty-nine years it remained. It was the beginning of the so-called Babylonian captivity. Avignon, technically an imperial fief held by the King of Sicily, was within French territory, and the succeeding Popes were Frenchmen, and under the King's thumb. France had triumphed, and the University of Paris had had its revenge.

Rome mourned its departed glory, and the rest of Europe looked askance at the French domination, but no chance offered to do anything about it until 1378. An Avignon Pope, while on a visit to Rome, had the misfortune to die there. His retinue of Cardinals, who were mainly Italians, were promptly seized by the Roman populace, and forced to elect an Italian Pope then and there. But Urban VI, unable to perceive on which side his bread was buttered, quarrelled with his electors. Whereupon the Cardinals, safely back on French soil, declared him no Pope by reason of the intimidation brought to bear, and proceeded to elect a Frenchman, Clement VII.

There were two Popes now, each declaring himself to be the only true and anointed successor to St. Peter. One resided in Rome and the other in Avignon. All the smouldering feuds of Europe were fanned into a roaring blaze. England, North Italy, Germany, Hungary, and Poland plumped for the Roman Pope; France, Spain, Sicily, and Naples for the Frenchman. The spiritual issues were wholly occluded by more practical considerations. It was the old political line-up with a new pretext. Each Pope fulminated against the other and ex-communicated him. The Church split in twain; passions ran high, accusations and counter-accusations filled the air; all the dirty linen of the Catholic Church was washed in the most public manner. Respect for the Papacy neared the vanishing point. Heresies multiplied in such a congenial atmosphere. The Lollards and Hussites started their sweeping movements. The Reformation was in the offing.

The University of Paris was by this time at the very zenith of its power and prestige. Its lightest opinion was heard with respect in the courts and camps of Europe. John Gerson, one of its most brilliant and able students, was Rector in 1398. Thoughtful men saw only ruin ahead unless the disgraceful Schism was composed, and at once. The University saw it more clearly than any. At first it was inclined to favour the Roman claimant, but John Rousse, who presented a petition from the University to the Court for the calling of a General

Council, was jailed, and freed only on recantation; the King would countenance no weighing of merits just then; it might have proved fatal to the pretensions of the Avignon Pope. The Rector of the University was threatened with a like fate, and both Rousse and he fled for safety to the Court of Urban VI. The King then ordered the University to declare for Clement, and with all the pressure he could bring to bear, he achieved his purpose only by a bare majority. The Nations of Picardy and England steadfastly dissented.

But this declaration did not end the agitation. The University continued to demand a peaceable solution of the Schism. It took the written opinions of all its members, and found that they boiled down to three ways of ending the Great Schism : (1) the concerted abdication of both Popes; (2) arbitration; (3) a General Council of the Church.

The University embodied these three suggestions in a letter, which it sent to every prince and king, every bishop and archbishop, every influential body in Europe. It threatened to declare the Pope who refused to abide by any of the proposed methods a Schismatic—horrendous word! In 1395, after due deliberation, the University declared itself publicly for the method of simultaneous abdication. This suited the fancy of neither Pope, and the Avignon pretender tried to deprive the University of its benefices; that is, of those ecclesiastical offices and livings under its control. There was no surer way of earning the everlasting enmity of the altruistic Doctors of Paris. King or no king, it was now war to the knife. For twenty years the University worked unweariedly, sending its envoys, like a veritable European power, to all the other powers of Europe. Their emissaries appeared at the courts of kings and princes, before the thrones of the Emperor and the Popes themselves; every Bishop and Archbishop and Cardinal was visited. The recommendation of the University was invariable, and everywhere it was heard with the profoundest respect. Compel both Popes to abdicate and call a General Council of the Church in the event of refusal.

Finally their efforts proved successful. The Emperor Sigismund, in 1414, summoned a Great Council at Constance to put an end to the Schism. Though no Pope had convened it, it claimed superiority to the Pope, on the ground that it was the supreme ecclesiastical authority. The University unearthed precedents to support its position, going back to the early Councils of the Church in the days of the Fathers.

From the very outset the University dominated the proceedings. Gerson, its Rector, wielded the power of a potentate. Never again was the University to exercise such influence. The very organization of the Council followed the University pattern. It was divided into four "Nations," in accordance with the arbitrary structure of the University of Paris: France, England, Germany, and Italy. Each "Nation" deliberated on its own and cast its vote as a unit. Just as the "Nations" of Paris, by this means, avoided the overwhelming preponderance of Frenchmen in the University, so did the Council avoid control by the numerical majority of Italian ecclesiasts.

Gerson's great influence, backed as it was by the power of the University, was unfortunately on the side of intolerance and conservatism. What might not have happened had a radical, or even a liberal, been in the saddle? Alas, the University of Paris, swollen with benefices and authority, was no longer the home of intellectual curiosity. The suppression of the Averrhoist heresy, the adoption of Thomism, had led to a self-satisfied acquiescence in things as they were.

This was the one opportunity of forestalling the Reformation, and it was not taken. The programme of the Council was threefold: to extirpate heresy; to end the Schism; to reform the crying evils of the Church. The first two objects were attended to with alacrity; the last, and most important, was forgotten.

Following the suggestion of the University, both Popes were deposed, and Martin V elevated to the Papal throne, which was promptly returned to Rome. Europe, including Paris by this time, wanted no more of French domination.

Then, in their capacity of smellers-out of heresy, the Council proceeded to an act which has made its name for ever infamous. John Hus, leader of the notable reform movement in Bohemia, was called to appear before the Council and expound his views. Relying upon the safe-conduct of the Emperor Sigismund, he came alone, and was promptly seized, tried for heresy, condemned, and burnt at the stake. This was not the first time a safe-conduct had been used for similar nefarious ends.

Prior to the middle of the fourteenth century, the University of Paris had meddled very little in local French politics. For one thing, it was concerned mainly with philosophical and theological questions, which inevitably centred its interest in the affairs of the Church and the Papacy. For another, its constituent masters and students were a great international corporation, citizens of the world. They came from every nook and cranny of Europe, and it is a remarkable fact that hardly a single Scholastic of the first rank, hardly a single great teacher in their midst, was a Frenchman. Abélard was a Breton, John of Salisbury an Englishman, Peter (he of the *Sentences*) was a Lombard, Albert the Great a German, and Thomas Aquinas an Italian.

Here, in the very midst of a city that had no privileges of its own, under the eye of autocracy, rose a veritable republic of letters. Its citizens were clerics in name, and as such, immune from civil process; educated men, in fact, whose presence brought glory to France. The King protected these foreigners, even when at war with the princes to whom they owed allegiance; and they, very sensibly, attended to their own proper business, and kept out of politics, which did not concern them. But as the privileges and the prestige of the University increased, it lost the first fine careless rapture of learning; priests and ambitious youths poured into Paris who sought this easy path to high ecclesiastical office; the Doctors waxed fat and wealthy with accrued benefices; and the blaze of intellectual life died down.

"The eldest daughter of the king" the University came to

be called, and like all daughters, she evinced an irresistible desire to stick her nose into the family business. The University demanded and obtained representation at all ceremonials, in the Councils of the National Church, in the assemblies of the Notables, in the States-General. It plunged into politics. The learned Doctors spent more time in settling the affairs of the State than in attending to the lectures which they were supposed to deliver to their pupils; the real business of the University, to wit, the transmission of knowledge, devolved more and more on the Bachelors, mere apprentices.

About 1357 the University became involved in the uprising of the burghers of Paris, led by Étienne Marcel. Twice it intervened to mediate between the temporarily successful Parisians and the Court party. Needless to say, it favoured the Court.

The University again entered the political arena in the long struggle between the Burgundians and the Armagnacs. Though in sympathy with the Burgundians, its good offices were on the side of mediation and peace for a war-racked country. It sharply admonished the Duke of Orléans to effect an immediate reconciliation with the Duke of Burgundy and reform the prostrate realm. Orléans, then in control, angrily retorted: "As you do not consult knights in questions of religion, so you ought not to meddle in questions of war; therefore return to your books and attend to your own affairs, for though the University is called the daughter of the king, she should not interfere with the government of the kingdom."

In spite of this rebuff, the University continued to labour in the cause of peace, and even won the thanks of the Duke of Guienne for its efforts. It also advocated reforms in the King's government, drafted lists of evils therein, and gave advice on the method of government. It took a prominent part in the procuring of the Cabochian Ordinance, the Magna Carta of mediaeval France.

It intervened also in the foreign policy of France. When Rouen was besieged by the English, the beleaguered citizens implored the University to intercede with the French King to send them aid, and the Parisian Doctors patriotically did so. But somehow, as the war progressed, and matters began to look black for France, the University executed a *volte-face*, and lo and behold, this French institution became violently pro-English. Charles VII of France was a fugitive, and English and Burgundian troops were victorious; the French masters and students were in hiding or discreetly silent. That is why in 1422 the University actually gave thanks because Henry of England captured Melun from Charles, and celebrated with solemn procession each further victory of the English arms. It must have been a strange and ignoble sight to the darkly muttering citizens of Paris, cowed though they were by the Burgundians.

By 1430 the English were in full control. Those patriotic Masters of Paris who had held out against the invader were in prison or had fled the country. Only the sycophants, the boot-lickers, had remained behind and, of course, those foreign Masters who were neutral amidst the clamour of war, or, like the English, patriotically in favour of their own country. We must realize this state of affairs before condemning too harshly what has been considered the most damnable and most infamous proceeding in the history of the University. In 1431, at the command of the English and Burgundians, backed up by threats and a show of armed force, the Sorbonnical Doctors, the Doctors of Theology, solemnly proclaimed Joan of Arc a damnable heretic and sorceress, thereby lending colour to the tragedy which was being enacted in Rouen.

There were other elements involved in this hideous act. In the first place a good proportion of the French people themselves sincerely believed Joan, their saviour, to be possessed of more than earthly powers; and who should say whether they came from heaven or from hell? The King whom she had crowned stood weakly by and refused to lift a finger in her behalf. The clergy of France resented her miraculous claims as they resented her emotional appeal to mass psychology; it cut the ground from under their feet. The theological Doctors, aloof in their cold intellectual rigidity, for whom every element of the Christian faith was neatly labelled and given its proper place in the scheme of things, naturally felt that this untutored maid, with her wild claims of heavenly voices, was a charlatan, or at least a person of disordered mind. And so the tragedy ended; and Joan, the Maid of Orléans, died in the roaring flames, reviled by the very people she had sought to save.

When the University swung away from the Papacy, it naturally looked more and more to the protection of the King. During the fourteenth century Parlement tried weakly to gain a certain measure of control over the University, but without success. The University, watchful of its privileges, claiming to be the "eldest daughter of the king," demanded the right to be heard only by the King himself. No taxes could be levied on the masters or students, or even on the tradesmen and servants connected with the University, and in the days when war had scraped the treasury bare, and the common people were staggering under intolerable burdens, many a fiscal officer cast longing eyes at this untouched source of revenue.

Finally Charles VII, in 1445, tiring of the University's constant appeals to privilege, and remembering with bitterness the ignoble part which it had played during the English occupation, decreed flatly that Parlement was to have jurisdiction in the suits of the University, and that no private appeals lay to the King. This was a terrible blow to the litigious and quarrelsome University, and marked the beginning of the end.

Yet the University, unabashed, continued to pursue its quarrels. Learning was a thing of the past; animosities and disputes were the breath of life to the Masters of Paris. On the slightest provocation a Cessation was declared. The lecture-halls were emptied; the pupils rioted in the streets; every preacher who was a graduate of the University, and there were few who were not, discontinued his sermons. Paris was filled with silent pulpits, and the Parisians were left without spiritual guidance until the University graciously deigned to resume its activities. And woe to the individual who aroused its ire, be he bishop, judge, court official or government officer, if he were a University man. The terrible "privatio" was exercised against him. He was an outlaw, an excommunicate; no University man held social, professional, or business intercourse with him; he was a perjurer, "an arid, rotten, and infamous member," and placards were posted in all the prominent public places of the city informing the world that he was such; indeed, the penalty was invoked against his children, even to the fourth generation. No wonder the highest heads in France bowed before its wrath.

But the end was in sight. Whom the gods wish to destroy, they first make mad. The Masters became more and more quarrelsome as time went on; privations and cessations were invoked for any fancied insult. The preservation of the ancient privileges of the University became a mania with the degenerate descendants of the once mighty scholastics. Learning dwindled; irritability and rancour increased. Every move by the civil or ecclesiastical authorities was an infringement to be resented.

In 1459, for example, the *Générales des Aides*, a Commission appointed by the King to collect a special war tax, while recognizing the University exemption from this as well as all other taxes, nevertheless asserted the right to judge of the *bona fides* of any claim by an individual that he was actually connected with the University. The Masters rose in their wrath and excommunicated all members of the Commission who happened to be University men. Easter Day was at hand, and these dignified, highly placed members of the Commission were compelled to leave the churches before the priests, also University men, would proceed with the Mass. A Royal Ordinance forbidding the "privation" meant less than nothing to the indignant University. The *Générales* was upheld in its contention, but to soothe the injured feelings of the University, the President of the *Générales* was given a special and high-sounding title, "Conservator of the Exemption of the University from the *Aides*," and he was compelled to take an oath to respect the privileges of the University.

When Louis XI, the spider autocrat, ascended the throne, he surveyed the situation with his beady, crafty eyes. The University constituted a menace to his absolutistic visions, and he set methodically about the task of draining the life-blood from its tremendous privileges. In 1467, on the pretext that the University was conspiring with his enemies, he sternly forbade any further meddling in politics, "even in letters to their relations." In 1474 he meddled with the most sacred right of the humbled University—the Rectorial election. Thereafter, he decreed, the Rector must be a subject of France. The University, with a flicker of its old defiance, promptly elected an alien Rector. The King struck back with lightning-like rapidity. He forced the Rector's resignation and suspended all University privileges until another election, by a tamed and cowed body of Masters, satisfied him of their obedience to his decree.

The last blow to the University, and it fell with crushing finality, was struck in the reign of Louis XII. He had promulgated an edict restricting University privileges and exemptions, notably those relating to taxation, to *bona-fide* students and Regent, or actual Teaching, Masters of the University. Serious abuses had arisen. The tradesmen who catered to University needs, and the very servants, claimed inclusion in the exemptions. So, too, did every graduate, teacher or no; in other words, the great majority of lawyers, doctors, government officials, and the higher clergy of France. The body of exempt citizens was enormous, and growing larger every year.

The University in 1499 ordered a Cessation. Parlement cited the University officers to appear before it. They refused. Thereupon Parlement ordered the withdrawal of the Cessation. The University sent a delegation to the King. They found him in a towering rage. The scholars of Paris had placarded the walls with seditious posters; he had been personally denounced from the pulpit by University Doctors. The delegation quailed before the royal anger, and returned to advise immediate surrender, if worse were not to befall. The Cessation was revoked, never more to be used. The University had lost its sharpest and most ancient weapon; the days of its glory were over. Mediaevalism had fled before the rising sun of nationalism. Paris had dwindled from a self-contained, self-governing republic of international scope to a mere local University, subject to King and Parlement.

See Nations P.78

CHAPTER XII

The Arts Course of Paris

THE University of Paris, as we have already noted, was divided into four Faculties: Arts, Medicine, Canon Law, and Theology. Arts was the lower, the preliminary Faculty; it constituted a pre-requisite to study in the superior or graduate Faculties. These, it will be seen, were strictly professional in character. Civil Law, the only other mediaeval Faculty, was not represented at Paris, for reasons which the Papacy had deemed good and sufficient, but at other Universities it was often the preponderating school.

Each Faculty consisted of the Teaching or Regent Masters as a body, and represented the purest type of democracy. The Congregation of the Masters of a Faculty, each with his equal voice and equal vote, was the sole sovereign and court of last appeal. There was no outside Board of Trustees, no group of wealthy benefactors, no rough-riding President, to interfere with the internal affairs of a Faculty, or with the University as a whole. Even the King or the Pope hesitated to intrude. The superior Faculties had their Deans, of course, but they were purely administrative officers, carrying out the will of the Masters.

By a curious evolutionary process, the Arts Faculty was almost immediately divided into four "Nations," and by an even more curious process, the Nations came to be regarded almost as independent Faculties of the University. Result— in the General Congregation of the entire University, where each Faculty voted as a unit, and unanimous decisions were the early rule, three of the four Nations of the lowly Arts Faculty could veto the expressed will of the superior graduate Faculties. The Rector, the youth of twenty-two or three, originally the representative of the Nations alone, came to represent the whole majesty of the University. It was only

I

the short tenure of his showy office, ranging from one to three months, that kept him from seizing almost autocratic power. As it was, he called the General Congregation of the University, announced the votes of the Faculties, administered the affairs, and executed the will of the University. He had his Court too, where he heard disputes about the rentals charged the scholars by the townsfolk, a perennial sore spot; took cognizance of complaints against overcharging or cheating tradesmen under the University jurisdiction; tried claims between scholars and Masters; heard complaints by injured students, or concerning scholars in jail, and took measures to avenge the insult and procure satisfaction; punished offences against the University Statutes, and administered the estates of deceased students. In short, he was a combination of judge, surrogate, executive officer, and avenging angel. From his decisions an appeal rested by the aggrieved party to the Congregation of the University.

The meetings of the University were rather turbulent affairs. In matters involving the interest of the Masters, parliamentary procedure went by the board. Shouts, hissings, and brandished fists were by no means uncommon means of making a point. Blows were exchanged freely, and on more than one occasion a Congregation ended in the drawing of forbidden weapons and the letting of blood. A Faculty or Nation, though internally divided, would nevertheless make common cause against all others.

In later days, when majority voting became the rule, many and ingenious were the methods employed by a Faculty or a Nation that had been outvoted and felt strongly about it. For example, the great seal of the University, essential for the official promulgation of its acts, was kept in a chest. Such was the brotherly affection and trust between the several groups that there were seven locks to this chest, and each of the Superior Faculties and the four Nations held a key to one of the locks. The Dean of the Faculty or Proctor of the Nation whose sensibilities had been lacerated would appear at the

General Congregation, and announce with simulated regret that he had misplaced the key, and would even intimate that it could not be found unless by some miracle the Congregation voted as his Faculty or Nation desired. This was a serious matter. Without the seal, a document was just so much paper; to break open the chest would mean faction fights, and at all events the ruin of a valuable piece of furniture. Besides, such physical methods gave the dissenter an excuse to appeal to Rome against the outrage, and while the appeal was rarely successful, it meant long and expensive delays. Somehow a compromise was usually reached; the methods of Tammany proving as effective then as they are in our own times.

The University proper had no buildings, no endowments. It was an intangible affair, a thing of the spirit, and therefore infinitely powerful. Wherever the Masters were, and the pupils gathered around to listen, there was the University. If the Masters and pupils packed their knapsacks and moved to another town, the University went with them. It was this foot-loose freedom that made effective the "cessation," or "strike," of an insulted University. From this ability to wander derived all the privileges and powers of Paris, Oxford, and Bologna. When, in the later Middle Ages, pious founders gave college buildings, and tied down the errant scholars, this meant the end of a period of rising power. The secular authorities had something by which they could enforce their will; buildings and endowments could be seized; scholars supported in the colleges on founders' bounties were unable to carry their perquisites elsewhere.

At first the Masters of Paris clustered around the Cathedral of Notre Dame, using their own homes or rented houses for schoolrooms. Then, as the fight waxed hot with the Chancellor of the Cathedral, the Masters began to drift from the right bank over to the left, where the Abbey of Ste. Geneviève was located, in order to escape his jurisdiction. As they went they rented the houses on the curious wooden bridge, the Petit-Pont. "The Petit-Pont," wrote Guy de Bazoches, a Latin poet of the twelfth century, "belongs to the dialecticians, who walk there deep in argument," and who, no doubt, when at loss for an answer, stared down through the chinks at the smooth-flowing Seine.

As time went on the Left Bank, the Latin Quarter, became the permanent home of the University. One street in particular was dedicated to the Arts Faculty and its constituent Nations—Rue du Fouarre, or "Straw Street." In this single, narrow street, overhung by dilapidated, crowded wooden houses, dirty, unpaved, roaring with student life, echoing with the cries of vendors, a bottomless quagmire in rains, thick with dust in dry weather, was the very heart and soul of the University. Here the Nations ultimately rented houses for their Masters from the bourgeoisie; here the rooms were crowded with students, sitting cross-legged on the damp, straw-strewn floors (benches were frowned upon as unmanly), hearkening to the drone of the Master lecturing from the only chair, hearing perchance the buzz of other classes through the walls; and here originated the riots and the calls to arms that spread like wildfire through the city of Paris.

The University revenues were intermittent and precarious. As with the Nations, its chief income came from the fees exacted from candidates for degrees, and from forced exactions from those of its members whom it had honoured with office. Then, as now, it cost money to be a politician; the only difference was that the payment was made publicly. As for the Rector, he had perforce to be a young man of great possessions. He paid heavily for the privilege, and the University insisted that he should maintain the magnificence of his office in proper state; at his own expense, of course. In Bologna the cost was so great that even the wealthy hesitated to incur it, and it was made a penal offence for the honoured victim to refuse the office forced upon him by his admiring comrades. The importance of the fees collected may explain the extreme brevity of office. The greater the number of Rectors per year, the more money in the Treasury.

Not that any moneys lay very long in the University coffers. These worthy philosophers, lawyers, doctors, and theologians suffered from an incurable thirst. The sight of gold in the chest drove them immediately to the nearest tavern, where food and the inevitable accompaniment of wine rendered the cupboard as bare as ever Mother Hubbard's was, until the next election of officers, or the inception of another batch of candidates for degrees.

The scholars of the University had their own peculiar privileges. As we have seen, they were clerics, and as such they enjoyed all the immunities that any parish priest or bishop might possess. But they had other privileges over and above those of benefit of clergy. They were entitled to two warnings before they could be excommunicated: they could not be fined for offences not relating to property; all civil personal actions were under the jurisdiction of the Rector's Court, while criminal offences were tried by the Bishop; yet even here an accused scholar might be freed from prison pending trial, on taking his oath to reappear.

The Arts Faculty was the fundamental school, and at the same time the most numerous in point of masters and students. Graduation from its ranks was, for the vast majority of scholars, the road to entry into the superior Faculties, though *Start here* it was not absolutely essential.

The young lad of fourteen or fifteen, fresh from the provinces, required very little preliminary training before enrolling under a Master in the Faculty of Arts. The ability to read and write, the alleged ability to speak Latin, as evidenced by a memorized speech addressed to the Rector on matriculation, and behold, the boy was a regularly enrolled University man. He entered upon a course of studies that in the early days of the University lasted for six years. This period was divided into two parts: one of approximately two years, in which the hopeful scholar was a pupil pure and simple, and the second, in which he became a Bachelor, or apprentice teacher. During this latter period, while continuing his studies under a regular Master, he was required also to do some teaching himself; being, in fact, a sort of pupil-teacher, who learnt the practical art by actual experience. The analogy with the trade guild of the time is obvious.

What was it that these youngsters studied so diligently? A strangely limited and, to modern ideas, an arid-seeming curriculum. Paetow has remarked that it is easier to define the mediaeval Arts course by what it did *not* contain. There was little or no science, for example, and experimentation was unthought-of, except by a few fanatics outside the teaching profession. Latin, of course, was taught, but no other language; a man spoke the tongue of his native country; others were acquired, if at all, only through actual residence. The ancient classics had died during the last half of the twelfth century; Greek was a thing of wonderment. As for the whole complex of modern university fare — history, economics, sociology, art, archaeology, government — a blank stare would have greeted the inquirer. The very names of most of these studies were as yet unborn.

There seems, then, to be very little left. The Universities, by their insistence on the all-important matter of Logic, tended to obscure most of the other subjects of the Seven Arts, which had at least been paid lip service in the preceding era. Grammar, which had been the most important, was contemptuously relegated to the elementary or grammar schools. If the aspiring student had learnt the rudiments there, and incidentally, something of the classical orators, poets, and historians in the process, well and good; if not, according to the University, there was no great harm done. The Arts course, they thought, was not to be considered as a medium of culture; it was something utilitarian. It was a means of learning the universal Latin and the rules of Logic, so that the student could enter the professional schools and hold his own in argument.

Grammar, what there was of it, was studied chiefly in the texts of Donatus and Priscian; the first a teacher in Rome about A.D. 350, and the second in Constantinople about A.D. 500. The "Barbarismus" of Donatus was elementary, while the two works of Priscian were for advanced students. But this was the "old grammar," badly adapted to the needs of the mediaeval student. Alexander de Villa Dei published his rhymed "Doctrinale" in 1199; and in 1212 Eberhard of Bethune brought forth his "Graecismus," also in verse, for the edification of the age. These proved so popular that the Universities adopted them wholly. It is curious to note how the mediaeval mind ran to doggerel. Grammars, medical advice, sermons, the Bible, chronicles, charters even, all appeared in atrociously bad Latin verses. The idea, supposedly, was to avoid the curse of aridity; and in an age of few books the jingles were an aid to memorization.

Even in learning the parts of speech the fatal Logic made its appearance. One did not clear up a doubtful point in syntax by a perusal of the best Latin authors to determine usage; one *argued* about it in syllogisms. Disputations were actually held in the Universities on moot questions. Imagine the furore in the schools when it was announced that William of Blois and John of England would dispute to the death on the proposition that a certain phrase was pure Latin, or in the alternative, a barbarism. Did they quote Cicero, who had used that very expression, or Tacitus, who had carefully avoided it? By no means! They set forth their universal major, submitted the particular minor, and triumphantly evoked the conclusion, to the accompaniment of a storm of cheers from their partisans.

Naturally, under these conditions, Grammar degenerated into a series of bare rules, unscientifically taught, without a vestige of the literary or human value that had formerly been attached to it. Even to this day the subject is a deviscerated, horrible affair, as a result of this revolution in mediaeval thought.

In 1215 the Statutes of the University of Paris prescribed "the two Priscians or at least one of them"; from 1250 to 1360 even Priscian dropped out of their requirements; he may have been studied, but, if so, only superficially. There was a slight revival in the middle of the fourteenth century; a few choice spirits actually read some classics, but in the next century, the period of final decay of the University, they were again forgotten.

As a result, the Latin language, which had been fairly pure and classical in Abélard and John of Salisbury's time, became unbelievably corrupt and barbarous. The technical lingo of Scholasticism added to the general *débâcle*. Aside from certain Oxford scholars—notably Grossetête, Bacon, John of Garland, Henri D'Andeli, and a few others—no one could write decent or vigorous Latin, or even protested against the neglect of Grammar.

Bacon's voice was raised in season and out. John of Garland, a Parisian Master who taught also at Toulouse, wrote a satire —in verse, of course—entitled "Morale Scolarium." The date was 1241, and its purpose was to inspire in the Logic enthusiasts of the day a retrospective fondness for the ancient Liberal Arts, as well as to convert the students to cleaner morals and purer Latinity. The real students, the real teachers (he complained) were thrust out into the cold; they were paupers. Law and Medicine were the fashion, and the real money-makers, and only those studies were pursued that had a tangible cash value. A lone voice crying in the wilderness, touting the value of forgotten wares. The logicians mocked and carried on.

Rhetoric, too, the study of style, of proper phrasing, was grossly neglected in Paris, though not in Bologna and Orléans. Logic, however, the third member of the Trivium, received overwhelming attention. The whole Organon of Aristotle was absorbed with pious reverence, and the Isagoge of Porphyry. Philosophy was a strange compendium of Logic and the whole of the Quadrivium—to wit, Music, Geometry, Astronomy, and Arithmetic. In this potpourri the Nicomachean Ethics of Aristotle (*toujours* Aristotle), and later his Metaphysics and his works on Natural Philosophy, represented the prescribed programme. There may have been other books for the diligent pupil under an extra-diligent master, such as the Summulae of Petrus Hispanus, the Little Logic of Marsilius, some Euclid, the Almagest of Ptolemy, and other rarities of which we have no present definite knowledge. But the point is that Paris was not interested in the Seven Liberal Arts, except for Logic and its companion, Philosophy. The instruction in them, if any, was extremely sketchy and hurried; the scholars were anxious to get on with their real business, to wit, a sufficient knowledge of disputation to achieve graduation and entry into the professional schools.

After two years of study in the Arts, the student, who must at least be over fourteen, could, if he so desired, become a Bachelor, or apprentice teacher. To achieve this particular dignity in his weary progress toward fame and fortune the student had to "dispute" publicly, or "determine."

The ceremony of "determination," an imitation of the coveted Master's initiation, took place annually during Carnival-tide and Lent. The candidate for Bachelordom, the "determiner," announced a thesis which he was prepared to maintain against all and sundry. Actually, his opponent was a mere student, lower than he, and there are grounds for suspicion that if proper influence were employed, the scholar selected as a stalking-horse, a foil, against whom the aspiring Bachelor could display his coruscating wit and subtlety in argument, would not be among the most brilliant.

In any event, it was a great day. The "determiner" rented a school in the Rue du Fouarre from his old Master, decorated it to suit his taste and pocket-book, and then tried to pack the house. He dragooned all his friends, his comrades in the schools; he wrote respectful notes to all the dignitaries of Paris, requesting the honour of their presence. Let but some bishop appear in the audience, and the delighted candidate would soar into the empyrean, employing every verbal pyrotechnic at his command in order to impress the great man, and perchance, insert the wedge that would open the way to a well-padded benefice in later years. In the case of students of noble birth and influential connections, the hall was crowded; even the King had been known to attend. But the obscure student from a far country, with few friends or connections, had to resort to "papering the house" if he did not wish to dispute before empty benches. His friends, noting the deadly gaps as the hour approached, ran out into the streets and waylaid the passers-by. Many a startled citizen of Paris, intent upon his business, found himself suddenly surrounded by a group of students and invited to enter. Expostulations that business required his presence elsewhere, that his wife was even then in labour, were unavailing. He was pushed, jostled, dragged into the neighbouring hall, there to add by his presence to the illusion of an overflowing, enthusiastic audience.

After the Bachelor had maintained his thesis, and the feeble adversary had been appropriately crushed in the rebuttal, to the accompaniment of stampings and cheerings from his loyal friends, he was given by his Master the round cap indicative of his new degree, and a procession was formed, that led inevitably to the tavern, where wine flowed freely, and the spits rotated merrily before the fire, all at the candidate's expense.

The celebration over, and his pockets well drained, the new Bachelor settled back into the rut of study under his Master. But now he had an additional duty: to instruct the freshmen students in a series of "extraordinary" lectures under his Master's supervision. To display his new dignity, he was sometimes permitted to sit next to the magisterial chair from which the Master delivered his lectures, haughty and aloof from his recent comrades, who were still compelled to sit cross-legged on the damp, straw-strewn floor.

After a further period, ranging from five to six years, though in the later, degenerate period of the University the novitiate was greatly reduced, the Bachelor was ready for his real goal: the entrance into Masterdom, graduation, the Licence to teach. This ceremony resolved itself into two sections: the receipt of the Licence from the Chancellor, and the initiation, or "inception," into the Guild of Masters.

For the Chancellor's Licence there was a formal, public examination, which consisted of another glorified dispute, or "determination." The subject was chosen by the candidate; and the disputation was therefore called the *Quodlibetica*. But this was a bare formality. The real test was in a prior, private examination, held before examiners appointed by the Chancellor from the Faculty of Arts. Almost invariably he was guided in his judgment by their advice.

Robert de Sorbon, eloquent divine of the day, and founder of the famous College of Sorbonne, compared the examination for entry into Heaven with the requirements for the Master's degree. Think you, he demanded of his University audience, it will be as easy to pass the vigilant eye of St. Peter as the lenient eyes of the Chancellor? The analogy is valuable for its information, if not exactly into doings in Paradise, at least for the *modus operandi* of more earthly affairs.

The examination, we are informed, was purely voluntary; the scholar was bound by no fixed term of studies; he might wait as long as he wished, or drift along as a student for ever. Once he made up his mind, however, he ate and drank sparingly, conned his books, and searched out all the authorities on his special topic; attending the lectures only of those professors who dealt with it. He then presented himself for examination. The examiners, and the Chancellor, questioned him on the books he had read, and were not satisfied with mere verbal knowledge; they actually demanded that he should understand the sense of what he repeated. Usually the questions were confined to seven or eight passages in the book, and the candidate was passed if he were correct in three out of four. Only one who attended the schools at least twice a week and heard the "ordinary" lectures was considered a student, and as such, eligible for examination and release from prison on demand of his Master when he fell foul of the law.

But this examination, which sounds so formidable, was not always very conscientious. By proper influence, or even bribery, it was not difficult to ascertain what the several propositions of the impending examination would be; and if the candidate were lucky enough to be a member of the nobility, or otherwise entitled to special favour, he might be exempted altogether from the tedium of an examination. Very few failed to pass, and as time went on, practically no one ever failed. It was sufficient in the eyes of the Chancellor that one had attended the Schools of Paris for the required period; *ipso facto*, the diligent scholar had absorbed learning. But even if the miracle happened, and a candidate was so palpably stupid that he had to be turned down, he could appear at the end of a year for further examination. But delay was too long for impatient students. The wisest course was to seek out friends with a little influence to intercede with the Chancellor, or, if none availed, to spend a little money on presents, to be judiciously distributed to the Chancellor's relatives, but not, of course, to that dignitary himself. Such little marks of attention usually worked wonders.

The private examination safely passed, the day of the Licensing arrived. The candidate, attired in full academic regalia, accompanied by the Rector of the University and the Proctors of the Nations, preceded by beadles to clear the way, the students and Masters following in a long procession, made his way from the Mathurine Convent to the Episcopal Palace, there to kneel and be solemnly invested with the Licence in the name of the Father, the Son, and the Holy Ghost. He was now a Licentiate, privileged to teach.

But that was not enough. He must be admitted into the Guild of Masters, failing which, if he dared to set himself up as an instructor, the wrath of the Nations, the Guild, and the University would descend upon his luckless head. No one dared to dispense with the ceremony; no one, that is, except the Mendicant candidates in Theology.

Usually half a year elapsed. Then the Licentiate appeared before his own Nation, and received the seal of its approval on the impending step. He swore obedience to the Rector, the Nation, his Faculty, and the Statutes of the University. On the previous day he took part in a disputation known as his "Vespers." On the day of his inception into the Guild as a full-fledged Master, he gave a formal inaugural lecture in the presence of the full Faculty, the Master's cap or *biretta* was placed upon his head, a book in his hand, and a ring on his finger, and the presiding Master bestowed on him the kiss of fellowship. He then took his seat in the Magisterial chair. He had achieved his goal; he, too, was a member of the proud and privileged order.

No ceremony of the Middle Ages was complete without a banquet. Accordingly they adjourned to an inn, and there sat late at feast, again at his expense. The next morning he started on his career as a Teaching, or Regent Master; teaching, in obedience to the oath which he was obliged to take, for at least two years. All that he had to do was hire a hall through his Nation—and look for pupils.

CHAPTER XIII

The Graduate Faculties

A GOOD many of the Masters in Arts were not content with their status; they proceeded immediately to study in the higher Faculties. One of these was the Faculty of Medicine. A physician in the Middle Ages, though ignorant of science, and full of superstitious maxims, usually managed to accumulate a sufficiency of money, a fine house, horses, servants, and a well-dowered wife. There was no lack of patients in those days; filth and garbage, disposed of by the simple method of emptying the refuse-bin or chamber-pot into the street, flies and offal, recurrent and devastating plagues, with sword and knife wounds, saw to that.

The Paris School of Medicine ranked low in the scale, even as mediaeval schools of medicine went. Salerno and Montpellier far outranked it in prestige. The standards were not high; it was almost impossible to fail, which was, of course, an inducement to study in Paris. Thirty-two months was prescribed for the Bachelor's degree, and five and a half years more for the Medical Licence, if the student was already a Master in Arts; otherwise, six years. The method of studying for these degrees followed approximately the Arts model, as did that of the other graduate Faculties. The would-be physician studied the Liber Tegni of Galen, the works of Theophilus the Byzantine; the books on General Diet, Particular Diet, Urine, and Fevers of the Jewish physician, Isaac, and his disciples; the Book of Antidotes of Nicholas, the Salerno physician, and the Theory and Practice of Ali ben Abbas, the Arab. Galen was represented by one book only, and Hippocrates by none at all.

It was a strange hodge-podge of learning and nonsense, drawn from a variety of sources. The Paris doctors were content with what was handed down to them, and did not strive

132

for any improvement. Whatever progress might be achieved was due to the southern Universities. In Paris the training was along strict scholastic lines; the learned doctors preferred to dispute about diseases in impeccable syllogisms rather than examine a live patient infected with a real disease. That would have been undignified and messy. As for dissection, the restraining hand of the Church was heavy. The body of man, made in the image of God, must not be violated, even in death. Yet some of the southern schools managed to obtain special dispensations for a dissection every year or so. Paris was not interested.

It must be remembered that the surgeons or chirurgeons (in Northern Europe), who might have been interested, were not physicians. They were a lowly tribe, and were snubbed by the lordly University-bred physician as artisans. They sawed bones and let blood under the supervision of, and only at the orders of, the physician. With increasing organization, however, they managed to worm themselves as actual scholars into the Faculty of Medicine, but only for the attendance of lectures. No degree was available. But the surgeons were ambitious. In 1491 they demanded full equality with physicians. The Faculty retaliated in kind. They permitted the barbers also, who let blood between haircuts, to enter for the lectures. The chirurgeons were not so democratic. They wanted equality with the physicians, but they did not relish the idea that humble barbers should rise to their level. They searched the University Statutes and flourished triumphantly that particular one which required all lectures to be in Latin. Inasmuch as the barbers were unlettered, Latin was so much Greek to them, and lectures had been given in the despised French. The ingenious doctors got round this difficulty. They gave the lectures twice; once in Latin to conform with the Statute, and then in French to conform with the meagre learning of the barbers.

That broke the resistance of the chirurgeons. Faced with the competition of the barbers, they sued for peace. Apothecaries also were subject to the jurisdiction of the doctors. No medicine, not even a laxative, could be sold except on a physician's prescription.

The Faculty of Canon Law was not much more distinguished than the Medical School of Paris. Civil Law, as has been noted, was a forbidden subject, and the Canon, or Church Law, derived in all respects from Bologna. No student who desired real instruction went to Paris; Bologna, Orléans, Padua, Laon, attracted the serious scholar. Nevertheless, the Paris School was well attended. There were plenty of ecclesiastics, exiled to comfortable benefices, who longed for the fleshpots of the capital, its life, its movement, its situation in the centre of things. Theoretically the holder of a benefice was supposed to reside in his living, but an ingenious cleric who was marooned in the country could find ways to circumvent the restriction. Attending a University was one of them. In the days when the Papacy was sincerely trying to raise the clergy from their gross ignorance and sloth, it had decreed dispensations from residence to beneficed clergymen who wished to study. It was thought that the devout priesthood would naturally flock to the Faculty of Theology. They did nothing of the kind. Theology was a long, tedious, profitless business. Canon Law was infinitely more to their liking. The course was fairly easy, failure was almost unknown, and a degree in Canon Law meant that numerous higher offices of the Church were open to an ambitious ecclesiast. The codification of the body of Canon Law by the monk Gratian had resulted in the rise of a large body of lawyers whose business it was to expound that code in all its intricacies.

The ecclesiast from the country might be hopelessly ignorant, but that was not an insuperable obstacle. The buying and selling of degrees became a lucrative business for examiners and candidates. Regent Masters could retire at an early age with their pockets well lined; and there was keen competition for teaching jobs.

The Church was well aware of this crying scandal, and legislated vehemently but vainly against bribery and the purchase of degrees. At no time in the history of the world has legislation corrected an evil while it was in the interests of all parties concerned to perpetuate it.

The ostensible period of study was four years for the Bachelor's degree and forty months for the Licence. The curriculum and the texts studied followed Bologna, and will be considered in detail in connection with that University.

But the School that was the particular glory of Paris, the one in which she rose pre-eminent over all Europe, and which had a practical monopoly in its own field, was the School of Theology. The reverend Doctors sat as on a throne, dispensing theological doctrine for the Church to ingest. The course was long and the way thorny; no poor student dependent on his own resources could hope to approach the far-distant goal. In the thirteenth century it took five years to obtain a Bachelor's degree, and three more to achieve a Doctorate; moreover, the candidate must be over thirty-five years of age. By the fourteenth century the requirements were increased to a total of *sixteen* years! This meant half a lifetime of study.

For the first six years the theological student was a simple *auditor*; for four more years he attended lectures on the Bible; for two years the lectures were based on the *Sentences* of Peter the Lombard. These were the only texts deemed worthy the attention of Theology, and it is a question whether the *Sentences* were not rated above the Bible. This influential book of the Middle Ages was modelled on the *Sic et non* of Abélard, as was the *Decretum* of Gratian in Canon Law. As a matter of fact, Peter the Lombard was a pupil and disciple of Abélard, and he followed the same method. He took seemingly discordant authorities on moot theological questions, and set them in parallel; but instead of leaving them contrasted, as Abélard had done, he reconciled and

K

harmonized the conflicts; at least to the satisfaction of the Middle Ages. They preferred to read his commentaries on what the Bible and the Fathers had said and meant, as they preferred the *Summulae* of Petrus Hispanus, the commentary on Aristotle's *Logic*, to the original itself; as in modern times we prefer the *Outline of History*, the *Outline of Science*, the *Outline of Art*, to any extended study of the subjects involved. Second-hand knowledge, it is true, but the commentaries told them what to think, and gave them ready-made ideas.

In his ninth year the Bachelor delivered himself of a Tentative Disputation, which rapidly degenerated into a farce. It was nothing more or less than a set of complimentary speeches about himself, the Doctors of Theology, the Church, Paris, or any high dignitary whose presence was expected in the audience. After this effort he was declared *ingeniosus et doctissimus*. The following year he started on the *Sentences*, which he studied for a period of three to four years. As each of the four books was finished, the candidate gave a public discourse on some theological problem involved; this lecture was attended by the entire Faculty, who listened somnolently, and woke up only in time to attend the "honest and moderate beer-drinking" (as the Statute naïvely puts it) that followed.

For the balance of the period, while awaiting the Licence, the Bachelor remained in Paris, taking part in public disputations, preaching an occasional University sermon, and, if he were not too serious, enjoying a taste of Parisian night-life.

One of these public disputations, however, was an ordeal. It took place in the Hall of the Sorbonne, and was known as the Sorbonic Disputation. The Bachelor stood alone on the platform—he was not permitted to sit even for an instant—from six in the morning until six at night, with only one hour's intermission for lunch; during which period a succession of opponents, working in relays, rose up to dispute with him, and the arguments ranged back and forth, while the audience stamped and applauded each rapier-like thrust, and cheered on the combatants.

The Licence was conferred in alternate years and only on All Saints' Day. The Faculty examination laid more stress on character, morals, and attendance at lectures than on the candidate's knowledge. In the early days the test was necessarily very strict, inasmuch as the number of chairs in Theology were limited by Papal decree, and admission to the Doctorate practically meant a teaching chair. The number of applicants was always far in excess of that of the chairs, so that a little moderate bribery or an appeal to influence usually worked wonders for the ambitious Theologian.

By the fifteenth century, however, standards became extremely lax; and there is no record of any candidate being rejected simply because of intellectual deficiencies. It was more important that he should not be a "bastard."

At those other few Universities that had Theological Schools matters were even worse. Toulouse permitted the Chancellor to dispense with any examination whatsoever in the case of a noble, and the test of nobility was the ability to support servants in livery. Cambridge had the same high-minded rule. At Leipzig all examinations in theology were suspended in 1444 because of evidence of wholesale bribery and corruption. And later a Statute was actually passed forbidding the Dean and Vice-Chancellor to give candidates private information of the questions in the coming examination.

Theology was thoroughly scholastic in character. Reason played its part as well as authority in the examination of traditional beliefs, but reason was carefully orthodox in its conclusions. To quote Clemengis, who was Rector of Paris in the fifteenth century: "The shrewd arguments of our theologians have at first glance something acute and ingenious about them; but if you cast away the husk and envelope of the words and seek the fruit, they vanish into smoke, being empty within."

In fact, most of the contempt and derision that has been

poured upon the Scholastic philosophy of the Middle Ages
was really meant for Theology. Take the classic example of
the supremely futile problem: "How many angels can dance
upon the point of a needle?" Or the grotesque matters
debated in all earnestness in the *Summa* of Albert the Great:
"What is the interior structure of Paradise?"—"What do
angels do with the bodies of which they have made use to
fulfil a mission upon earth?"—"What was the colour of the
Virgin's skin?" And, of all things: "Whether the most
sainted Virgin suffered any pain or achieved pleasure while
conceiving!"

All theological problems these, and in such a bewildering
maze there was little room for authentic religious emotion
or passionate belief. The whole science was an elaborate
syllogism, with something of the mathematical about it.
Anticipating Spinoza by centuries, the mediaeval theologians
employed axioms, theorems, and corollaries to unveil the truth
that was already inherent in the Catholic dogma.

The Bible, except for the Mendicant Friars, who actually
studied that strange document, was obscured by the mass of
commentaries, of which the *Sentences* was naturally the chief.
By Wyclif's time it was a forgotten book, and his naïve
suggestion that people should read it afresh was tantamount
to sacrilege.

The Theological Doctors of Paris stood at the pinnacle of
mediaeval life; they were famous, and proud of their privileges; their profession was lucrative, and their number limited.
Having created a monopoly, they grew lazy. Even the necessary teaching required of all Masters grew to be a burden.
They turned it over more and more to the Bachelors, and
gave a perfunctory annual lecture in order to maintain their
professional standing. Their smug self-satisfaction, together
with the general low standards prevailing throughout the
University by the fifteenth century, contributed largely to the
final decay and intellectual suicide of the once great institution.

CHAPTER XIV

Rise of the Colleges

IT was chiefly on account of Theology that the college system was first evolved in Paris. Transferred to the English Universities, it completely changed the course and structure of University life.

In the great struggle between the Mendicants and the secular University for control of the Theological Faculty, one of the great advantages possessed by the Friars was the possession of disciplined monasteries, in which the students of Theology were housed, fed, tutored, and generally guided through the long years of study, all at no expense to the ambitious scholar.

The secular student might well draw back in dismay from the prospect of studying five to six years for an Arts degree, and then devoting an additional eight to sixteen years to the subtleties of "the queenly science." This was a drain on a man's time and his purse that could be viewed with equanimity only by the very wealthy. No wonder the average man turned with something of eagerness to Medicine and the Law, where the course was shorter and the financial rewards far more immediate and certain.

A good many of the secular clergy, themselves possessed of what passed for comfortable fortunes, viewed the approximate monopoly of the Friars in Theology with dismay. It meant control of the sources of authoritarian dogma, and the overlordship of the hated Regulars over the more easy-going, urbane clergy of the realm.

There were other influences working in the minds of the early college founders. Vanity, for instance—the desire to have one's name and fame immortalized as that of a benefactor; anxiety for the salvation of one's own soul, as witnessed by the minute instructions in many a charter of foundation for perpetual masses and prayers to speed the founder's spirit through Purgatorial fires. And lastly, on the part of a not inconsiderable minority, genuine charity, and the sincere desire to promote scholarship.

The first Arts students who flocked to Paris were entirely independent. In spite of the extreme youth of the majority—fourteen to fifteen being quite a normal age—the University paid no attention to their private lives outside the lecture halls, except to see to it that they were not cheated by unscrupulous citizens or injured in the numerous broils of the day.

The young lad, far from home, and free from parental influence for the first time in his life, sought quarters where he could find them, looked at the roaring gaiety of the capital and found it good; the brightly-lit taverns with their odours of wine and roasting fowl; the bawdy, rousing choruses; the rattle of leathern cups, and the click of the dice as they rolled across the tables; the slow, tantalizing smile of what was beauty to untutored eyes: all this was a heady brew for the provincial youngster. Only too many deserted their studies for the lures of gambling, bawdry, cut-pursing, and pimping. In later years François Villon, the immortal, was but one of a numerous band of castaway scholars, his rivals only in vice.

The more serious students early began to band themselves together for the purpose of hiring a communal house. A Bachelor or Master ordinarily agreed to take care of the financial arrangements, and to exercise some measure of control over the comings and goings of the inmates. Such a community residence was called a Hospicium at Paris; at Oxford, a Hall.

According to the earlier authorities, these Halls were purely democratic, self-governing societies. The students who footed the bills chose the older man who was to be their Head, and deposed him at their pleasure. They made their own house rules, and in all respects conducted themselves like an autonomous republic.

It is a pleasing picture, this one of fourteen-year-old boys governing themselves, liberty-loving in a great city; but there has been a disposition of late to question the veracity of this view. These authorities, with a show of reason, claim that certain Masters, at the instigation of alarmed parents, or with an eye to increasing their income, organized the Halls on their own initiation.

Whichever view is correct, it is certain that by the middle of the thirteenth century the great majority of middle-class students resided in such Halls, and that the self-governing democracy was a thing of the past. The Masters or Principals in charge had evolved their own iron-clad rules for their charges. Only two classes of scholars still lived outside the Halls: the very rich, who could afford a house of their own and private tutors; and the very poor, who begged their food from door to door. At best their lodgings consisted of a miserable, dark, ill-ventilated garret with a straw pallet for a bed. In France these garret lodgers were called "martinets" (from the martin's nest under the eaves); at Oxford, "Chamberdykens."

The Colleges were at first merely endowed Halls whose function it was to provide shelter for the poor scholars or "martinets." Charitably disposed founders left funds for the provision of the plainest of board and lodging and apparel. The Hall was the pattern followed; except that the Master or Head was paid out of the Foundation, and naturally, his authority over his charges was considerably greater than in the voluntary associations. Yet there was at first no disposition to tyranny; and the scholars usually had a certain voice in the management of the College.

The first College foundation was exceedingly humble. In 1180 a pious Englishman, one Josse de Londres, newly returned from a pilgrimage to the Holy Land, purchased a room in the "Hospital of the Blessed Mary of Paris," to be used for ever for the lodging of "eighteen scholar-clerks." The Hospital in return agreed to furnish the beds and provide the cost of the scholars' food out of the alms collected for the poor. Obviously only the poorest and most desperate of scholars would avail themselves of such meagre charity; yet, such as it was, the "Collège de Dix-huit," so named from the number of the pensioners, was the beginning of a great system. Neither founder nor Hospital laid down any rules apart from certain religious obligations: to wit, the scholars had to bear the cross and holy water at funerals, and every evening to repeat the seven penitential Psalms and other regular prayers.

In 1186 the second College was founded by Count Robert of Clermont; and the year 1204 saw the foundation of the College of Constantinople, doubtless for the purpose of training missionaries to teach the heretic Greeks the pure Catholic doctrine.

From this time onwards the Colleges rapidly increased in numbers. The Mendicants were quick to see the advantages of this new type of institution, and founded several Colleges. Robert de Sorbon, the King's chaplain, and a staunch defender of the Seculars against the inroads of the Regulars, conceived the idea of founding a College to combat their influence. The result was the Collège de Sorbonne, the greatest and most famous of all Colleges, afterwards to become identified with the Faculty of Theology.

The purpose of the Sorbonne differed from that of previous foundations. It was intended primarily for students who desired to study Theology, but who had not the means to undertake the arduous task. It was for mature students, Masters of Arts, seculars, who might otherwise have yielded to the temptations of the Mendicant Orders, or have transferred to the more lucrative Canon Law. It was the Sorbonne, and the Sorbonne alone, that kept Theology from becoming a Mendicant monopoly.

The College was designed for sixteen students, four to be chosen from each Nation. But others of the secular clergy found the purpose praiseworthy, and contributed generously, with the result that the number was finally increased to thirty-six. These were full Bursars, and were treated in far better fashion than the poor devils who were compelled to suffer the charity of the Collège de Dix-huit. Their food was good and plentiful, their lodgings fair, and each Fellow was entitled to a "poor clerk" as his personal servant! These clerkly servants were also University scholars, but were not students of Theology, and were therefore unable to share the benefits of the Bursars. They did the dirty work, and in return were offered rude pallets and broken meats from the Hall table.

The government of the Sorbonne was in the hands of external Governors, appointed by the terms of the Foundation. The ordinary administration of the Hall, however, was left mainly to a Provisor, appointed by the Governors, and to the Fellows of the Sorbonne themselves. In time this College became almost the whole University. It grew in fame and in privileges beyond all others; and to this day it exists as a University in its own independent right.

In 1304 came the College of Navarre, founded by the Queen of Navarre, and in quick succession followed a host of others, taking their names in the main from their founders or the countries from which their inmates hailed. Thus there was the Collège de Cluny, founded by the Abbot of Cluny; the Collège de Narbonne, founded by the Archbishop of Narbonne; the Collège de Lisieux, founded by the Bishop of that diocese; and the Collège de Danemark, the Collège de Linckoping, and the Collège d'Upsal for Scandinavian students, founded by patriotic Northmen.

Some of the Colleges were good; some were fair; some were wretchedly bad. The Collège de Montaigu, founded in 1314, had a most unenviable reputation for abominable living and savage discipline. Rabelais has immortalized the College in a vitriolic passage. Ponocrates, tutor of Gargantua, tells his pupil's father: "My sovereign Lord, think not that I have placed him in that lowsie Colledge, which they call Montague ... for the Galley-Slaves are far better used among the Moores and Tartars, the murtherers in the criminal Dungeons, yea the very Doggs in your House, than are the poor wretched Students in the aforesaid Colledge."

But for better or for worse, the College as an institution had come to stay, and in so doing, had profoundly modified the organization of the University.

The Collège de Harcourt was the first College that had a provision permitting of the reception of paying Scholars. Later the other Colleges all followed suit. At first, no doubt, the paying resident student was the exception; the scholar who could afford his own board and lodging, either alone or in a Hall with congenial companions, treasured his freedom. The discipline and restrictions of a College naturally irked the liberty-loving, reckless young man. But gradually certain advantages which the College possessed over the Halls impressed themselves, if not on the scholar's mind, at least on that of his parents, who footed the bills, and could therefore compel acquiescence.

For one thing, anxious fathers and mothers in remote hamlets of Ireland, Spain, Brittany, and Hungary, no longer need fear for the immortal welfare of their offspring in the sinful capital, nor quail before the constant stream of appeals for money. At the Colleges there were regular hours; the gates were closed at sundown, or not much later; discipline became increasingly exacting; the studious were encouraged in their studies, and the idlers sternly reminded of their obligations. Further, the Head Master, or his assistants, acted the part of tutor, helped the scholars with their lessons, chose their University Masters for them, and lectured with increasing frequency in the privacy of the College.

At Navarre, for example, the Master was required "diligently to hear the lessons of the Scholars studying in the Faculty of Arts and faithfully to instruct them alike in life and in doctrine." Latin was spoken exclusively, and disputations were held almost every evening in the College Hall.

Very gradually the University evolved to meet the changed conditions. More and more the lectures and the repetition of lessons in the Colleges, originally intended to be merely subordinate to the University teaching, assumed an independent character. The Colleges hired more Masters to assist the Head Master. The lectures were fuller and more complete; the resident Scholars spent more and more time in the College grounds rather than in the public Schools. The more competent Masters drifted into the Colleges for full-time jobs, and those who remained outside were either lacking in ability or were content to give an occasional lecture in order to comply with the regulations. By the fifteenth century the Colleges provided full and regular courses of lectures with all the activities of a University; in 1445 the University itself, in a petition addressed to the King, stated that "almost the whole University resides in the Colleges." In 1457 the University suppressed the poor "Martinets," requiring residence in a College or Hospicium; by the sixteenth century the famous "Straw Street" was deserted except for the public disputations and inceptions, and the Schools were nearing ruin.

From a voluntary association of Masters, each with his individual School, and his own quota of pupils, whose fees belonged to the Master, the University had become an association of Colleges, with full-time Masters, supported partly by the original Foundation, and partly by the regular fees of the paying Scholars.

The old University had prescribed the curriculum for the Master's degree, but had not interfered with the personal liberties of the masters and scholars. The Colleges changed all this; both were now amenable to varying degrees of discipline. From a few rented rooms masquerading as schools in "Straw Street," the University became an aggregation of College buildings, sprawling in an immense arc over and across the Seine.

The University had gained in order and discipline; doubtless, too, it had gained in solidity and regularity of teaching; but it had also lost much. For one thing, it was now tied down;

choked into submission to royal authority by the value of its possessions. No longer could a poverty-stricken, yet irresponsible and foot-loose University thumb its nose at authority and move to more congenial quarters if it had a quarrel with King or Parlement or townsfolk. There was a substantial stake to be left behind, which could be burnt down or expropriated.

Again, the brilliance of the early teaching was gone for ever. Those silver-tongued, eloquent, free-speaking Masters of an earlier era, whose magnetic influence drew thousands from the farthest limits of the Western world to sit at their feet, had been replaced by dull, plodding instructors. In the old days a Master *had* to be good, or his School was empty; now he had to know the right people, and the unfortunate students were compelled to listen to him, willynilly. Something of intellectual freedom went out of the teachers as well; they had to conform to the prejudices and beliefs of the Governing Board of the College; radical teaching might lead to instant dismissal. Then, too, the adventure, the colour, the glamour of University life were things of the past. The students had become more like the "college men" or undergraduates of today.

So shed a tear for that mediaeval University of Paris that astounded the world with its magnificence, with its swarming cosmopolitan body of scholars, its resplendent Rector and disputatious Masters, its impecuniosity, its brawls, and straw-strewn floors and keen intellects; its inordinate privileges, its touchiness, its democracy and independence; done to death by the inexorable march of the times, the growth of royal authority, the inner decay of Scholasticism, and not the least, by the drab conservativeness of the Colleges!

CHAPTER XV

Bologna—A University of Students

THERE were two great Mother Universities in the Middle
Ages—Paris and Bologna. Separate and distinct in almost
every respect, they dominated the intellectual life of Europe;
from these fertile centres proceeded the quickening influences
that gave rise to almost all the Universities of Europe.

Paris has already been described: the sprawling University
of Masters in the capital of France, under the autocratic eye
of king and bishop; the home of subtle dialectic, of philosophy and theology, beloved of the Pope, for ever meddling
in matters spiritual and political. It was the pattern for all the
Universities of Northern Europe.

But Bologna, emerging from the mists of time, was opposed
in its form and structure and its very essence to its great rival
on the banks of the Seine. Southern Europe followed in its
track. Bologna, the city, was a free municipality, a Lombard
town of Northern Italy, bowing its head to no outside master,
a republic surrounded by other republics. Bologna the University meddled little with Pope and Church, and demanded
like treatment in return; not Philosophy, not Theology, but
the Law was its *raison d'être*: Civil Law and Canon Law;
while Rhetoric, the despised of Paris, superseded Logic. But
there was a still greater difference. To us a University of
Masters, like that of Paris, is understandable enough; but
what shall we say to Bologna, a University, a Society, a
Guild, a Trade Union of Students! A University in which the
pupils govern the teachers, in which freshmen and sophomores
walk with arrogant step to the humble salutations of grey-
bearded doctors, a University in which the students dictate to
their masters what lectures shall be delivered, what hours shall
be kept, what absences permitted, what penalty inflicted.
To us it may seem a topsy-turvy situation, in which the

147

oppressed of all ages have become the oppressors. With what longing must the historically-minded undergraduate of today, who has come into conflict with any one of the innumerable Faculty restrictions, look back to the halcyon era of Bologna and her daughter Universities!

Yet in the retrospect of history, Bologna was no miraculous phenomenon; on the contrary, it was the natural, logical child of its environment, of the influences in which it was bathed. Northern Italy had retained, even during the darkest centuries, some measure of the ancient traditions of Rome. North of the Alps the influx of barbarians almost completely extinguished the great system of Roman jurisprudence and education; and when Charlemagne reorganized education in his realm, it was already in the hands of the monks, and inevitably followed ecclesiastical lines.

In Italy, however, the remnants of the Roman schools had lingered on much later; the Latin classics had managed to survive through the tumult of the centuries. Ecclesiasticism, the spiritual domination of the Church, had never taken root in the practical, slightly sceptical soil of Italy, as it did among the more mystically-minded, brooding barbarians of the North. Lay teachers persisted, concentrating on lay subjects; the Church schools never had a chance to monopolize education as they did in the North.

The Italian was practical by nature. His forbears were citizens of Rome, and the Romans were nothing if not practical. They kept their feet firmly on the solid ground; they had an eye to the main chance. They were warriors, organizers, administrators, traders, dealers in grain and oil; their literature is a literature of sanity and common sense; their law was the very essence of their practical genius. Their descendants laughed at the subtle disputations of the North and concentrated on the things that really mattered (or on what they thought were the things that really mattered).

The Lombard cities had evolved rapidly during the eleventh century. By the twelfth century they had wrested their free-

dom from the domination of the German Empire, and had
entered upon a period of unexampled growth and vigour.
Commerce, trade, and politics were their gods; the Church was
a necessary but incidental feature in the life of the busy citizen.
He made money in trade; he speculated in cargoes that sailed
the Adriatic and the Mediterranean; he guarded with fierce
turbulence his hard-won independence, and fought against
internal and external enemies alike. Philosophy and Theology
were vain pursuits to men like these; Law, however, was a
matter of supreme practical importance. His contract rights
depended on the proper interpretation of the law; his privileges in the municipal assembly were based on ancient Roman
privileges, and the very independence of the State was inextricably bound up with the intricacies of the law of nations
and of the Empire. Law! That was what he wanted and clamoured to be taught. Grammar and Rhetoric too; for they
taught him how to draft his legal documents, his contracts
for merchandise, his leettrs demanding payment on delinquent
accounts. Even Logic was of value in the preparation of
arguments to be adduced in a court of law.

Moreover, the Lombard nobility, imbued with the old
traditions, actually read the classics, and gave their sons an
education in literature, whereas the feudal lords of Northern
Europe looked with contempt upon all such womanish and
monkish pursuits.

Accordingly the subjects of the Trivium were well regarded
in Italy; those of the Quadrivium not so well, but more highly
than in France. The vital differences resided in the completely
secular character of the education, and the emphasis laid on
Law and Medicine in the professional schools, as against
Philosophy and Theology.

The old Roman genius was essentially legalistic. From the
earliest times their codes went far beyond the fragmentary,
inconsistent codes of the Greeks. Then came the five great
jurisconsults of the Roman Empire: Gaius, Julian, Papinian,
Ulpian, and Paulus. These learned lawyers, members of the

Imperial Auditory, judges in the Court of Appeals, took the vast body of former decisions and theoretical considerations, perfecting, polishing, and revising them, until there emerged a vast system of law, embodied in legal propositions of universal validity, logically consistent, and applicable to the decisions of actual cases before them.

Future courts and future Emperors recognized the binding force of their decisions, and the doctrine of *Stare Decisis* was born. It led to stability, to order, to a prior knowledge of one's rights, but at the same time it made for a fixity that has played havoc with modern law, especially in the United States today. Law has become a laggard, limping fifty years behind the rapid advance of modern conditions; frozen, instead of flexible, deferring too often to the incompetent or prejudiced opinions of some venal judge of a bygone era. The Romans had not contemplated such a rigidity of mould (a passage in the Codex commands the judge, in deciding a case, to follow the principles and reasoning of the great jurists rather than the actual decision in a like issue); nor, for that matter, had Aristotle when he formalized his knowledge.

Justinian codified the whole body of the Law in what was known as the *Corpus Juris Civilis,* and digested, sifted, and arranged the decisions in the *Digest* or *Pandects.* When Rome went down in ruins, the invaders set up their own crude law; but they permitted the subject races to continue locally under the Roman Law, provided their rulers were not injured thereby. Indeed, the Visigothic king, Alaric II, in the year 506, adopted to some extent the Roman Theodosian Code, interlarded it with Teutonic comments, and applied the *mélange* to his provincials in Gaul. This *Breviarium* became standard law for the Merovingians and Carolingians; of course, after the inevitable work of glossing, digesting, and interpreting in which the Middle Ages delighted.

In Italy the Justinian Code underwent a similar transformation; distorted almost out of all recognition, it became the law of the land. By the tenth century the Codes were being used

chiefly as Latin texts for the study of grammatical construc-
tions and the meanings of words, and only in a secondary
degree for the law contained in them. The most ambitious
shied from the task of delving into such an amorphous mass.

By the twelfth century, however, there already existed
schools of law in certain centres of North Italy—or rather, a
few scattered, independent teachers who were willing to impart
their legal knowledge. Ravenna had such teachers as far back
as the ninth century; Pavia at the beginning of the eleventh
century, and Bologna about the same time.

In the twelfth century something seems to have happened;
it was as though a catalyst had precipitated the study of Law
into a widespread intellectual Renaissance. At a time when
students were flocking to Paris to study Logic and Philosophy,
there was a similar mass movement developed for the study of
Roman or Civil Law in Italy. It concentrated on Bologna, and
that School, hitherto a School of Liberal Arts, became primarily a School of Law, and soon outshone all its rivals and
predecessors.

Various explanations for this sudden resurgence have been
advanced. The romantic story of the discovery of the Pandects
of Justinian on the capture of Amalfi in 1135 has been ex-
ploded. Pisa had the manuscript long before this date; it had
simply been neglected. The other alleged explanation dies
harder. Taking an analogy from the brilliant presence of
Abélard in Northern Europe, there has been evolved the myth
of a great teacher of law at Bologna, one Irnerius, who by his
own unaided efforts caused Law to be born Minerva-like in
the Italian consciousness. Now it is quite probable that
Irnerius existed, and that he was a famous teacher in his day.
Dates have even been assigned for him: A.D. 1050 to 1135. But
it is not true that he was solely responsible for the revival of
Law; there had been teachers and schools before him. In the
year 1100 one hears of a professor named Pepo, "the bright
and shining light of Bologna."

L

Nevertheless, Irnerius' influence, if he really lived and had his being, was undeniably great. The soil was fertile; the economic, political, and legal problems of the Lombard cities *demanded* Law. The *Summa Codicis Irnerii*, the book that marked the beginning of the professional study of law in the Middle Ages, was probably his work. He took the new parts of the *Digest* of the Justinian Code, hitherto neglected, collated them with the Code itself, and arranged them in order, in the form of a textbook and compendium. It was not the complete Corpus Juris Civilis, but only an extract of those topics that were interesting to the mediaeval mind. Roman Law had definitely become exact and professional, and the method employed by Irnerius in "glossing" the text, became the standard for following generations.

Of Irnerius himself we know very little. The chief source of information is the garrulous and untrustworthy Odofredus, a jurist of the thirteenth century. According to him, Irnerius was a Bolognese citizen, a Master of Liberal Arts; and "when books of Law were brought from Ravenna, he began to study in them by himself, and by studying to teach the Laws, and he was a man of the greatest renown."

From approximately the period of his alleged activities, however, Bologna rose into European fame. Apart from the presence of such a famous teacher, in an age when famous teachers were the only essentials of a School, Bologna had other attractions that made for its choice as the site of a great Law University. It stood at the crossroads of the great highways that crossed the Alps from Northern Europe to Central Italy.

Now the Lombard cities were fiercely patriotic; it was almost sacrilege for a citizen of one to seek instruction in a neighbouring city if there were any teachers in his birthplace. Accordingly, most of the early schools were purely local affairs. But with the great intellectual reawakening of the twelfth century, when men were hungry for learning, for any kind of learning, the North Europeans, less locally minded, came through the Alpine passes to the sunny plains of Lombardy, seeking the Law. There stood Bologna, conveniently at hand; there was the semi-mythical Irnerius and his compatriot professors; there exact and codified instruction was available.

So here these alien thirsters for knowledge halted, and more and more teachers gathered round them. The foreigners had money, and spent it freely; and the townsfolk and the native lawyers opened their arms to welcome their guests, and their pockets to receive their gold. Before long a flourishing School had sprung into existence.

For these strangers were not the youthful students of fourteen or fifteen who had flocked to study Logic in Paris, too often without a penny to their names, and only the clothes on their backs for capital. The foreign scholars in Italy were mostly men, often of mature years, usually wealthy in their own right, and of considerable social standing in their home communities. They were ecclesiasts, many of them, with lucrative benefices at home, and dignitaries of the Church, who felt that the Law opened even higher preferments in the power of the Church. There were high officers of State, too; and lawyers who wanted the prestige of a Bolognese degree to give them the needed impetus in their private practice.

There was another attraction that brought students across the mountains: namely, the rise of Canon Law. This was the Law of the Church, its Constitution, the rules and decrees under which it was governed. And inasmuch as the Church was the greatest of mediaeval governments, with an infinitude of powers, political, social, governmental, regulatory, in which the powers purely spiritual were almost unheeded, it is understandable that the complexity of its regulations gave birth to a body of ecclesiastical lawyers, whose business it was—and a very lucrative business it proved to be—to decipher and interpret the Canon Law for the benefit of Bishop, Archbishop, Cardinal, and Pope—and for litigants, office-seekers, and claimants for special privileges.

Originally, the Church sought the solution of all disputed

constitutional questions in the Bible. But gradually, through the centuries, that sacred book was overlaid by the commentaries of the Church Fathers, the pronouncements of the Councils, and the decrees of the Popes. The additional matter grew and grew in volume, until it became so unwieldy that something had to be done about it. There had been partial codifications from time to time, notably that of Dionysius the Scythian in the sixth century, the infamous pseudo-Isidorean decretals of the ninth century, and an attempt at codification by the Bishop of Worms in the eleventh century. But these were unscientific, haphazard, and worthless almost as soon as formulated. The material was increasing apace.

The rise to power of the Papal monarchy in the twelfth century called for a firm and stable body of law. The pseudo-Isidorean decretals had strengthened the claim of the Papacy to supreme power, but with such a mass of material still undigested, the Papal hierarchy felt insecure. Who could say what explosive matter it contained—when some too ambitious marplot might unearth a passage from an Early Father that would rock the foundations of the Papal power, and give rise to endless controversy? The Middle Ages delighted in texts and compendiums; the written word of authority had almost a hypnotic effect on the reasoning faculties. Very well, then! Let the miscellaneous mass of writings, dicta, decrees, rescripts, what not, be put once and for all into definite, written form, and properly arranged; let the Law of the Church be ascertained, and thereafter there would be no further disputing, no searching of old manuscripts.

An unknown monk in the Camaldunensian Monastery of S. Felix in Bologna rose to the occasion. It was a mere happy chance, we are to think, not instigated by the Pope or the monk's superiors; as fortuitous, no doubt, as the discovery of the forged decretals of the pseudo-Isidore. Gratian was the monk's name, and he was not even, seemingly, a teacher; just a penman, a diligent copier of manuscripts. About 1142 he completed his monumental work, the *Decretum,* or *Concor-*

dantia discordantium Canonum. A Concordance of discordant Canons.

This monk, of whom little else is known, owed his entire method of approach to Abélard. The Scholastic method is everywhere palpable. Even as Peter the Lombard was later to organize Theology in his *Sentences*, so did Gratian put Canon Law into negotiable form. Gratian presented all the authorities he could find on either side of every disputed point in Canon Law. Then he extracted, from this welter of opinions, those which seemed to him most reasonable, or supported by the greater authorities; and these opinions, he said, were to be accepted as the ascertained law of the Church.

Such dogmatism and self-assurance on the part of an obscure monk is literally startling; yet almost immediately the *Decretum* of Gratian sprang into a position of recognized, definitive authority in ecclesiastical Courts and in the Schools. Is it not permissible to suspect the fine Machiavellian hand of the Papacy? In any event, it was hailed by all Europe as a great achievement; Gratian's opinions had practically the force of binding law; and his *Decretum* became the sole source of study in Canon Law for the Schools.

It did not pretend to independent thinking; it was merely a compilation, an organization of ill-digested matter. Gratian almost invariably bowed to authority; yet, significantly enough, he did one peculiar thing. He placed the decrees of the latest Pope, no matter how venal or incompetent, on a parity with the considered declarations of the General Councils of the Church or of the most venerable and venerated Fathers. With all Europe bowing down to this new Bible, the cause of the Papacy was immeasurably strengthened; a new power deposited in its hands. Canon Law had become as rigid and unyielding as Theology and Scholasticism. The Church had emerged from a certain fluidity of doctrine into a condition approximating to a spiritual arteriosclerosis.

The two studies, Civil and Canon Law, usually went together. The methods of Civil Law were employed in

Church Law; the laws of Constantine and other Christian Emperors were laws for both Church and State. The Canon Law grew by fresh accessions from the Civil. Finally, except in Paris, where the Civil Law was forbidden, the Canonist was also a Civil Lawyer, with two strings to his bow.

The inrush of students into Italy gave rise in 1158 to the grant of rights and privileges to the scholar class by the Emperor Frederick Barbarossa. This was a general grant; no town or University is mentioned. Yet in the same year, according to Otto of Freising in his *Deeds of Frederick*: "During the impressive diet at Roncaglia in 1158 the Emperor Frederick I . . . had four judges, Bulgarus, Martinus, James, and Hugo, well educated in jurisprudence, doctors of law in Bologna, who advised him."

This, however, does not mean that a University existed. These doctors and teachers were private and unauthorized, belonging to no organized institution, enjoying no special legal privileges, influential only by virtue of their acknowledged reputation for learning.

The Charter of Frederick Barbarossa took the general class of students under his wing; gave the scholar the option, when sued, of being judged by his own teacher or the Bishop, and was the basis of all future privileges. Yet this very permission to have one's teacher act as judge indicates that the teacher could not become a professor of law merely by opening his doors. It implies recognition of professorial standing by other professors similarly constituted, by the townsfolk, and by the student class itself. While no licence was demanded, while there was no formal initiation, we may suppose that custom and the weight of public opinion set up certain standards and qualifications. There may even have been about this time—that is, the middle of the twelfth century—a loose organization of Masters, rather similar to that in the process of formation in Paris. It was not until 1215, however, that there is written evidence of such an organization, when Boncompagno's *Rhetorica Antiqua* was read before "the University of Professors of the Civil and Canon Law." Remember that *University* meant simply Trade Union or Guild; nothing more.

Very early at Bologna, and elsewhere, trouble arose between the students and the townsfolk. The trouble was solely financial. These scholars were men of mature years; men of wealth and position at home. They did not riot in the streets like their more youthful confrères in Paris; gambling, drinking, and wenching would necessarily be indulged in with a greater regard for the outward decencies. On these scores there were no causes of friction.

But these alien scholars, unprotected by the legal safeguards that surrounded the citizens, were fat pullets, ripe for the plucking. The city of Bologna, with its crooked mediaeval streets, and its few inns, found its population almost doubled. The law scholars overflowed into the private houses of the burghers, seeking board and lodging, each negotiating for himself. The townsfolk welcomed them—and increased their prices unconscionably. The meanest garret, in the eyes of its proprietor, became a vision of dripping gold.

The indignant foreigners protested; the natives smiled. Even the municipal assembly chuckled sardonically. Then came the Charter of the red-bearded Emperor. That was a blow; but after all, a contract was a contract, and the student could be sued before his Master. The Master, too, was almost invariably a citizen of Bologna, who would naturally be chary of giving a decision against a fellow-citizen.

The students thereupon put their heads together. Frenchmen consulted with Englishmen, Scots with Germans; mass meetings were held. Someone made the inevitable suggestion. Let us organize to protect ourselves, he proposed. Look at the Guilds of barbers, of carpenters, of dyers and weavers.—The Guild was a universal mediaeval institution. The idea caught on; the worldly-wise ecclesiasts, nobles, and lawyers saw its advantages. Aliens had no legal rights in Bologna; very well, they would achieve rights by the force of numbers. Thereafter their demands and complaints came from the whole body of students.—Prices will not be reduced? We have no standing in law? In that case, said the spokesmen for the students to the city fathers, we shall leave Bologna. Bologna is not the only town in the world; other cities have professors of the law just as good, perhaps even better. Their citizens would be glad to grant our demands in return for our custom.

The citizens saw the point. Bologna, denuded of its student class, would lose in wealth as well as in status; the goose that laid the golden eggs would have taken wing. An agreement was speedily concluded. Rents for students were to be fixed by a Board of four arbitrators, or taxors; two to be appointed by the students, and two by the city.

At almost the same time the scholars of Paris were obtaining similar concessions; but note the difference in the means employed, and in the outcome. In Bologna it was the *students* who banded together and enforced their demands; in Paris it was the *Masters*—acting in their own interest (for they, too, were being overcharged) and only incidentally on behalf of their pupils. There is this distinction also! The Masters of Paris were chiefly foreigners; they hailed from the same parts of the world as their pupils; they were subject to the same legal disabilities. In Bologna, on the other hand, the professors of law were natives, or at least, were legally citizens, and had no need to fight for their rights. Their students were as alien to them as to the other citizens. The interest of the professors was purely financial; if the students left Bologna, their custom and their fees went with them.

CHAPTER XVI

The Students are Masters

THUS it was that the "Universitas" of students was born, a banding together, or guild, for mutual protection and resistance to inordinate demands. It was the organization of a state within a state, an independent republic with its own laws and customs, treating with the city as with a foreign power.

The municipality of Bologna resented this abrogation of its cherished powers, and fought against it as long as it could; but the arguments of the student body were unanswerable. As in Paris, they had no buildings, no possessions, not even the physical ties that a Master might have, to hold them back. Foot-loose, ready to travel, they could denude a city of half its population overnight, taking with them three-quarters of the trade and income of the native inhabitants. There were a few such migrations, even as from Paris, and in practically every case the Student University was requested, indeed begged, to return.

Two points must be noted in connection with this rising Student University. Firstly, only the alien students belonged to it. Those students who were native citizens of Bologna were not members of the University, and were not subject to its laws. There was no necessity for their adhesion. As citizens of Bologna they had all the rights and privileges they required; they were fully protected from fraud; they could not, as a matter of fact, take the requisite oath in the Student University without violating their oath as citizens of Bologna.

Secondly, the professors, the teachers, were also outside the pale. They, too, were citizens of Bologna, and as such, natural enemies of the students. It is a moot question whether it was possible for a foreigner to set himself up as a teacher. In later years it was definitely prohibited. There was not that community of interest between master and pupil that existed in

159

Paris, where both were aliens, where both were considered "clergy," where both suffered the same disabilities. The Doctors of Bologna were generally laymen, to whom the students owed no ecclesiastical or other obedience; in the beginning they were simply private adventurers who had set up schools for pay, and depended solely on the fees of their pupils for support. Gradually, in order to avoid cut-throat competition, and to establish certain rules and conditions as prerequisites to recognition as a Master, they, too, organized into a Guild of Law Doctors, which came to be known as a "College." Note the difference between their terminology and that of Paris. There the University consisted of Masters; in Bologna, of students. The College, in Paris, was a charitable boarding-house for poor students; in Bologna it was the Professorial Guild.

This College of Doctors examined all candidates who desired admission to the teaching profession, and granted the licence to teach, without which, eventually, no one was permitted to set up a school in Bologna. They were the sole judges of the candidate's qualifications; there was no Chancellor or other ecclesiastical person to interfere. Only later did the Bishop of Bologna enter into the picture; he came to grant the licence; but this was purely a formality; the real power rested with the Doctoral College.

The student body did not interfere much with these Doctoral privileges, nor, at first, with other strictly academic matters. They were interested only in obtaining political, legal, and financial security from the townsfolk. But once victorious in that direction, attention was inevitably turned to the professors. The student body was conscious of its power, there were clashes of temperament, and the Doctors may have felt a certain jealousy when they saw their pupils organized and independent. They pursued a selfish and short-sighted policy. They sided with the town in all conflicts; they tried to restrict the Doctorate to fellow-citizens. The students began to harass the unfortunate Doctors, and assume more and more authority over the academic Studium, over lectures, over courses of study, hours, and methods—all the matters normally within the sole jurisdiction of a Faculty; even over the private lives of the professors, until the grave and reverend Doctors of Civil and of Canon Law were reduced to a state of servitude, of slavery to their pupils, unparalleled in the history of education before or since.

It must not be assumed that the College of Doctors submitted without a struggle. They did resist, and vehemently. But the Student Universities were possessed of a powerful and terrible weapon, against the Doctors as against the municipality. They could migrate, for one thing, or they could boycott the obstreperous professor. No pupils would attend his lectures; he would find himself facing bare benches; and woe to the student who violated his oath and sought learning under the boycotted instructor.

The Doctors of Law were practical men. Dignities and powers were pleasant things, but without profit in the face of a boycott. Their livelihood depended on the fees of their pupils; no pupils, no fees. There was nothing for it but to submit with as good a grace as possible. The students, flushed with victory, were not inclined to be merciful; they exacted hard and degrading conditions. Pupils became masters, and Masters an inferior class.

The Doctors were compelled to swear obedience to the students' Rectors, and to obey all the regulations of the Universities; a professor might not absent himself from the city without permission of the students, even for a single day. When and if he obtained such permission he was compelled to sign a bond that he would return within a certain time-limit; he was fined for unauthorized absences; if he failed to secure an audience of five at a regular lecture, or of three at an "extraordinary" lecture, he was fined as though he had been absent; and he—not the pupils—must be punctual. He must begin his lecture promptly when the great bell of St. Peter's began to ring for mass, on pain of forfeiting twenty *solidi* per offence, and he must finish it within one minute after the bell began to ring for tierce. If the students delayed after that, they themselves would have to pay a fine, but only half as much as a delinquent professor.

The hurried professor who skipped a Chapter or a Decretal in his lectures was fined; he dared not postpone dealing with a difficulty in the text until the end of the text was reached, in the manner of certain modern teachers, who then conveniently forget all about the knotty point. He was required to be abreast of definite portions of the law text by definite dates, and to complete his schedule of lectures by the end of the year. Ten Bolognese pounds was deposited as security for the proper completion of the course.

These minute regulations may excite our astonishment; it is hard to conceive that respected and influential citizens should submit to such degrading and humiliating conditions. For the Bolognese Doctors were powers in their own municipality; they possessed important privileges in the Constitution of the Republic; they were not required to bear arms; and they were *ex-officio* members of the governing Council of Six Hundred. Their reputation was international; their considered opinions in Civil and Canon Law were as greatly respected as those of the Paris Doctors in the rival field of Theology.

However, their pupils wanted their full money's worth. For these far-travelled, middle-aged students of the Law were in earnest; they were spending their own money, not that of complaisant parents. They were not adventurous youngsters, eager for the glamorous delights of Paris, and pretending to "scholarity" in order to obtain them; their regulations were directed towards obtaining a full measure of lectures.

The organization of the students into Universities took place at some time during the last quarter of the twelfth century. According to their nationality, they were divided into several Guilds or Universities, much like the "Nations" of Paris. Rashdall claims that there were originally four such

Universities: the Lombards, the Ultramontanes, the Tuscans, and the Romans. But no documentary evidence is adduced for such a view, and his arguments are not convincing. In any event, if there ever were four Universities, they were quickly reduced to two: the Universitas Citramontanorum, and the Universitas Ultramontanorum. In other words, the Guild of students hailing from this side of the Alps—the Italians; and the Guild of students from beyond the Alps.

Only the Law Students were involved, and no Bolognese. The Arts followers were in the main young men, as in Paris; they were numerically inferior, and unimportant. The Arts Studium was chiefly a local affair; it had no international reputation.

These two Societies of Law Students neither sought nor obtained any charters or privileges. The Pope may have cast longing eyes at this secular Studium, but he was not invited to assume control. His aid was not wanted. To the very last these two Universities existed side by side, each modelled upon the lines of the Guild, each headed by a Rector, but working harmoniously together for the common benefit of their respective members.

The Societies made their own laws, and bound all members by oath to obey the Statutes and the Rectors. The Bolognese students took no oath of obedience, had no vote in the University Congregations, were ineligible for University offices, and were apparently quite content with this arrangement. There was no nonsense about college spirit in those days.

The Popes finally saw their chance to insinuate themselves into the situation. After the students had effectually subjugated both the city and the professors, the Papacy confirmed their statutes and privileges in a series of Bulls, subjecting offenders to ecclesiastical punishments; but the independent student body, though it consisted very largely of ecclesiastics, was inclined to ignore the proffered aid. The students preferred to manage their own affairs and exact their own discipline. Very few appeals were taken to Rome by the University, whereas the Paris Masters were constantly appealing against infringements of their rights.

The Bolognese government recognized the student University, and treated with it as with an equal power. But there was one right to which they strongly objected, and for obvious reasons. This was the right of the University to declare a secession. On the most trivial pretext, the municipal authorities felt, a hot-headed council of students might bind the entire body to a mass migration, and thereby deprive the city of its most important source of revenue. Consider Atlantic City or Blackpool suddenly deprived of its visitors, and you may realize what secession would mean to a mediaeval University town.

Yet, strangely enough, it was not the students who instituted the fatal custom of migration; it was the teachers themselves, citizens of Bologna though they were. Prior to the thirteenth century individual Masters or groups of Masters, discontented with the prospects of teaching in their native city, or feeling they were not receiving sufficient recognition from the authorities, or possibly seduced by rival municipalities, migrated and set up as teachers elsewhere. The great majority of the Italian Law Schools resulted from such secessions of Doctors—and later, from secessions of student bodies, or from both causes.

Bologna frowned on this practice. The departure of a famous teacher meant one magnet the less to attract outsiders. The city authorities compelled professors who wished to teach in Bologna to take an oath that they would not teach anywhere else. Even the oath, however, with its tremendous mediaeval penalties, did not always avail against the lure of larger fees and greater opportunities. Student mass migrations were, of course, much more serious in their consequences.

In 1204 the University, as the result of some grievance, went off to Vicenza. Bologna was swept clean of students. The University of Vicenza dates from this migration. The townsfolk were in despair; the civic authorities had no power over the alien students. But they could control their own citizens. Accordingly they forbade such students as were citizens of Bologna to follow the University, or to aid or abet future secessions.

After the next secession—to Arezzo, in 1215—they went further. They forbade, on pain of banishment and confiscation of goods, *any* scholar to administer an oath to another, binding him to leave the city if so commanded. This ordinance brought the students up in arms; it was manifestly hitting below the belt. Its purport was clear. It was the Rectors who administered the oath, and the city was assuming summary jurisdiction over them.

The University promptly appealed to the Pope—it was one of the few occasions of such an appeal. The Pope as promptly sided with the students. Honorius III commanded the repeal of the ordinance, but the City Fathers chose to defy the Bull. For when the Rectors proceeded to exact the usual oath from newly-arrived scholars, the city took immediate action.

It decreed that the office of Rector be suppressed, and that all scholars who took the oath be placed under the ban of the city, subject to loss of civil rights and confiscation of their worldly goods. The University as promptly retorted by dispersing. For three years the scholars fertilized the infant Studia of other Italian cities, and Bologna lamented her deserted schools and her lean purses.

In 1220 the Pope appealed once more to the city—probably as a face-saving device—and this time it gracefully yielded. It repealed all the penal clauses and invited the scholars to return, but it stubbornly insisted that the Rectors must take an oath of non-removal from the city. So matters rested until 1222, when a fresh clash occurred. Regardless of their oath, the Rectors issued a clarion call for secession. The University obeyed *en masse*, and thousands of students flocked after their leaders to the neighbouring city of Padua. The famous Uni-

versity of Padua—where Galileo taught for a generation—
dates from these troublous days at Bologna. Though by 1224
the Bolognese were recalled, after yet another Papal intervention, a good number of students preferred the more
salubrious air of Padua, and there remained.

But Bologna, whose pride was touched, yielded in the matter
of the oath only by making the law a dead letter; the law
itself was not repealed until 1288. By the middle of the century
the city went so far as to grant civil, though not political
rights, to the alien students, and directed its Podestà to enforce
by appropriate measures the decrees of the Rectorial Court in
so far as they affected University students.

In 1321 occurred the last important secession from Bologna,
and, strangely enough, the only one involving a crime of
violence. A scholar abducted the daughter of a wealthy and
powerful citizen—his object being honourable matrimony,
doubtless with an eye to the father's wealth. The indignant
Bolognese complained to the authorities; the fugitive pair were
pursued and captured. The daughter maintained that she was
the victim of a forcible abduction. In any event the penalty
was death, and the unfortunate scholar was duly executed,
despite the protest of his University. The outrage was too
great to be borne in silence, and once more the students
streamed out of the city gates, this time followed by a great
number of their professors, who for once cast in their lot with
their pupils. Siena was the beneficiary this time.

A reconciliation was effected the following year, in token
whereof the city elders publicly rebuked the Podestà, and the
humbled citizens built a chapel for the University—thereafter
known as "The Church of S. Mary of the Scholars in the
Borgo of S. Mamolo."

Thereafter City and University dwelt in a fair degree of
amity for several centuries, until, paradoxically enough, the
enormous strength and prestige of the University sowed the
seeds of its own decay. For the City, anxious to propitiate her
famous daughter, began to pay regular salaries to the pro-

fessors, thus reducing the students' fees. But by so doing it gradually acquired the power of supervision, until eventually the student Universities became mere shadows of their former selves, empty shells without substance. But of this more anon.

M

CHAPTER XVII

Cismontane and Transmontane

THE School of Law was the School *par excellence* of Bologna. It overshadowed in fame all the other Schools of Europe, and cast the other Faculties of its own Studium into the shade. There were two separate and distinct Law Universities: one of the non-Bolognese Italian students—the Cismontane University; and the other of all other European students—the Transmontane University. Each elected its own officers, was headed by its own Rector, and attended to the welfare of its members, even as the "Nations" of Paris did. But they worked in unison against the common enemy—whether City or Professoriate—and by the fourteenth century they acted to all intents and purposes as one body. At that late period Congregations were held in common; Statutes applied equally to both bodies, and either Rector could act on behalf of the other in the event of absence. The other Faculties—Arts, Medicine, Theology—had little to say in the government of the whole; they were content to follow in the footsteps of their brilliant brethren. In Paris, on the contrary, it was the four "Nations" of the Arts Faculty that lorded it over the rest.

The supreme governing body of each University was the Congregation, or General Assembly of all the student members. Every Cismontane or Transmontane scholar was entitled to a vote. The Bolognese students were, of course, left out in the cold. There was another class, too, who had no say: poor scholars who lived at the expense of others. It was not quite a democracy; wealth already played a necessary part in the affairs of these budding lawyers. Attendance at the Congregations was compulsory, and everyone had a right to speak. The Rectors moved the question, and votes were decided by a majority. Inasmuch as the Universities had no buildings, a

Convent or a Church was usually borrowed for the occasion; if a splendid ceremony was in prospect the great Cathedral was used. As in Paris, there was no tangible property; the lectures were held in the private homes of the Masters or in schools rented for that purpose. Thus for the students a cessation was merely a matter of packing their private belongings and taking to the road. Therein lay the tremendous strength of the mediaeval University.

The Rector had to be a student and a clerk. The clerical status was essential, if he was to possess jurisdiction over all the clerks among the students. Canon Law was strict in its insistence that no layman should have power to try the sacred person of a "clerk." The Rector was elected for a term of two years by the body of ex-Rectors, the Council of the University, and an equal number of special delegates elected from the student body.

Together with the Council, he made up the executive authority of the University. This Council, seventeen in number in the fifteenth century, was elected from the local subdivisions of the University. Inasmuch as the student body was almost too large for frequent assemblage, the increasing tendency was to leave matters in the hands of the Rectors and the Councils. The effect of the longer term of office was to increase the power of the Rectors.

Yet the Rectors could not legislate; they could only enforce the Statutes passed by the general Congregations. Where a fine was imposed by Statute, it was their duty to collect it. If they failed in that duty, it became chargeable as their own debt to the University. They sat as judges in cases involving the members of the University, and in later years their sentences could be executed by the City authorities. As in Paris, the University claimed jurisdiction in cases where a student was either plaintiff or defendant, but Bologna always denied such a right as usurpation, and there were many disputes in this connection. By 1432 the University provided that no student was to be arrested for any crime, except that of high treason, without the consent of his Rector; that he was not to be dragged through the streets in the good old mediaeval way, and that, if he infringed the law against carrying arms, he was to be permitted bail.

The Rector also exercised control over the landlords of the houses in which students resided, and over all tradesmen and booksellers who dealt with the University. He could fine a delinquent student; he could expel him for a serious offence, and declare the malefactor "perjured." All students, with the exception of Bishops and other high dignitaries, were required by oath to inform against their fellows who had offended in any way against the law of the University. This was a pernicious custom that infested all the Universities of Europe, and gave rise to a class of backbiting, blackmailing informers and spies who played havoc with the morale of the students in general.

There were adequate safeguards against a too arrogant use of power. In serious cases the consent of the Council was necessary; after the Rector's term of office complaints could be lodged against him before the full Congregation by any scholar or professor who felt himself aggrieved by his act, omission, or decision. The Congregation could hold him personally responsible and require him to pay damages to the injured party, and also to the University itself for malfeasance or non-feasance in office.

But during the tenure of his office the student Rector was a most magnificent individual, hedged about with privileges and immunities, invested with all the gorgeous trappings so dear to the mediaeval heart. Rector Magnificus was his title; he walked in dignity ahead of the most powerful in Church and State; Bishops, Archbishops, even Cardinals, were compelled to yield precedence to this scholar. Only the Bishop of Bologna enjoyed a special exemption.

His salary was elastic; it was a proportion of the fines which he collected. Yet he dared not be too harsh, for fear of retribution and damages. As a matter of fact, his emoluments were small compared with his heavy expenditure. The Statutes provided that he must live in state, to uphold the honour of the University. He must keep at least two liveried servants; he must serve a lavish table, and impress all comers with his wealth. In the sixteenth century the new Rector had to submit to a friendly mauling; the clothes were torn off his back and rent into little pieces, and he was expected to redeem every fragment at an outrageous price. At Padua he had to bear the cost of his own installation, at which no expense was spared. It took place in the Cathedral; he was invested with due pomp and ceremony in the Rectorial hood by a Doctor before the assembled University, who then escorted him in procession to his own house, where all were served with "wine and spices," food and sweetmeats. Then a tournament was held, in accordance with the rules of chivalry, all in his honour and at his expense. Two hundred lances and a like number of pairs of gloves were his particular contribution. The Statutes regulated his affairs with meticulous detail; cost being no object to his fellow-students. His liveries had to be of a specified fine cloth; the wine he served must be of a particular quality; he must comport himself in such and such a manner.

It followed that only the most wealthy students could achieve the doubtful honour of Rectordom. Probably the lucky candidate was selected only after an exhaustive study of his financial condition; what benefices he enjoyed, what broad fields and castles he possessed, what ships laden with spices and silks were sailing the sea for him.

Even the wealthiest shrank after a while from assuming such exorbitant burdens, such a drain on the fattest purse. The student body countered by making the honour compulsory. The recipient of their esteem *had* to accept office willynilly. This was the first adumbration of the modern doctrine of the particular duties of the rich to the general public, exemplified in philanthropic outbursts and largess to institutions of various kinds. Then, to prevent the unlucky Rector from absconding after his election, he was forbidden

to leave the City without the Council's permission, or without
putting up a substantial bond to secure his return.

It grew more and more difficult to find students to take
office, even under compulsion. Scholars concealed their
wealth, even as men do in these days of crushing income-tax;
shabby garments and well-worn shoes became the fashion.
There was the City to contend with, too; every secession or
threat of secession meant that the Rector might be held personally responsible for the injury to the citizens. By the
sixteenth century the two Rectorships were usually held by one
individual, and in spite of the loud protests of the scholars,
who loved display that involved them in no expense, the office
was gradually shorn of its outward glories, and its executive
functions began to devolve upon deputies. In the end the
Rector Magnificus was but a pale shadow of his former self;
and as he declined in prestige, the City grew bolder in usurping
students' liberties.

Not much is known of the individual lives of the students
of Bologna, their manners and customs. This is understandable. The chief sources of information are the University
Statutes, and as they were drawn up by the students themselves, they were naturally not as strict or meticulous as those
drawn up by Masters, as in Paris.

The Bolognese scholars rented their own houses from the
townsfolk, individually or in groups. The rentals were fixed
at a fair sum by the Taxors; otherwise there was complete
liberty of action. The student regulations were directed chiefly
against the carrying of arms—to ensure that verbal disputes
should not suddenly turn into more serious affrays—and
against gambling. Especially at a General Assembly the carrying of weapons was forbidden, but eventually the law was
more honoured in the breach than in the observance. For
another Statute naïvely permits anyone who fears the stiletto
of his enemy to inform his Rector privately to that effect;
when the Rector, instead of taking active measures, granted

the intimidated student the right to stay away from the Assembly.

Gambling also was strictly disciplined. It was an offence against the University not only to play at dice, but even to watch the dicers. It was an offence to maintain a gaming-house, or to enter one, and this former prohibition included even the Law Doctors. Evidently some of the professors, in those bad old days, had eked out a meagre income by enticing their students into games of chance, where locked purses opened much more readily than in the lecture hall. As a matter of fact, the student Universities, as we have already seen, were at pains to discipline the masters rather than the students.

The student, newly arrived at Bologna, took the oath of obedience to his Rector, and paid his matriculation fee. There were three lectures daily. The first began at about 6.30 a.m., when the bell rang for mass at St. Peter's, and lasted until about 9 a.m., when the bell ringing for tierce brought it to an abrupt halt. The second began at 2.0 p.m. and ended at 4.0; the third from 4.0 to 5.30 p.m. This, at least, was the winter schedule. In the summer the afternoon classes were slightly earlier. It may be seen that a student's life at Bologna was no sinecure; it meant early rising and application.

The lectures were given in the home of the professor or in a rented school; if a teacher happened to be so popular that no dwelling-house was large enough to contain his auditors, he might use a public building, or even lecture in the great open squares of the city. The student paid his fees directly to the professor, and the amount was a matter for private negotiation. That students were reluctant to pay high fees is made evident by the complaint of Odofredus, Professor of Law at Bologna about the year 1250. He closed his season's course of lectures with the following pithy words:

"Now, gentlemen, we have begun and finished and gone through this book, as you know who have been in this class, for which we thank God and His Virgin Mother and all His

Saints. It is an ancient custom in this city that when a book is finished mass should be sung to the Holy Ghost, and it is a good custom, and hence should be observed. But since it is the practice that doctors on finishing a book should say something of their plans, I will tell you something, but not much. Next year I expect to give ordinary lectures well and lawfully as I always have, but no extraordinary lectures, for students are not good payers, wishing to learn but not to pay, as the saying is: All desire to know but none to pay the price. I have nothing more to say to you, beyond dismissing you with God's blessing and begging you to attend mass."

The textbooks in Civil Law were chiefly the Digest and Code that together made up the Corpus Juris Civilis, and Irnerius' minute gloss thereon. In Canon Law, Gratian's Decretum was the text of texts. In 1234, Gregory IX added five more books of Decretals, representing the latest decrees of the Popes, and ordered that they should be studied in Bologna and Paris. Subsequent Popes followed suit, until there was a complete Code, the Corpus Juris Canonici, which set up the Papacy and Papal authority as the final word on almost any matter. Arrogance was the keynote of the Canon Law; if secular laws conflicted with it, so much the worse for them. No wonder the Canon Lawyers, accustomed to such outrageous pretensions, became the staunchest bulwark of the Papal hierarchy. Their livelihood, their very reason for existence, depended upon the blindest loyalty to the ecclesiastical system they had helped to rear. Even when the Theologians themselves resisted the Papal pretensions, the Faculties of Canon Law could always be counted on to come to the rescue. And in return, a grateful Papacy, while exalting Theology, was careful to award the most lucrative posts to the Canon Lawyers.

The Civil Lawyers, on the other hand, were essentially secular in character. They mingled actively in the political life of the times, and held positions of honour in every Italian municipality. In the great life-and-death struggle of the Guelfs and the Ghibellines at least as many sided with the Empire as with the Pope. Justinian was their oracle, even as Aristotle commanded obedience from the Philosophers. Gradually, as in Theology, the glosses overlaid the original text. First it was Irnerius; then came Accursius with a witless selection from all former glosses. Accursius was studied, and Justinian neglected. Civil Lawyers grew more and more narrow and sterile in thought, discussing vain distinctions with dialectical subtlety, contributing nothing to what after all is a social science, capable of progressive growth to meet the conditions of new times, new *mores*. But we can ill afford to cast stones at these ossified mediaeval lawyers. One glance at our own vast body of law should convince us that there has not been much change in method.

After five years of study, the student of Civil Law, at the discretion of the Rector, might lecture on a single title of the Law, or after six years on an entire book. For a Canonist these terms were rather shorter; four and five years respectively. The privilege of lectorship constituted them Bachelors, or apprentice lawyers. To become eligible for admission to the Doctorate, the Bachelor must have completed six years in Canon, and seven in Civil Law, or a combination course totalling ten years. He must also have given a full course of lectures. This was the most difficult task of all. For to lecture presupposes an audience, and students were naturally sceptical of the prowess of one who was actually their fellow. It was all practice for the Bachelor, but hard on the students. Not even the Bachelor's friends would suffer too long in the name of friendship. The unfortunate Bachelor was therefore compelled to exercise certain blandishments to attract an audience, and the most effective of these was found to be a discreet distribution of gifts or loans of money to needy students.

At last came the day for the bestowal of the Doctor's degree. Here the suppressed and downtrodden Doctors of Law held unlimited power. Their College had laid down strict rules for admission to their ranks, and the student Universities never attempted to regulate or limit its prerogative.

There were two stages in graduation: the first a private examination, and the second the public ordeal of the *Conventus*.

The anxious candidate rose betimes and attended the Mass of the Holy Ghost to strengthen himself for the ordeal. He then appeared before the entire Doctoral College, and listened while the Doctor under whom he had sat vouched for his qualifications. The College thereupon assigned to him two passages in the Law. He was permitted to retire to his own quarters, there to study these knotty passages, and was at liberty to obtain whatever assistance he desired. Later in the day he appeared again before the College and gave an extended exposition of the assigned passages. Two Doctors questioned him closely on the passages in question, while others subjected him to a running fire of questions on related points of law. After the examination was over a ballot was taken; a majority vote was sufficient to pass him. The Bachelor was now a Licentiate.

It took the *Conventus*, however, to make him a full Doctor. This was a solemn and colourful ceremony. The candidate rode round the city on horseback, accompanied by beadles, and issued invitations to his friends, and various public officials and church dignitaries, to attend his *Conventus* and the ensuing banquet. On the great day he was escorted in state by his Doctor and all his "socii," or those fellow-students who lodged in the same house with him. With a fanfare of trumpets and much cheering and music the procession made its way to the Cathedral. There the candidate delivered a speech, and advanced a thesis on a point of law. This thesis he defended in the manner of the Paris disputation against all comers. Probably the whole argumentation was a formality. Friendly students in the audience fed him with questions and objections which he was prepared to demolish with a flourish of wit. Read what a vainglorious candidate of Bologna wrote home to his trusting relatives:

"'Sing unto the Lord a new song, praise him with stringed instruments and organs, rejoice upon the high-sounding cymbals,' for your son has held a glorious disputation, which was attended by a great multitude of teachers and scholars. He answered all questions without a mistake, and no one could prevail against his arguments. Moreover, he offered a famous banquet, at which both rich and poor were honoured as never before, and he has duly begun to give lectures which are already so popular that other classrooms are deserted and his own are filled."

The disputation over, the candidate was presented to the Archdeacon, who also delivered an oration, and then conferred the licence to teach the Law by authority of the Pope and in the name of the Holy Trinity. Thereupon he was invested with all the trappings of his new office. He took his seat in the Magisterial Chair, an open law book was placed in his hands, a gold ring on his finger, and the biretta on his head; the Archdeacon embraced him, and gave him the final kiss and benediction; and behold, he was a Doctor!

The Universities escorted him in triumph through the town, and if the new-fledged Doctor were wealthy he was attended by a mounted escort; while three pipers and four trumpeters squeaked and blasted to wake the dead. The tables were laid, the banquet prepared, and all set to with a right good will. The newly-fledged Doctor distributed presents to all and sundry—to the Archdeacon, the Prior of the College, and each of the assembled Doctors. And if he were very wealthy, the rejoicings might be capped by a tournament, though this was forbidden by Statute. Graduation, in short, was a costly business. The poor student had sometimes to wait indefinitely for his degree, until he and his family could scrape together the wherewithal. At some of the Spanish Universities matters were even worse: a bullfight was an almost indispensable part of the ceremony.

Now the ritual of Bologna has certain points of resemblance to that of Paris, and also certain marked differences. The procedure of the private and public examinations, and the ceremony of investment, are approximately alike, and have much in common with the rites of initiation into a trade guild, or even into the order of knighthood; though at Bologna, as many of the students were wealthy, the whole affair was considerably more expensive than in Paris.

But as regards the licence itself, and the ceremony of inception, the procedure was quite different. In Paris, the Chancellor ostensibly conducted the private examination, and granted the licence, and then followed inception into the University of Masters. At Bologna the Doctoral College conducted the examination, without interference from the Archdeacon; their approval was a sufficient inception into their College, and the final Licence of the Archdeacon was a pure formality which was not required until the year 1219. The Doctors of Bologna never had to fight for their very existence against ecclesiastical control as in Paris, and the students did not object to the Archdeacon's moderate fee. That seemed to be the extent of his interest in the matter.

In Bologna a teaching Doctorship was much more valuable than in Paris. Here the Masters of Arts were numerous, and each had the right, and indeed was required, to teach. Bologna, however, had many incepting Masters who did not intend to, or were unable to teach. The teaching Doctorship was a prize of considerable value. The number of such degrees was limited and the reward in fees large.

The Doctors jealously restricted admission to their ranks, especially after salaried chairs were endowed by the City. Bologna had been reluctant to take this step, but was compelled to follow the example of rival cities, if she wished to keep her most famous teachers. The Italian cities, anxious to annex some of Bologna's prestige, would tempt the Doctors with promises of fixed contracts, lodgings, bonuses, exemption from taxation, and immunity from the process of the lower courts.

Accordingly, in 1280 the students of Bologna themselves made a contract with the Canonist Garsias to lecture to them for one year at a fixed salary. When it came to payment, however, they skilfully persuaded the City to foot the bill. Nine years later two permanent chairs were endowed, the salaries were increased, and the City had a say in the nomination of professors.

Before that happened the Doctoral College, by its own pettiness, and its short-sighted and selfish policy, had destroyed itself. Not content to leave the power of control in the hands of the College, a clique was formed to assume for itself a complete monopoly of admissions. This clique, small in numbers but all-powerful, made itself self-perpetuating. Eventually it *was* the College; the other Doctors found themselves shouldered out. There were sixteen in the Civil Law College in 1397, and twelve in the Canon Law College in 1460.

Quite early the Doctors confined membership in their College and the right to receive the best of the salaried chairs to citizens of Bologna. In this the municipal authorities supported them. But the students objected in so far as the salaried chairs were concerned, and as they had effective means of enforcing their will, in 1255 they compelled the Doctors to swear that they would not refuse permission to foreign Doctors elected by the students to fill any chair.

In spite of the opposition of the students, and later, of the City, the clique of incumbent professors manœuvred themselves into an even more impregnable position. They actually claimed the right to reserve the emoluments of professorial office for themselves, their sons, and their families *in perpetuum*. The right of the son of a Doctor to succeed to any vacant chair was expressly maintained by the jurist compiler, Accursius. (In codicem, L. 4.)

This introduced a new note into educational methods. A hereditary aristocracy of professors! Yet why not? It is no madder than a hereditary ruling class, or hereditary wealth. The City itself intervened in 1295, possibly at the instigation of resentful fellow-citizens who were not members of the clique, and forbade the exclusive promotion to vacant chairs of sons and nephews, cousins and relatives twice removed. But in spite of prohibitions and protests, the Professoriate managed to ride its uneasy seat. In course of time, their blood ran thin; imbecile sons found the chairs which they inherited too much for them, but they clung to them none the less, and Bologna rapidly lost prestige. Other Universities made their way to the front; notably the French Schools of Angers, Orléans, and Laon. The City, too, helped on the decay of its greatest glory, by undermining the independence of the students. The salaried professors were partly responsible; for the authorities, as the paymasters, thought it only right that they should have some measure of control. This was exercised by a Board appointed by themselves. This Board assumed greater and greater powers, until by the sixteenth century it was omnipotent in University affairs. The students had been ousted from control.

CHAPTER XVIII

The Letter-Writers of Bologna

THE Arts School of Bologna played no such prominent part
in the affairs of the Studium as the same Faculty in Paris; yet,
strangely enough, the Seven Liberal Arts were always much
more highly regarded at Bologna, with the single exception of
Logic. At no time were the classics altogether neglected. In
1321 one Antonio di Virgilio was given a substantial salary
for lecturing on such *démodé* poets as Virgil, Statius, Ovid, and
Lucan. A Compendium Grammaticae, written in the latter part
of the thirteenth century by one Caesar, was profusely illustrated with quotations from the classics. Cicero and Latin
composition was taught at the University even in the fourteenth century; but the revival of learning then in progress,
and intimately associated with Petrarch, was taking place
outside the Universities.

In Bologna, more especially, there was no independent
inquiry, no intellectual curiosity, eager for the lore of the new
humanism. There all was formal, crystallized. The Law overshadowed all else; even Rhetoric was formalized, and, in
accordance with the practical spirit of the age, exceedingly
lucrative.

Rhetoric, the art of eloquence, of mouth-filling, noble-
sounding phrases, of literary style and elegance, now underwent a remarkable change, becoming almost exclusively the
Ars dictaminis, the art of writing—letters, documents, charters,
papers both public and commercial. This transformation was
in progress in and around Bologna, in the little city republics
that covered the plain of Lombardy. There was a vast growing
commerce that called for the inditing of correspondence, bills,
and contracts; the ecclesiastical chanceries, which had a complicated mass of affairs to be handled; the municipal councils,
with their charters and statutes, their correspondence with

Papacy and Empire; the increasing number of Papal decrees on every conceivable subject; and the rapid progress of the law with its infinitely ramified forms: all contributed to swell the demand for ready letter-writers, and men skilled in the drafting of documents.

Such a demand, coupled with the ability to pay for services rendered, always creates its own supply. There arose a huge industry—one can call it only that—of professors, who, for a consideration, wrote and wrote, and taught others how to do the same. They drew up manuals, explaining the principles involved in this noble art; they even published collections of model letters and documents for every occasion, for the use of those who were too lazy or unskilful to create their own forms. The correspondent who wished to congratulate his friend on the birth of a son, or condole with him for the loss of a wife; the student writing home for money; the creditor seeking payment of a long overdue bill; a city in need of a charter; a lawyer in search of the correct wording for a title-deed; the prince anxious to draft an unequivocal statute; the Pope polishing up his latest Bull and hesitating over the turn of a phrase: all would find what they wanted in such a compendium.

The new art was not only practical; it was immensely popular. In Bologna, in the year 1200, it had become a separate and dignified branch of study. And from Bologna, as from other Lombard cities, self-appointed masters migrated to France and set up at Orléans a secondary centre of radiation. They invaded Paris, where they drew up wills, contracts, and other legal papers, gave legal advice for fees, and acted, in short, as unqualified lawyers. But the University of Paris, although there is some evidence that the *Ars dictaminis* was taught there as an incidental subject, was greatly inclined to be superior in respect of this "Lombard" art.

The most famous, or shall we say notorious, of all the masters of the *Ars dictaminis* was Boncompagno, who dates approximately from 1165 to 1240. He was a most arrogant fellow, shouting his own praises from the housetops, and advertising himself with a skill that would have shamed a modern publicity agent. His enemies and his envious imitators he denounced as "numberless scorpions . . . trying to sting him with their venomous tails, and countless dogs . . . barking at his back, but when they were face to face with him the lips of the envious trembled." He announced the advent of a famous foreign doctor, who had challenged the mighty Boncompagno to a public trial of wits; and when half Bologna was impatiently awaiting the arrival of the unknown scholar, he blandly admitted that the foreign doctor was merely a figment of his imagination.

He acknowledged no predecessors, claiming to be the sole originator of the art. His one extant work, *Rhetorica antiqua Boncompagnus*, is divided into six books: (1) On student letters; (2) Forms for the Roman Church; (3) Letters to be addressed to the Pope; (4) Letters to and from emperors, kings, and queens; (5) Letters to the clergy; (6) Letters to noblemen, cities, and peoples. According to him, this work was publicly crowned with laurel at the University of Bologna in the year 1215, in the presence of all the Doctors of Civil and Canon Law and a multitude of cheering onlookers.

Yet in spite of all this publicity, the art had run its course before the end of the thirteenth century; though the *Ars notaria*, its sister art, exclusively concerned with the drafting of legal documents, continued its uneventful career, with real Doctors of *Notaria* to teach its intricacies at Bologna.

The School of Medicine, while completely subordinate to the Universities of Law, was well attended, and of a higher grade than the Medical Faculty of Paris. It was a practical study, like the Law, like Letter-Writing, and hence was well regarded by the Italians. In other words, there was money in it.

The Quadrivium, the second section of the Arts course, was regarded as almost a branch of Medicine. Mathematics flourished; Astronomy, in the habit of Astrology, was fundamental.

N

Your well-instructed physician considered it essential to know what were his patient's critical days, and treatment was given only in accordance with the favourable or unfavourable aspect of the heavens. Astrology was in good repute at Bologna; as a matter of fact, there were Chairs in the Faculty of Astrology. It was the duty of one of these professorial Astrologers to cast gratis the horoscopes of inquiring students. Nevertheless, it was a ticklish trade. If the predictions were untrue, the Astrologer was an impostor; if the percentage of guesses proved unduly accurate, the ever-suspicious Church was ready to accuse him of necromancy and black magic. The most distinguished member of the Astrological Faculty of Bologna, one Cecco d'Ascoli, fell in between the horns of this dilemma. He erred on the side of predicting only too well. As a result, he died at the stake in 1327, a victim of the Inquisition.

But Medicine at Bologna was more than mere superstition. The medical student was supposed to know the *Liber Tegni* of Galen, the *Aphorisms* of Hippocrates, the *Canon* of Avicenna, and the medical treatises of Averrhoës. What set Bologna apart from Paris and the Northern Universities in general was her special attention to anatomy and surgery. The surgeon in Italy was also a Doctor of Medicine; he was not degraded as in Paris. Dissection was practised, too, in spite of the vehement opposition of the Church. Mundinus, the father of modern anatomy, taught surgery at Bologna. His *Anatomia* was the standard text on the subject for several centuries. Dissections of corpses of executed felons were not practised more than once or twice a year, but even this limited number of autopsies made for the understanding of the human body. The dissections were barbarously done, and the corpses stank unconscionably. The Statutes of Florence required that wine and food be proffered to both professors and students in the course of a dissection, to keep them from fainting during the grisly ordeal.

Theology was ill-regarded at Bologna, and generally in

Italy. The Italians had no stomach for its abstractions and metaphysical discussions. Besides, there was little money in it. The Papacy, too, in pursuance of its considered policy to restrict the sacred science to Paris and one or two other Universities, like Oxford and Toulouse, frowned upon its installation too near home. As a result, there was in the beginning no School of Theology at Bologna. Only the Mendicant Friars undertook to study the subject. Other and more worldly ecclesiasts preferred the study of Canon Law, which brought them honours and preferment. The Regulars studied and taught Theology in their own Convent Schools, but they had to go to Paris if they wanted a degree. In the year 1352 Innocent VI constituted a Theologic Faculty in Bologna. But it did not mean anything. The Regulars were practically the only ones to take advantage of its courses; it saved them the expense and danger of a trip to Paris.

CHAPTER XIX

Oxford

WHILE Paris and Bologna were the great archetypal Universities of Europe, another University of almost equal importance was evolving in the realm of England. Together with Cambridge, Oxford secured a complete monopoly of the higher education, a monopoly that has lasted almost to this very day. Paris was the model, yet the checkered career of Oxford is distinctive and fascinating. In theology it proved a worthy rival of Paris; in the natural and mathematical sciences it far surpassed all other Universities; in philosophy it began where the Parisian Scholastics left off; and it housed the Wycliffite movement, the greatest of pre-Reformation revolts.

Like its forbears, the University of Oxford was a gradual growth, spontaneous and free; no pope or king or municipality had a hand in its foundation, though both king and pope were deeply interested once the Studium had reared its head. Some time in the twelfth century the scholars gathered, a trickle of enthusiasts inhibited by poverty or other reasons from crossing the Channel, where the well-advertised Abélard was addressing the scholars of Europe.

Oxford was not a Cathedral town, and there is some doubt as to why it should have attracted any scholars at all. Possibly its accessibility, its thriving commerce, and the accidental presence of one or two eminent teachers had something to do with it.

At all events, when Henry II quarrelled with Thomas à Becket, he initiated a train of events that raised the tiny Studium almost at once to the dignity of a *Studium Generale*, a place of international importance. Enraged by the aid and comfort which his adversary was receiving from his fellow-clergy, Henry, at some time between 1165 and 1169, declared an embargo on ecclesiastical traffic. Henceforth no cleric was

186

to cross from the Continent to England, or from England to the Continent, without the permission of the king himself, or of his Justiciar. Furthermore, he decreed that all clerks abroad who possessed revenues from English holdings be peremptorily summoned by the Sheriffs to return to English soil within three months, "as they loved their revenues."

As a climax, it seems that the King of France, righteously indignant at Henry's cavalier treatment of Holy Church, and always eager to make trouble for his hereditary enemy, helped the good work by expelling the English scholars from Paris. For John of Salisbury in 1167 writes that "France, the mildest and most civil of nations, has expelled her alien scholars."

There must have been wailing and gnashing of teeth among the English scholars at Paris. They were clerics one and all, wearing the tonsure, as did every scholar in Northern Europe, and hence theoretically on Becket's side. But many were possessed of benefices from which they derived the income that made their comfortable sojourn in Paris possible, and they surely "loved their revenues." They had no illusions as to Henry's readiness to carry out his threat; for them it was "return or starve." The passion for learning was not strong enough to overcome the cravings of a hitherto well-fed body. So, reluctantly and with bitter thoughts, the English contingent in Paris, scholars and masters alike, packed their gear, bade farewell to their fellow-scholars of more fortunate realms, and crowded into boats that plied across the Channel.

Dumped on English shores, that had grown alien in the years of absence, these beneficed scholars pondered on their future course. They could, no doubt, return to their benefices and endeavour to earn the incomes which they derived from them, but the prospect was not attractive. They were homesick for the intellectual, heady atmosphere of Paris, the keen disputations, the give and take of the Schools.

The little Studium of Oxford attracted their attention. It was conveniently near the metropolis, London; scholars and masters gave the city an aura of learning. Many of the returned students drifted thither, found the place to their liking, and recommended it to hesitating friends. Exiled Masters from Paris set up their schools as on the Seine, and their old students flocked to them again. The Schools grew rapidly in reputation. New scholars, prohibited by the troublous times from travelling to the Continent, joined them. A *Studium Generale* was in the making. Another daughter of Paris had been born.

Inasmuch as these masters and scholars were chiefly from Paris, it was only to be expected that they should set up an organization similar to that of the parent University. In other words, a Guild of Masters to run its affairs, a course of studies and a manner of living modelled on what they had been accustomed to.

The first definite reference to Oxford as a home of scholars is contained in the contemporary account of the vainglorious yet sprightly Welsh traveller, Giraldus Cambrensis. According to his Autobiography he visited Oxford about 1184-5, and decided to try out his newly-written *Topographia Hibernica* on the assembled scholars. His account of the experience, written in the third person, is a masterpiece of naïve egotism:

"In course of time," says he, "when the work was completed and corrected, desiring not to hide his candle under a bushel, but to place it on a candlestick so that it might give light, he resolved to read his work at Oxford, where the clergy in England chiefly flourished and excelled in clerkship, before that great audience. And as there were three distinctions or divisions in the work, and each division occupied a day, the readings lasted three successive days. And on the first day he received and entertained in his Hostel all the poor (scholars) of the whole town; on the second, all the Doctors of the different Faculties, and such of their pupils as were of greater fame and note; on the third, the rest of the scholars with many knights, townsfolk, and burghers. It was a costly and noble act, for the authentic and ancient times of the poets were thus renewed, nor does the present or any past age recall anything like it in England."

By 1192, according to Richard of Devizes in his *History of Richard I*, the scholars were so numerous that "Oxford barely keeps its clerks from starving." By 1209 it was estimated that there were 3000 students in the town; a number practically equal to its native population. It was no doubt a serious problem to feed and lodge this tremendous influx of celibate non-workers and non-producers. It taxed the town's economy to the utmost, even though most of the scholars had sufficient money to pay their way.

The masters and students lived scattered throughout the town as tenants and lodgers in private houses; their food came from local sources, hitherto just about sufficient for local needs. As in every other nascent University town, the inhabitants seized upon the situation as a tempting opportunity to profiteer. Rents of dwellings went sky-high, food prices reached hitherto unheard-of levels. The scholars protested, but they had as yet no strong organization. Nor had they any other protection, except that of their "clericality"; neither pope nor king had taken official cognizance of the inchoate assemblage of scholars. The townsfolk turned the screw a little tighter. It was good business, for one thing; and for another, there was no particular love lost on clerics in England. The broad acres and easy lives of the ecclesiasts evoked the resentment and envy of those who toiled for a bare pittance. Moreover, the students, mere youngsters, as in Paris, released from the restraints of home and filled with the lust of life, were running wild. The shadowy organization of Masters had as yet evolved no system of control over their pupils. There were clashes with the townsfolk, drinking and gaming, sudden flurries of hatred between the two classes, women to be pursued. The students fought even among themselves. They divided into two "Nations," geographical in character, as in Paris. But the divisions were of the British Isles only. There was the "Northern" Nation, comprising all the North English counties and Scotland; and the "Southern" Nation of South England, Wales, and Ireland. The antagonism between the two was deep-seated; the divisions of local England hated each other with more venom and deadliness than the representatives of disparate and alien nations in Paris.

Paris was the great model in everything, even for the riots of Oxford and the tremendous results ensuing therefrom. In 1209 a scholar killed a woman of Oxford—accidentally, say the clerical chronicles of the time. It may have been so, but the town thirsted for revenge. The Mayor and burgesses attacked the offender's Hostel and arrested him. And on the principle that one clerk was as bad as another, they arrested other scholars found on the premises. The time was ripe for drastic measures. King John, that bad egg of English history, was in the midst of a tremendous quarrel with Innocent III, the most able and ruthless of Popes. The king was excommunicated, the entire country lay under the ban of an interdict. It is understandable that clerics were a little less than loved.

The Mayor of Oxford petitioned the king for permission to hang the imprisoned scholars. John thought he was striking back at the Pope and gave his instant consent. Two, or possibly three of the scholars were strung up. If we are to believe the chronicles—written by clerks—these had nothing to do with the original offence.

The Masters and students of Oxford, some three thousand of them, in their natural resentment against the outrage, and probably fearing the temper of the aroused populace, packed up and left the town. A good number went to Reading, some to Paris—the early restriction had long been removed—but most of them removed to Cambridge, where another tiny Studium was in formation. Cambridge got its start from this migration, and Oxford was deserted.

So far the picture parallels almost exactly what happened in Paris about the year 1200. As regards the *dénouement*, the parallel is even more exact.

A few years later, John, unable to keep up his unequal combat with the Papacy, and in mortal fear for his immortal soul, backed down. His submission to the Pope was grovelling in the extreme. It happened that the Holy Father had heard of the indignity suffered by "clerics" at the hands of the laymen of Oxford. Further, his far-sighted policy involved the encouragement of the nascent Universities all over Europe; he regarded them as so many pillars of the Papal throne. Accordingly he forced upon the suppliant John the Ordinance of 1214, the first great charter of privileges that Oxford possessed.

It provided that the whole town, its Mayor and burgesses, should march in procession, barefoot and coatless, to the graves of the victims buried in unhallowed ground, disinter the mouldering remains, and convey them to a cemetery sanctified by the Church for proper burial. For a period of ten years all existing Hostels and Schools occupied by clerks were to be let at half rates; for ten years more, rents could not be raised above what they were prior to the secession. More, the offending town, now humble and penitent, was required for ever and a day to pay the sum of forty-two shillings annually, to be distributed among the poor scholars on the feast day of St. Nicholas, patron saint of scholars—and of rogues; and in addition, it was to feast 100 poor scholars with bread and plenty of beer, pottage, meats, and fish. While the Pope was in this mood the scholars, taking another leaf out of the book of Paris, demanded the settlement of other grievances: the exorbitant charges for food, for instance. Hereafter provisions were to be sold at fair and reasonable prices, and fifty of the most prominent citizens of the town were compelled to take an oath to enforce such prices, and to renew this oath annually. Further, any clerk arrested by the townsmen for any offence had to be surrendered to the Bishop of Lincoln on demand, or to the Chancellor whom the Bishop was to appoint. This was the first mention of a Chancellor at Oxford; the institution and the office were previously unknown. This was another idea which the Pope had borrowed from Paris.

At one stroke Oxford was elevated to the rank of a great University; the Papal protection had been actively enlisted, and privileges had been granted to the scholars which were more far-reaching in effect and more onerous to the town than those granted on a similar occasion, only a few years earlier, to Paris. The conditions were rigidly enforced. Thus, the annual fine to the town has been exacted from that day to this; probably the longest period in all history over which any fine has ever been paid. In the year 1240 the forty-two shillings a year was diverted to a fund from which loans were made to poor students without interest. Later the Abbey of Eynsham undertook its payment in exchange for certain favours. And later still, the monks, repenting of their bargain, inveigled the Crown into the assumption of the burden, and there it rests to this day.

The thoughtful student of history finds food for thought in the fact that a weak, evilly-disposed ruler like John should have been unwittingly responsible for two great Charters of liberty—the Magna Carta that relieved the barons of England, and incidentally, the commoners, from the pressure of autocracy; and in a lesser field, the privileges and immunities accruing to Oxford, the educational centre of his kingdom.

Up to this time there had been very little organization of Masters; what little there was related merely to their own professional concerns and not to the benefit of the Studium as a whole; and there was practically no outside interference with them, apart from the general jurisdiction of the Church over all clerics. It is quite probable that a Guild of Masters existed, and that they had laid down certain conditions and qualifications for entrance into their body, which corresponded in effect to a licence to teach. The fact that Oxford was not a Cathedral town meant there was no Bishop on hand to assume general jurisdiction, and no Chancellor or other official on the ground ready and willing to assume authority over the Studium.

Now the Pope had decreed that the Bishop of Lincoln should take hold, and set up a Chancellor corresponding to the Chancellor of Paris. But the situation was entirely different from that of Paris, and it is no wonder that the constitutional development of Oxford proceeded along different lines.

In the first place, the Schools existed before the advent of Bishop and Chancellor; in the second, the diocese of Lincoln was some 120 miles away; no inconsiderable distance in those days. It was inevitable that the Bishop, even if he desired, could not maintain as close and sharp a supervision over a turbulent, independent University as was possible in Paris. Then, too, the Bishop was in no hurry to select a Chancellor. He might prove a veritable Frankenstein-creation, being in a sense forced on him by the Pope. In 1221 the University was still managing to exist without one. Finally pressure was brought to bear, and behold, there was a Chancellor.

It took him a long time, however, to gain any measure of control. His powers were originally merely those of a superior ecclesiast over clerics; the University itself was not involved. He could only judge the masters and scholars as clerics, and enforce his decrees by the usual excommunication and penance, and deprivation of "scholarity." The fact that in 1246, more than twenty years after the founding of the office, it was deemed necessary to issue a Bull forbidding teaching at Oxford "unless according to the custom of Paris he (the prospective teacher) shall have been examined and approved by the Bishop or his representative," shows that the fundamental job of a Chancellor, the issuing of teaching licences, was still undefined.

The Masters' University was slow in making a start. It followed closely along the lines of the Parisian pattern, but there was naturally a time-lag between the two institutions. Gradually the Faculty of Arts evolved, and divided into two "Nations," Northern and Southern, with Proctors and other officers, oaths, and funeral obligations, dues, Statutes, and other evidences of a complete organization. In one most important particular, however, the Parisian model was not followed, *i.e.* the institution of Rector.

The reason for this very grave omission lay in the peculiar character of the Chancellor himself. He had not existed from the beginning; he was, so to speak, an interloper. While it is true that ostensibly he was the Bishop's personal representative, the Bishop was a hundred and twenty miles away, and busy with what to him were more important problems. The Chancellor was alone in the midst of a rough-and-ready University, only too eager to defend its rights with vehemence. Accordingly, he felt that it was wise to live and let live.

Most important of all, at the very outset, the Masters had achieved a victory. The Chancellor was no outsider; he was a Master; in fact, one of their own number, and elected by the vote of his fellow-Masters. Thus there could be no such inevitable antagonism as existed on the Continent; the Chancellor was their own man, to all intents and purposes their Rector. Gradually he identified himself more and more with the Society of Masters, became their head, and forgot that he was the Bishop's representative. The Bishop might fume and fret, but he was far away. Both Chancellor and Masters were more and more inclined to ignore the Bishop; and in their usurpation of powers both king and Pope assisted.

The history of the Chancellor of Oxford is a long record of grants of power, until he grew to dominate the University as no other official dominated any other institution in mediaeval times. Henry III, for instance, in 1244 conferred on him the right to try all debt actions, rent cases, actions involving food, horses, clothes, or other forms of personalty in which a clerk was a defendant. In 1260 his jurisdiction was extended to contracts with the Jews of Oxford, a numerous and flourishing colony, with the exception of land claims and matters pertaining to the Crown. For the Jews had been considered wards of the Crown and not ordinarily amenable to the courts. Which meant, in plain language, that if there was any mulcting of this unfortunate race to be done, the Crown wanted the first pickings.

In 1275 Edward I went still further. He granted full powers to the Chancellor in all personal actions where a scholar was a party, whether as plaintiff or defendant, and the very important right to imprison as well as excommunicate, and to call upon the constable of the Royal Castle to enforce his mandate.

This comprised the whole sphere of civil jurisdiction. In criminal matters Henry III, in 1248, was heavy-handed. If a scholar was injured by a townsman, the inquisition into the deed was to be conducted by the representatives of neighbouring villages as well as the burgesses of Oxford. If, perchance, he had been slain, the whole town was called to account, on the ancient principle of community blood-guilt.

In 1251 two scholars were arrested and clapped into jail by the town authorities. The king commanded their release, and ordered that thereafter all clerks charged with lesser offences should be turned over to the Chancellor for judgment; those guilty of more serious crimes to be haled before the Bishop of Lincoln himself. But in 1290, on the occasion of a dispute that reached Parliament, King Edward intervened and gave the Chancellor full power over all crimes in Oxford in which a scholar was the aggressor or the injured party, with the exception of homicide, mayhem, and freehold trespasses. There must have been complaints from harried townsfolk as to the exorbitant fines imposed on them by the Chancellor, for the king added a postscript that he was to exercise moderation in fining laymen—that they were not to be ruined financially for trivial offences against the sacred persons of the scholars.

In Paris it was the Pope who was the most sedulous protector of the University's liberties; at Oxford the King stepped into the position of defender. Not only to the Chancellor, but to the University itself in its long bitter struggle against the town, he was a source of comfort and a tower of strength.

The Society of Masters had been slow in forming. By 1252, however, it was fairly complete. In that year it enacted that no one should receive the licence in Theology who had not passed his Arts degree, a requirement that even Paris, that home of Theologians, had not seen fit to impose. In the same year the long-standing antagonism between the Nations of the North and South had broken out in a series of bloody riots. The University was divided into two armed camps, and it was suicide for any of the combatants to venture out alone. Cooler heads eventually intervened. Twelve arbitrators were chosen by each side to settle all matters in dispute; forty wealthy men of either Nation were sworn to observe the conditions of the treaty of peace. Even this did not help. War broke out again, and another peace had to be concluded in 1267. This time four Captains were selected, three from the North and one from Ireland, the most pugnacious tribe of the South, whose duty it was to settle all disputes and maintain the peace—with force if necessary. But again there was trouble; and this time the war was fought to a finish. The Faculty of Arts met in 1274—that Faculty whose two component Nations were responsible for the fracas—and came to an agreement. The two Nations were to be for ever obliterated; Scots, Irish, Welsh, and plain English were to be one great family, with one Congregation and one set of officers. It may sound strange, but the arrangement worked; without the separate organization of Nations to intensify and stir up racial antagonisms, there were no more student riots. Thereafter their superabundant energies were satisfied by uniting to harry the natural enemy—the people of the town.

As in Paris, it was the Faculty of Arts that ran the University, and for the same reasons—the numerical preponderance of the young Masters of Arts, and the readiness with which they entered into all disputes whereby the privileges of the University were increased. The position of the Faculty was even stronger than in Paris, because the superior Faculties of Paris were organized, and had fought strenuously against submission to the lower Faculty; in Oxford they were never so completely organized.

All proposed Statutes for the governance of the University as a whole had first to be submitted to and discussed by the Arts Faculty in Congregation, before submission to the University as a whole.

There were three Congregations. First came the "Black" Congregation, the assemblage of the Regent or Teaching Masters of Arts. They initiated all legislation, elected Proctors —two of them, to correspond to the division into two Nations —and supervised inceptions of new Masters. Second came the "Lesser" Congregation, the assemblage of Regent Masters of *all* the Faculties. Its duties were to take charge of the finances of the University, and the control of ordinary educational matters, such as lectures and degrees. The third and supreme governing body of the University was the "Full" or "Great" Congregation, to which all the Masters who had ever graduated from the University were summoned, whether still teaching or not. In this great body voting was by Faculties, and doubtless the consent of all was necessary. To this Assembly alone was given the right to enact permanent Statutes, after they were initiated by the Arts, in "Black" Congregation assembled.

Technically the Arts Faculty of Regent Masters had no control over proposed legislation, other than the doubtful right of prior discussion. But practically it was in a position to exercise a power of veto. For the two Proctors of the Faculty, being its only representative officers, alone had the right to call a meeting of the Congregation. The Chancellor, technically an outsider, had no such right, nor had anyone else. Hence it was a simple matter, if obnoxious legislation was to be proposed for discussion by the "Black" Congregation, for the Proctors to refuse to call the meeting. No meeting, no promulgation; no promulgation, and the "Great" Congregation of all the dignitaries of the realm could only sit and fume helplessly. Here, of course, the Arts Faculty had a power that it never had in Paris, nor did the Faculty of Paris invite the non-regent Masters to partake in its deliberations.

CHAPTER XX

Town and Gown

WE have seen how the Chancellor of the University gradually acquired the right of jurisdiction, both civil and criminal, over the townsfolk of Oxford, in all cases where scholars were involved. This control by a University over an independent, prosperous town, inhabited by sturdy English burghers, as a rule only too touchy in respect of any diminution of their hard-earned rights, was destined to increase until the last vestiges of independence were gone, until the Town had become a mere appendage, a chattel of the alien scholars squatting within its walls. It was a situation unique in Europe. It may be explained in several ways: the greater interest of the English kings in the almost solitary claim to educational prestige within their borders; the fact that Oxford was not a royal capital in which the king himself would naturally rule; the lack of a local Bishop to ally himself with the town in the struggle for power over an errant University; and the bad blood which was early generated between the townsmen and the scholars.

The first riot of 1209 had already caused the town to be subjected to humiliating conditions, such as had never before been imposed on any body of citizens. But the University was not content; it never ceased to complain. Thus, the nostrils of the fastidious scholars discerned certain foul and stinking odours on the Oxford air to which the sturdier townsfolk were completely indifferent. For example, the good old custom of slaughtering sheep and cattle within the city walls and dumping the entrails and other offal in heaps on the public thoroughfare for flies and vermin to dispose of. Slops and chamber-pots, of course, as in all mediaeval towns, were dumped from the windows into the gutter, and the passer-by could look after himself. Garbage and other filth accumulated, and recurrent

O

plagues developed to decimate the inmates of the crowded houses. But this was all in the natural, orderly process of Nature. What did these too delicate scholars of Oxford mean by their constant complaints? sniffed the honest citizens. Why, even in Paris, the model which these clerics affected to follow, conditions were exactly the same, and the University did not complain!

But the King and his Council gave heed to these owners of fastidious noses. A Royal letter, dated 1300, informed the local Sheriff that the air is so corrupted and infected by the filth and refuse in the streets, that "an abominable ague . . . is diffused among the aforesaid Masters and scholars." On other occasions it was commanded that streets be kept properly clean, and certain sanitary measures be observed in the butchering of cattle.

In spite of the royal interest, in spite of the steadily growing powers of the University and its Chancellor—or rather, because of these—the ill-feeling between the two combatants increased. The town was exasperated to find that its precious liberties were gradually being undermined in favour of a set of upstart clerics; and it is conceivable that the students may have swaggered a little and presumed on their privileges.

The next migration from Oxford, however, after that of 1209, was the result not of a conflict with the Town, but of a quarrel with a fellow cleric. This began innocently enough. In 1238 the Papal Legate, Otho, lodged at the monastery at Oseney, outside Oxford. A party of students came to pay their respects, and it seems they were a trifle boisterous in demanding admission to the noble presence. The Legate's servants refused them admission, and angry words were exchanged.

As always happens, it was the innocent bystander who got the worst of it. A poor Irish chaplain, begging peacefully at the gates just as the quarrel began to get beyond the stage of mere words, was the recipient of a pail of boiling water thrown by the "Master of the Cooks," who happened to be the

Legate's brother. Now whether he got in the way of a token intended for the scholars clamouring around the gate, or whether the "Master of the Cooks" was venting his rage vicariously on the body of a poor and friendless beggar, as a person less able to retaliate, will never be known. The result, however, would have been exactly the same.

The scholars took up the quarrel of the poor scalded chaplain as their own, and killed the offending Cook, forgetting, perhaps, that he was the Legate's brother. Then they went after the Legate himself, and that pompous individual was compelled to leave the monastery by the postern gate, and seek protection in town. Even there he was not safe. The scholars marched back to town and roused their fellows, and soon the trembling Legate heard them clamouring for his blood. In the friendly darkness of the night he fled the town. Note the resemblance between this incident and the adventure of another Papal Legate in Paris who had dared to offend the University.

But this Legate's courage revived in direct proportion to the distance between himself and Oxford. From his secure retreat he thundered and roared until his voice was heard in Rome. The Papacy itself had been insulted. Wires were pulled, and for once all forces worked in harmony against the offenders. Oxford town was laid under an interdict, the University was suspended by decree, and the king dealt sternly with those who had taken part in the affray. To all this the University could only interpose its time-honoured defence. It dispersed. And sure enough, matters presently quieted down, the interdict and ban were lifted, and the University was itself once more.

In 1260 there was another exodus, this time resulting from a fight with the town. Practically the whole body went to Northampton, and attempted to establish a new University. At first it received the King's blessing; it might do no harm to set up yet another centre of learning. But he was in the midst of the Baron's War, and Northampton was in enemy hands. He besieged the stronghold and, to his rage and consternation, the ungrateful scholars of the infant University sprang to the defence of the beleaguered town. These clerics, who had always insisted on their immunity from military service of any kind, now seized their crossbows and inflicted severe punishment on the royal forces. When the town was finally captured it was with the greatest difficulty that the enraged monarch was dissuaded from his avowed purpose of hanging the entire University. The punishment finally enforced was extremely mild. He dissolved the University, and ordered the renegade scholars back to Oxford.

Another attempt was made to form an outside University, this time in 1334, and in the town of Stamford. The old quarrel between North and South had broken out again, and the Northerners, who had suffered several sound beatings, left Oxford to set up on their own. But the Crown had had its lesson. The king sent the scholars back to Oxford, to the relief of the two old Universities. They desired no further competition. After the Stamford affair was ended, as that town seemed a favourite refuge for deserting scholars, Oxford thereafter made it an article of the oath of a candidate for the Master's degree that the new Master was never to lecture or in anywise teach at Stamford. With true British tenacity this oath survived as part of the ceremony of graduation into the nineteenth century.

To return to the relations of Oxford town and the Frankenstein monster which it had evolved. The Chancellor's Court was constantly increasing its jurisdiction over the townsfolk. In a dispute with a scholar a townsman had not a chance. The scholar's word was always better than his; the student accused of the gravest crime was viewed with a fatherly and lenient eye; but a layman, for the pettiest offence, was cast into jail, there to kick his heels in vain until the injured cleric and the Chancellor were satisfied, which they seldom were until a heavy fine was paid.

A clerk, even if guilty of murder or mayhem, crimes which came within the Bishop's jurisdiction, was not harshly handled. The law for ecclesiasts applied. Usually he was admitted to "purgation." This was a ceremony very agreeable to ecclesiastics. The accused, even though there were a hundred eyewitnesses to the crime, could gather together a few ecclesiastical companions, to whom in time of need he would render a similar service. They would join him in swearing blithely that he had not committed the crime. Thereupon the testimony of the eyewitnesses was disregarded, and the happy scoundrel was liberated, to join his fellow-perjurers in a stoup of wine at the nearest tavern. And even if no boon companions stood ready to swear for him, or if the offence was so horrible that the Bishop, for once, refused "purgation," the punishment was not severe. Execution was not a punishment in the ecclesiastical code; a penance, or at most a short imprisonment, was imposed. It is no wonder that the Middle Ages show such a long list of clerkly crimes. The records of coroners' inquests, of jail deliveries, tell the tale of Oxford. They disclose the appalling number of clerks accused of arson, highway robbery, rape, and murder. In almost every instance against the name of the accused is the significant abbreviation: "lib. epi." (delivered to the bishop).

The most serious riot of all, however, that occurred in the annals of Oxford was the battle of St. Scholastica's Day in 1354. The word "battle" is no misnomer, considering the number of combatants involved, and the list of dead and wounded, not to speak of the tremendous damage to property. It originated, as did most of the University affairs, in a tavern quarrel. Certain scholars, having called for good red wine, suspected its goodness, and told mine host of their suspicions in no uncertain terms. Thereafter events followed their usual course. The host retorted, and the scholars emptied the lees of the disputed liquor on his head. This was an outrage not to be borne, and the innkeeper's friends ran to ring the bell of St. Martin's Church. A mob of citizens appeared as if by magic, each man with cudgel, pike, knife, or bow. Meanwhile the befuddled clerks had discreetly disappeared.

The mob was not to be balked of its prey, and proceeded to attack every scholar who happened to be in the streets. The Chancellor of the University came out in splendid array, hoping to pour oil on the troubled waters. But the irreverent mob would have none of this dignitary, and he saved his life only by a most uncanonical burst of speed. Gone were all thoughts of peace in the ecclesiastical bosom, and the indignant Chancellor ordered the bell of St. Mary's to be rung to rouse the University. The University roused with a will, and the scholars, armed to the teeth, poured out of the University precincts to do battle. Now scholars were expressly forbidden, under the severest penalties, to carry arms of any kind, and it was the Chancellor's duty to enforce this law. But it does not seem that at this particular moment he was perturbed by the infringement of the prohibition. The battle in the streets of Oxford raged all day until darkness made it impossible to distinguish friend from foe. The respective forces retreated to their sanctuaries to lick their wounds. What puzzles the modern investigator is the fact that in all this first day of battle between armed men no one was killed or mortally wounded. But this was soon to be rectified.

All night the citizens from surrounding towns and villages poured into Oxford, thirsting to crush the hated clerics once and for all. The students naturally received no access of reinforcements. The next day the battle was resumed, the townsmen again being the aggressors. They caught "certain scholars walking after dinner in Beaumont," killing one and wounding others. Then on into the University quarter itself, where the scholars defended themselves desperately, fighting from street to street, pouring their bolts and arrows from the windows of beleaguered houses. But the army of townsmen was not to be denied. The students were overwhelmed; their ranks broke, and the fight developed into a total rout. Whoever could, fled the town; others attempted a last stand in their houses, and still others sought sanctuary in the churches and monasteries of the quarter.

For two days the mob rioted and pillaged and slew. There was no glutting their bloodlust and their hatred of all clergy. The poor scholars were dragged out of their hiding-places and ruthlessly butchered; the houses were literally torn down and the schools wrecked. Even the churches provided no sanctuary, nor did the appeals of the monks avail, even though the Regulars were held in far greater respect than the secular clergy. Trembling clerics were torn from the altars, and there is testimony to the effect that two chaplains were flayed alive, the mob having suddenly reverted to the practices of their barbarous ancestors. When the pillage was over, the University had vanished, seemingly never to return.

But one marvels at the immense vitality of these mediaeval Universities. The fleeing masters and students reassembled in distant places, and promptly the air of England was laden with their outraged cries. The King heard and gave them a terrible revenge. From that day onwards the liberties of Oxford were irretrievably broken.

Henceforth, said the royal decree, the University was to have full jurisdiction over the town in so far as the following matters were concerned: the regulation of all food supplies, market-places, weights and measures; cleansing and paving of streets; authority to fix rents for schools and halls housing scholars; punishment of all citizens caught bearing arms contrary to law; and power to decree forfeiture of unwholesome or "incompetent" victuals, which, it was decreed, were to be turned over to the Hospital of St. John! Which last astounding provision speaks volumes for the care given to the sick of the time. No longer was Oxford a royal town; it became a hostage to the University, whose Chancellor possessed more power than its own Mayor and Council.

Nor was the Bishop of Lincoln a laggard in revenge. The town was laid under an interdict, removable only on condition that the Mayor, the Bailiffs, and three score of the chief burghers of the town appeared as humble penitents each St. Scholastica's Day in St. Mary's Church, to attend mass for the souls of the slain scholars. This quaint revenge also persisted down to the nineteenth century, when the University finally decided that it need not be pursued any further.

Yet it must not be supposed that street battles were a thing of the past. In spite of the terrible punishment suffered by both sides, in spite of the complete subjugation of the town, political and economic, the warfare continued. There were constant outbreaks. In 1526 one of the University proctors, the highest official next the Chancellor himself, "sate upon a blocke in the streete afore the shoppe of one Robert Jermyns, a barber, havinge a pole-axe in his hand, a black cloake on his backe, and a hatt on his head," and therewithal organized and directed a student riot in which many townsmen were "striken downe and sore beaten."

Nor did intramural squabbles cease. The Irish contingent in the University continued to display a degree of belligerence and nationalist rancour toward their fellows that was astounding even for that age. Parliament was finally goaded into action by the constant turmoil, and in 1413 decreed their banishment from the University. Only Irish members of the religious orders and graduates were exempted from the sweeping terms. Thereafter the Irish were compelled, for want of better exercise, to quarrel among themselves.

Now the Chancellor's Court had obtained extensive jurisdiction over University and Town alike. All sorts of queer fish came up before its tribunal. It set itself up not merely as a court of law, but also as an ecclesiastical tribunal, with a special interest in the morals and manners of the browbeaten townsfolk. A combination of Comstockery and the Inquisition made their lives a burden. Now and again a general inquiry was held into the state of morals of the inhabitants; districts were marked out, with a Doctor of Theology and two assistant Masters as a board of judges. Before this inquisition were haled for justice all evil-livers, all night walkers, all common scolds. No inhabitant's private life was exempt from his neighbours' gossip and accusations. Prostitutes especially came under the ecclesiastical frown. They were solemnly banished from the confines of the city on penalty of imprisonment. This, however, was as ineffectual as all former and later attempts to regulate their trade. Instead of being scattered, these obliging ladies were now concentrated in a compact red-light district immediately outside the city walls, and beyond the Chancellor's jurisdiction. There the business throve, what with burghers slipping away from shrewish wives and lusty scholars feeling their oats.

The varied fare of a Chancellor's Court was most interesting. A merchant who attempted to corner the fish supply received due punishment; so did the sellers of rotten meats; brewers were put in the pillory for brewing bad beer, and bakers for giving light weight; a Canon accused a schoolmaster and his wife of abusing him and making faces at him—such practices were sternly forbidden, and all parties sentenced to unite on a goose for dinner. A Friar was degraded and banished (the severest punishment in the whole armoury of penalties) for daring to libel two Bachelors of Theology in a sermon. A vicar of St. Giles "forfeited his club and paid two shillings" for an assault with that weapon. A scholar of Civil Law was accused of entering a servant's house and knocking his wife about. A vicar was made to swear that he would cease his suspicious visits to a tailor's wife. A schoolmaster was imprisoned for inciting his scholars to drag a priest out of the pulpit while engaged in reading his, the schoolmaster's, excommunication. The bellicose youngsters tried to rescue their teacher from jail, and were sent to join him. An organ-player who was convicted of fornication and sentenced to imprisonment, wept so bitterly that the Chancellor's heart melted and he was released forthwith. Two townsmen were put in jail, however, whether weeping or not, for uttering scornful words against the office of University Proctor. There was the case of a student who

drew a dagger against the Proctor; it cost *him* only fourpence.
A master, falsely defamed as a Scotsman (in those days a cause
for resentment), went to the trouble of producing witnesses to
prove his English birth. A Warden of Canterbury, who incited
his scholars to raid the beer supplies of the town, paid twelve
farthings. Breaches of the peace were subject to a graduated
system of fines. It is interesting to note the mediaeval concep-
tion of the relative gravity of offences as evidenced by the
amount of the fine assessed. For instance, "nocturnal wandering" was discouraged by a heavy fine of forty shillings, but
for "shooting an arrow with intent to injure" the penalty
was only twenty shillings.

On the whole, the sentences of the Chancellor's Court were
mild enough, especially where clerks were involved. Clerks
were usually punished by small fines, or excommunication
terminable by light penances; in the most serious cases a few
months' imprisonment or banishment from town sufficed.
The townsmen were fined more heavily, they frequently went
to jail, and often sat in the pillories. But even the townsmen
were treated more leniently than in the lay courts. Hanging
was practically unknown. And promises of reform, and solemn
oaths never to do it again, went a long way with the Chancellor. The second chance, a doctrine now advocated by the
most advanced criminologists, was a regular part of the
routine of the mediaeval ecclesiastical court. So, too, was the
giving of sureties by substantial citizens for one's future good
conduct. Thus, to a great extent, the horrible savagery and
barbarous punishments of the king's courts were offset by the
extreme mildness of the church law, to which everyone who
could claim "clericality" was subject.

CHAPTER XXI

The Struggle over Wyclif and the Friars

IN the early years of the University of Oxford the Masters were remarkably free from ecclesiastical interference, in which respect Oxford resembled Bologna rather than Paris. We have already discussed the reasons for this strange state of affairs. For one thing, there was no Cathedral in the town. But this neglect was rectified by the Pope in 1214. The Bishop of Lincoln was placed in control, in an effort to make Oxford conform more closely to the model of Paris. Conditions, however, were very different. The Bishop, as has been stated, was far away; the Chancellor, who should have been zealous in his interests, by reason of the way in which he was chosen —a Master elected by the other Masters—tended to side with the University rather than with his ostensible lord.

Now the first Bishop of Lincoln to control the affairs of the University was Robert Grossetête, a former Franciscan friar, and himself a graduate of the University. The fame of this most distinguished son of Oxford is gradually emerging from the obscurity in which it has been shrouded; not even Roger Bacon was superior to him in knowledge and attainments, in broadness of vision and nobility of character. More will be said of him later. As Bishop of Lincoln, the function in which we are at present interested, he protected and cherished his mother University. During his long tenure the relations between the two were most cordial.

But when in 1254 he was succeeded by Henry of Lexington, the complexion of matters changed almost at once. Henry was the typical narrow-minded Bishop, fretful of his rights, insisting on the letter of the law, having no admiration for learning *per se*. Squabbles arose; the University claimed certain rights and the Bishop was eager to restrict them. The Crown, however, intervened, and by a series of charters rendered the

Chancellor practically an independent official. A provincial synod held in 1280, to which an appeal was made against further control by the Bishop, decided in favour of the University, even to the extent of permitting appeals from the Chancellor's court direct to the University Congregation instead of to the Bishop. Thereafter the Bishop, knowing that he was beaten, kept his hands off University affairs. The formality of confirming the election of the Chancellor by the Masters was also dispensed with by the Pope in 1368. And in 1395 the final blow to episcopal authority was given, when by Papal decree Oxford was granted absolute exemption from the supervision of all ecclesiasts except the Pope. Thereafter the Bishop of Lincoln was just another Bishop to the University. Nor did the Pope fare much better, in spite of the exception.

It is remarkable how little the Papal influence, so potent in the establishment and regulation of Continental Universities, was evident in the affairs of England. The autocratic line of kings, the strong hold they had on the compact little isle, the sagacity of monarchs who realized the need of nationalist as against ecclesiastically dominated Universities, all played their part. The Pope could only follow in the steps of the royal protector.

But in two matters the Papacy really attempted to put up a fight. One was the question of the Friars Mendicant, which had played havoc at Paris; and the other was the Wycliffite movement, which involved profound heresies and threatened the very foundations of the Catholic Church.

The Dominicans, clothed in black, and the Franciscans, clad in grey, came very early to England to save souls and convert the heathen to their particular brand of missionary faith. In 1221 the Dominicans opened a school in Oxford town. This was in the heart of the Jewish quarter, the intention being to make converts among that stubborn folk. Three years later the Franciscans followed suit. Years afterwards the minor Orders established themselves, but they did little to influence the main stream of events.

At first Oxford welcomed the Friars, and for good reasons. The finest intellects of the age were found in these two Orders; at Oxford, notably, among the Franciscans. Scholars, philosophers, and scientists like Robert Grossetête, Roger Bacon, Duns Scotus, Adam Marsh, Thomas of York, John Peckham—these men were the intellectual glory of the Middle Ages; it was their work and their teachings that gave Oxford a position equal almost to that of Paris. As a matter of fact, Paris would have been hard put to it to show an equal number of scholars of equal attainments.

But even as in Paris, the Friars soon showed the cloven hoof beneath the corded gown. The heads of the Orders were ambitious. They wished to dominate the University, and at the same time to stand outside its laws and its organization. Dissension grew, and soon flared to open enmity. Yet at no time was the controversy as bitter as it had been in Paris, nor were the Friars so successful at Oxford. In Paris they had the complete and unqualified backing of the Pope; to a great extent they had it at Oxford also, but as we have seen, the Papal influence was weak in England.

The University opened hostilities by demanding that the Friar Theologians should first obtain the University degree in Arts. This was against their Rules. They were forbidden by their Orders to study Dialectic or the *Sentences* of Peter the Lombard. They were simple-minded, or intelligent enough, to prefer the direct study of the Bible. Now Dialectic was an indispensable part of the Arts course, and the *Sentences* were prescribed for the study of Theology. Even Paris, in the heyday of its strife with the Friars, had not dreamt of demanding inception in Arts of the budding Friar Theologians.

But the battle was not yet joined. In 1253 Thomas of York, a Franciscan, petitioned the University for leave to "incept" in Theology without a previous degree in Arts. Such a dispensation was within the powers of the Chancellor and the Regent Masters. They listened, and graciously consented, and at the same time laid down the general rule.

Thus matters rested awhile. The Friars petitioned regularly for exemptions, and almost as regularly they were granted. But early in the fourteenth century the University suddenly changed its mind. It ruled that before a Friar could lecture on the Bible, he must take the degree of Bachelor of Theology. This meant a series of lectures on the *Sentences*, which presupposed a thorough logical and scholastic training. This the Friar Theologians did not as a rule possess.

Further, the complaint was made that it had become the regular practice for a single Regent Master to block the granting of the dispensation in Arts. One vote was sufficient. Again, the University required the oath of obedience from incepting Friars, and even insisted that existing Friar Masters should take the oath to obey all Statutes, past and present. A Dominican Doctor, who refused to take the oath, was excluded from the University Congregation; others were excommunicated by the Archbishop of Canterbury, at the request of the University, for contumacious conduct (note that in England, as elsewhere, the secular clergy had no love for the pushing, usurping Friars), and the students belonging to the Orders were driven from the Schools. The excommunication brought the secular pulpits gustily into the fray. The clergy thundered against the outlawed Friars; their confessionals, schools, and pulpits were deserted as though infected by the plague.

The University alleged that the Friars had made a practice of enticing young and unprotected boys into their Orders, offering as inducements a life in which shelter, ample food, and plenty of books were normal concomitants. Once inside the Order, said the University, righteously indignant, it was "ill work to get clear of it." Youngsters were snatched "before they could well distinguish between a cap and a cowl."

The Friars, excommunicate and embittered, appealed to Rome, their invariable succour in times past, and the fountain of all their privileges. But the Masters of Oxford proved of sterner stuff than their brethren of Paris. When the Proctor of the Friars attempted to serve notice of appeal on the Chancellor of the University, whom he accosted outside the Schools, that worthy took the offending document and threw it into the mud, using most uncanonical language in the process. The undaunted Proctor thereupon tried to serve the Congregation in the church where it was assembled, and was immediately thrown out by the wrathful Masters. Dizzy, but still undaunted, the brave Proctor mounted a tombstone outside the church, and shouted the notice of appeal through the open window. Then he prudently decamped. The servants of the Masters, enlisting in their superiors' quarrel, armed themselves and marched in a body to the Friaries, which they threatened to burn to the ground.

After some debate, the controversy was turned over to a board of arbitrators. In an English dispute the Pope dared not decide out of hand, as he had done in respect to Paris. The King of England was in the background, watchful of his own and the University's rights. The award of the arbitrators, confirmed by the King in 1314, was in effect a substantial victory for the University. The statutes aimed against the Friars were upheld almost *in toto*. Certain concessions were made to the injured Friars; for example, any Master refusing to vote the dispensation for a Friar incepting in Theology without an Arts degree was required to prove to the Theological Faculty that his objection was not due to personal malice, but that he had well-founded reasons. One may suspect that such reasons were never hard to find under the circumstances.

The Friars continued to hold on to their precarious foothold, but they were present on sufferance. Oxford was very different from Paris, where for years they had dominated the Faculty of Theology, until the rise of the Sorbonne. In England, as elsewhere, they had only themselves to blame for their growing unpopularity. The first fine ideals of the Orders had been conveniently forgotten; for organizations vowed to poverty, they had managed to accumulate an inordinate amount of worldly gear; their rivalries with each other and within their own ranks were an international scandal; they interfered arrogantly in the work of the secular priests and refused all offers of co-operation; they poisoned the minds of the Popes against the lower clergy; they laid claim to a superior sanctity. And at Oxford, at least, retribution followed.

Just as Paris had suffered from a rash of heretical teachings, mostly under the guise of Nominalism and Averrhoism, so Oxford had its outbreak. But the movement at Oxford went far deeper and proved of immensely greater importance than in Paris. It was a true reform movement, which, had it proved successful, would have anticipated Luther and the Protestant Reformation by centuries. The Pope and the vested clerical interests were not unaware of the true significance of the Oxford movement. They moved heaven and earth to crush it, and Oxford found itself for years a battleground of diverse, inimical interests, in which the University, after a brave and gallant start, was shattered almost beyond repair.

John Wyclif, of whose private life little is known, studied and taught philosophy and theology at Oxford. In 1358 we hear of him as Master of Balliol College, and in 1372 he took the degree of Doctor of Theology. It was the time of the "Babylonian Captivity," the period of the French Popes at Avignon. The sanctity of the Papacy had fallen to a peculiarly low ebb, the enormous wealth of the church was exciting more and more resentment among tax-oppressed commoners, the Mendicant Friars, with their fall from grace, had aggravated the feeling against the clergy as a whole, and theology was a weird assortment of subtleties far outside the ken of the simple layman.

Wyclif was anti-papal, anti-clerical, and a reformer to boot. At first he fulminated against the generally acknowledged abuses of the Church. Here he was on solid ground. Oxford, his University, and England generally agreed with most of his theses; the Church was corrupt, and must be brought back to her ancient standards of purity. His fame increased; he built up a large body of adherents.

But his teaching grew more and more revolutionary. It was no longer concerned with superficial sores; the evils it attacked were fundamental and deep-seated now. His treatise, *De dominio divino*, struck heavily at every kind of privilege based upon the claim of authority. He was attacking now the primacy of the Pope, the very foundations of the wealth and vested interests of the priestly hierarchy; going even further, he insisted that the State might lawfully seize the property of "habitually delinquent" priests. In the abstract realms of faith, he was even more explosive. The doctrine of Transubstantiation, the battleground of centuries, was vehemently denied; so, too, was the Sacrifice of the Mass and the theory of "dominion by grace." These theses he maintained openly and publicly at Oxford, and aroused much partisan enthusiasm. Nicholas Hereford, in 1382, violently defended Wyclif and his doctrines in a sermon before the entire University, and excoriated the Friars. For the Friars, as usual, had risen in defence of orthodoxy, and were attacking Wyclif with every weapon at their command.

The storm was gathering. It was felt by many who had sympathized with Wyclif in the first phase of his movement that he had gone too far. The cry of the prudent liberal of all ages was heard: we must proceed cautiously; we must not offend vested interests. And vested interests were not merely offended; they were alarmed. For in 1381, inspired by Wyclif's teachings, and taking them literally, John Ball, the Communistic priest, and Wat Tyler, headed an army of peasants in a short but bloody revolt.

> "When Adam delved and Eve span,
> Who was then the gentleman?"

The loudly-sung query horrified all right-thinking citizens; that is, all those who had built up a system of privilege on the basis of fortuitous birth and accumulation of property, or had taken refuge in the sanctity of the Church. The Peasant Revolt was crushed in brutal fashion; Crown, nobility, landed gentry, and merchants alike arrayed themselves against the dangerous implications of the Wycliffian heresies; the Pope, and all the hierarchy of clerics who saw their livings in danger, fulminated against him. As for the Friars, here was work after their own hearts: denouncing, inciting, conspiring, and persecuting.

Even at Oxford, where the great majority of Masters and scholars had enthusiastically followed Wyclif, there was some drawing back. After all, a good number of the students were themselves men of property, and "Lollardism" aimed at property as well as at spiritual rights. But to the eternal glory of Oxford, the University manfully supported its radical son, and so did many a man of wealth and position.

When in 1377 Wyclif was summoned to appear before a Convocation to answer charges of heresy, John of Gaunt and Henry Percy, the proudest and greatest of nobles, stood on either side of him and defied the Bishop to harm him. A Papal Bull to the Chancellor of Oxford, demanding the silencing of Wyclif's adherents at the University, received scant consideration. A mandate from the Archbishop of Canterbury to Robert Rugge, the Chancellor, requiring him to publish a condemnation of Wyclif's theses, was also refused. Wyclif's followers continued to teach and inflame public opinion under the benevolent protection of the University.

For this refusal the Chancellor was forced to beg pardon of the wrathful Archbishop on his knees, and even then, he exclaimed, he dared not, for very fear of his life, publicly to condemn the theses at Oxford.

From now onwards the opposition, backed by King and Bishops as well as the Pope, gathered speed. A Church Council was held at Blackfriars in 1382 which officially condemned the heretical teachings of Wyclif. In July of the same year the Crown peremptorily ordered the University, not merely to silence him, but to expel him from their precincts and from the city. The King meant business, and Oxford knew it.

Reluctantly it complied, and Wyclif was driven from the very seat of his movement. A few months later a Convocation in the nature of an Inquisition was held at Oxford. Wyclif's principal lieutenants prudently accepted the inevitable, and made humble submission. Wyclif himself, though threatened innumerable times with imprisonment and ecclesiastical penalties, lived out the two years of his exile unharmed, an officiating priest of the Church to the last.

This was the beginning of the end of the great liberties of Oxford, though the struggle of the Wycliffites against both Church and State continued for a considerable period. In 1395 the Pope actually exempted the scholars of Oxford from the last traces of ecclesiastical jurisdiction, in spite of the smouldering Lollardism at the University. It is hard to understand just what was in the mind of Boniface IX. Was he less concerned with the Oxford heresy than Bishop, Archbishop, and King in England? Or was it a subtle method of binding the University more closely to himself at a time when its former protector, the Crown, was hostile? As for the Bishops, their tendency was at all times to cast in their lot with the English Crown rather than with the Papacy. Whatever the Pope's intention may have been, it gave the University a breathing spell, enhanced the power of the Chancellor, and failed in its presumed object of attaching the body of scholars to the Papacy. The Papal Bulls continued to command very little respect from the University; and if it yielded eventually to Archbishop and Crown, it was only because it must.

At the Convocation of 1396, where complaints were heard from the orthodox minority of the University against the continued teaching of the Wycliffite doctrines, the University Proctor brought the Bull of Exemption into play. He maintained that the Archbishop had no further jurisdiction. The Archbishop brusquely disregarded the Papal command, and forced the Proctor to renounce the privilege of exemption. The University rose in arms against the weak-kneed Proctor and refused to abide by his renunciation. The Archbishop thereupon obtained a Royal writ requiring the University to surrender its "unwonted and unheard-of exemption." Matters looked black for the defiant University. Fortunately, just then the Archbishop suffered impeachment on political grounds, and he was too busy with his own troubles to bother any further with Oxford. The University was left alone for some years. The curious part of the whole business was the apathy of the Pope in the face of Wycliffite heresy on the one side, and the slap in the face administered by the Archbishop of Canterbury on the other. The secession of the Church of England was already foreshadowed.

In 1409 hostilities were once more reopened. During the interim the University was a hotbed of Lollardism. Even though Wyclif was dead, his adherents were numerous and well established. Once more a Convocation called on Oxford to abjure the damnable heresies. Once more there was a refusal, but steam-roller methods were employed, and the University was compelled publicly and solemnly to burn the Wyclif manuscripts. Devoted adherents managed to secrete the originals, and they appeared a little later at the Bohemian University of Prague, there to fan into flame a movement even more formidable than its English predecessor. It is remarkable to note the continuity of communication and influence between the two Universities, so far apart from each other in space, so different in background. In the second half of the fourteenth century scholarships were granted to assist Bohemian students to attend Oxford; and the Statutes of the University of Prague specifically recommended the books of the Oxford Masters to its students.

Though compelled publicly to go through certain motions, the majority of the Oxford scholars were Lollards at heart. In 1411 the Archbishop, to enforce his jurisdiction in spite of the Papal exemption, demanded that the University should receive him as a Visitor. The University barred the streets of Oxford against his coming; St. Mary's was hastily fortified, and armed students patrolled the streets and gates to resist his entrance.

The Archbishop prudently decided not to attempt the use of force; instead, he laid the town under an interdict. The University defied even this spiritual thunder. It used violence to enter St. Mary's and heard mass as though it were not outlawed.

Now the King entered the arena, in support of the Archbishop. Under the threat of dire penalties the Chancellor and Proctors were compelled to resign. The University rose to new heights. It decreed a cessation and held a new election of officers. Defying the power of the Crown, the rebellious Masters re-elected the deposed officials. The King's wrath increased; there is no telling what measures he might have adopted against these obstreperous scholars, had not the Prince of Wales interposed; and the matter quieted down, with the ousted officers still in office.

This was the last great stand for liberty and freedom of thought in Oxford. The University had blazed into glorious revolt against all the constituted authorities, and now the end was near. For the Papacy, disgruntled, no doubt, by the failure of the belligerent University to bow to its influence, took action. In 1411 John XXIII revoked the Bull of Exemption granted by Boniface IX, and the University found itself stripped of any vestige of a legal pretext for rebellion. Parliament joined the allied forces, and upheld the Archbishop's right of Visitation. The whole world was against the valiant rebels. There was nothing to do but submit. They yielded to the demands of the triumphant Archbishop; all Masters were compelled formally to abjure Wycliffism, and spiritual darkness fell. Church and State had set their seal upon the University.

Not only were the liberties and privileges of the great University gone, but Lollardism as a force in English life was definitely broken. Free speech and freedom of thought, that had held sway so long in the Schools of Oxford, were things of the past. Church and State had triumphed, but at what a cost! The liberty, the intellectual ferment of Oxford, the ardent spirit of speculation and scholarship, were gone.

Henceforth, for the balance of the mediaeval period, Oxford was a poor, timid, submissive thing, fleeing from its own shadow. The home of Grossetête, Bacon, Duns Scotus, Wyclif, haunted by the pale ghosts of departed giants, contributed nothing to the intellectual life of the time.

By the fifteenth century a somnolence had descended upon the once bustling Schools; the students dwindled in numbers; in 1450 only twenty Schools out of two hundred remained. The tamed remnant hearkened to Bishop and Archbishop alike; so much so that in 1479 it was thought safe to restore the old Papal exemption. The Chancellor, once the bulwark of Oxford liberties, had become a non-resident, with the consequent loss of interest in the affairs of the University. The Court ruled the University with an iron hand, and the Chancellor developed into a submissive Court official. And as he did so, he lost influence with the University itself, until he became what he is today, purely an honorary officer, without real power. Pestilence, the Wars of the Roses, the poverty of the times, all contributed to the decline. Students received licences to beg for bread.

Not until the late fifteenth and sixteenth centuries, when the Renaissance was in full swing, did Oxford revive from its torpor. Only then, with William Latimer, Thomas More, Grocyn, John Colet, Linacre, and the great Erasmus, did it emerge once more into the full blaze of intellectuality, rivalling if not surpassing, the great mediaeval days of its youth.

CHAPTER XXII

The College System in England

THE most characteristic of the Oxford institutions, one that developed to such an extent there, as well as at Cambridge, that it eventually overwhelmed the University proper, is the College. While it achieved its final and definitive form in the English Universities, we have seen that it was originally an importation from Paris, and that the College system flourished in the Mother University as well. But neither in Paris, nor elsewhere, was the College to become *the* University, until today, in England, the Colleges are all-important, and the University merely a name, a shadow.

In the beginning, as the Schools that developed into the University took form and being, there was the Hall. The evolution of the Hall was much what it was in Paris. The students soon found it mutually advantageous, for economic and social reasons, to dwell in groups. The rents averaged less per scholar; food bought in quantities was cheaper; there were greater possibilities of defence against the impositions of the Town, and the society of their fellows was grateful and comforting.

The Halls originated with Masters who set up a house for boarding of their pupils, thereby eking out a precarious income with the more substantial profits of a hostelry. Shrewd, business-like graduates, adults who could command the respect and confidence of parents, saw the financial possibilities, and followed suit. They rented a large house, and persuaded the parents of the youngsters who would soon be exposed to the temptations of Oxford, that the boarded students would be under good moral supervision, their bodies and souls being equally safeguarded. The system was successful, and a huge number of Halls sprang into being, draining the private houses of their student lodgers.

At first there was no supervision by the University. The

self-appointed Principals built up a flourishing business. They, or some of them, squeezed the last penny of profit out of the system. They trafficked in Principalships, buying and selling at a profit; they conspired with the landlords to declare spurious rentals, so as to elude the Chancellor's taxation of rents; they profiteered.

The scandal grew until the University was compelled to act. Thereafter a Principal was required to register with the University, and have his licence renewed annually, subject to good behaviour. To prove his financial responsibility, he had to deposit security with the University. The Principal must live with his charges, and no one was permitted to hold more than one Principalship. In the good old days a profiteering graduate could hold half a dozen such lucrative positions, and derive a substantial income from them without losing any sleep over the welfare of his boarders.

In spite of grasping Principals, however, the advantages of the Halls as places of residence were too obvious to be neglected. They became almost official in character, especially after the University began to exercise a measure of control. After a time very few students lived on their own. These were of two classes: the very rich, who could afford luxurious lodgings and private servants; and the very poor, who could not afford even the moderate Hall charges. When the Colleges were founded, and the wealthy were admitted to what had originally been charitable institutions, only the poor were left to shift for themselves. And they did so, in wretched garrets, sleeping in the icy cold and blazing heat on the same prickly pallets of straw, eating the scraps and broken meats they could beg or purchase with their few pence. This wretched tribe of scholars, known in Paris as "martinets," here suffered under the opprobrious name of "chamber-deacons."

But even then poverty-stricken scholars were not left in peace. For the rascals and cut-throats, the robbers and pimps, the gamblers and frequenters of brothels, who were found in every University town, where they preyed on honest citizens under the guise of scholars, soon adopted the name. Every murderer caught red-handed claimed to be a "chamber-deacon," and therefore immune from punishment at the hands of the municipal authorities.

The scandal finally became so intolerable that in 1432 the University enacted a Statute abolishing the tribe:

"Seeing that the peace of this kindly University is seen to be frequently broken by divers persons who, under pretence of being scholars, wait and lurk within the University and its precincts, but outside the Halls and under tutelage of no Principal—men known by the abominable name of 'Chamber-dekenys,' who sleep all day and by night haunt the taverns and brothels for occasions of robbery and manslaughter—therefore it is decreed by the said University that all and every scholar do dwell in that Hall or College wherein his common contributions are registered, or in Halls thereto annexed, which share with the aforesaid in commons, or battels, under pain of imprisonment for the first offence. . . ."

In the early days, when Masters were hard put to it to find buildings for Schools at Oxford because of the exorbitant rents, there grew up a custom that acquired all the force of law; to wit, that once a building had been used as a School, it could never be rented to a layman as long as any Master desired it; the rental to be fixed by a joint Board of citizens and Masters. Landlords were naturally reluctant to rent under conditions that smacked of expropriation, and schools became harder and harder to find. The advent of the Halls proved a godsend to harassed Masters, for Schools could be held in the Halls without any such complications. But eventually the advent of the Colleges, with their foundations and subsidies, their magnificent buildings, and their system of tutorial instruction, drove the private Halls out of existence. Everyone who could flocked to the Colleges. Only those Halls which were associated with the monasteries managed to linger on.

The first true College to be established at Oxford was

Balliol. Its *raison d'être* is interesting. About 1260 Sir John de Baliol, regent of Scotland, a father of one of her kings, had "unjustly vexed and enormously damnified" the Church of Tynemouth and the Church of Durham. His offence must indeed have been "damnifying," for the penance imposed on him was as humiliating as it was unusual. He was compelled to kneel at the door of Durham Abbey and there take a public scourging from the Bishop himself. Further, he was charged with the perpetual maintenance of a number of poor scholars at the University of Oxford. In this left-handed way was Balliol born. But the noble knight, smarting under his hurts, conceived an ironic revenge. No sum had been stipulated in the penance. I give, said he with a gesture, the sum of two-pence per scholar, and let the dogs make the best of it. So the College was a rather ghostly affair until Sir John died and went to his just reward. His lady, terrified by the thought of what that might be, and loving his memory in spite of his faults, hastened to raise the amount devoted to the poor scholars to a more substantial and practicable sum. Whatever the result of the pious lady's intercession for the soul of her lord, in 1282 Balliol became a College in reality. It proved to be a fair imitation of the Parisian type.

It was a genuinely charitable institution; only poor scholars were expected to take advantage of its hospitality, and it owned no land. In fact, it was a Hall with free boarders, the Principal of which was elected by the inmates. Two outside Proctors governed its affairs and finances, much after the Parisian fashion.

Merton College, the next to be founded in point of legal existence, though the first to get actually under way, was by far the most important in the history of Oxford. For Merton was the model which most of the succeeding Colleges followed. It, rather than Balliol, or any of the Paris Colleges, proved to be the true, distinctive Oxford institution.

Merton was founded in 1263-4 by Walter de Merton, ex-

Chancellor of England. He provided for the maintenance of
twenty poor scholars and some two or three priests. What was
unique in his arrangement was that he turned over to the
scholars themselves, in their corporate capacity, his manors of
Maldon and Farleigh, in Surrey. This endowment of land,
owned and controlled by the scholars, had no counterpart in
Paris. There were conditions, of course. His own blood-
relations were to have first claim on the scholarships, and
after them, natives of the diocese of Winchester, in which he
was interested. This was a second departure from the norm,
for there was evidently no intention of casting the opprobrious
mantle of charity and alms-giving over the College. It was to
be a place for men of birth and breeding, and no questions
were to be asked as to their resources. Each scholar was to be
granted an allowance of forty shillings per annum; they were
to live together in a Hall, and wear a distinctive uniform.
The management of the property was placed in the hands of
a Warden, who was to be a member of the Society, but without power over the scholars, except in the case of a disputed
election. The government of the College was left to the senior
students, and every year they journeyed down to Surrey to
make sure that their property was being properly managed
by the Warden. If it were not, they could depose the Warden,
with the consent of the Bishop of Winchester, and elect a
new one.

In 1270 Walter de Merton looked at the child of his generosity and saw that it was good. Accordingly he added to its
endowment by granting the scholars his large estate near
Cambridge. The College was now a wealthy landowner, and
required more detailed Statutes for its governance. He gave
the Warden wider powers in the management of the property
and the conduct of affairs in the Hall. He added sub-wardens
to assist him, and threw in a few deans to guard the morals
of the students. The senior scholars, too, were to be responsible for the studies of the juniors. From now onward
the scholars, originally Arts students, were to proceed to

Theology; only four or five were permitted to study Canon Law; as for Civil Law, it was regarded askance. The Warden's consent was required for the study of that pagan subject.

In other words, Merton had the same idea as Robert de Sorbon in Paris: he sought to provide a constant flow of secular graduates in Theology to combat the stranglehold which the Mendicant Friars were securing. No one, unless extremely wealthy, and extremely diligent, could hope to last out the sixteen odd years required for graduation in that arduous subject.

In return for his benefactions, the scholars were supposed to say mass several times a year for the soul of the Founder and his family, by no means an arduous task. But in 1274 he revised the Statutes. This time he made the rules almost monastic in character. The Warden was created a full Superior, and only the Patron of the College or his Visitor could question or depose him. Thirteen senior scholars still assisted in the government of the College, but their powers were sadly shorn. Scholars who were incorrigibly idle or depraved were to be expelled. Meals were silent, except for the clatter of dishes and the dulcet voice of a reader expounding some good, heavy text. Only Latin might be used, on penalty of a fine.

The policy adopted in the organization of Merton College proved so successful that all future founders hastened to reproduce its Statutes almost verbatim. Oriel College, founded in 1324, and the next important College, was an example. It consisted of ten scholars and a Provost as well as a Dean. The Scholars, called "Fellows," were to be at least Bachelors of Arts, who on graduation were to continue in Theology. Only three were to be allowed to study Canon or Civil Law instead. These Fellows enjoyed a completer autonomy than the seniors of Merton. They voted in the election of the Warden and enjoyed self-government. Even the legislative power was in the hands of the Seniors and the Provost. The Fellowships were wisely left unrestricted by ties of blood or other degrees of favouritism, and eventually they were thrown open to public competition. Accordingly an Oriel Fellowship was a sign of superior abilities, a badge of distinction in the University. It is not to be wondered at that Oriel, even far beyond the mediaeval period, played a leading part in the intellectual and religious life of the University.

Queen's College was founded in 1341 by the Chaplain of Queen Philippa, wife of Edward III. His Statutes are a masterpiece of minute detail. Nothing was left to chance or to the scholars' initiative; all was regulated: what was to go into the College pottage, and how often the Fellows' heads should be washed. He had some original ideas. The Society was to consist of a Provost and twelve scholars, representative of Christ and His Apostles. At meals they sat around the table dressed in blood-red garments, in imitation of the Last Supper. The sound of a trumpet ushered them to the festive board. To a modern, the whole procedure seems faintly sacrilegious; but mediaeval susceptibilities were far less squeamish than ours.

Nevertheless, the Queen's man enjoyed many advantages. The maintenance allowances were remarkably liberal; ample provision was made for servants; French, instead of the universal Latin, was permitted at the table. The purpose of this College, too, was definitely ecclesiastical. It was meant to maintain a supply, not only of theologians, but of actual practising priests. The Fellows were expressly required to enter holy orders. All twelve were to graduate in Theology or Canon Law; Civil Law was taboo. Canonists had to take orders within a year, and qualify as priests within three years. If the scholar was illegitimate, however, the time-limit was extended by another year, to give him a chance to obtain a dispensation. This was a most unusual provision, and spoke volumes for the courtier-Chaplain's wordly liberality. Illegitimacy was not ordinarily frowned upon in mediaeval times, but the Universities were very strict on the subject. In Paris, and most of the other Universities, proof of legitimate birth was a prerequisite to graduation; and the College Statutes usually were quite definite that no bastards need apply.

In addition to the twelve lordly Apostles, twelve "poor boys" shared the advantages of the College. These were grammar-school youngsters, who received some instruction and their board, and in return, sang in Chapel and waited on the table of the Last Supper on Sundays and holidays when the regular servants had their days off.

New College, the next important foundation, dates from 1379, and its benefactor was William of Wykeham, Bishop of Winchester. This was a large undertaking, accommodating as it did some seventy scholars, all to come from Winchester School, also the child of William's generosity. The good Bishop did not spare expense. He donated a magnificent residence, a lordly chapel and hall, a library sumptuously equipped, a garden, and a cloister for religious processions and funeral services. It was indeed a magnificent gift, and far outshone all other Foundations. Nor were the buildings all; the upkeep was provided for with a lavish purse. The Fellows of New College lived luxuriously; this was a far cry from the alms bestowed on charity students in the Parisian Colleges. Oxford was well on its way to become the home of aristocracy and wealth that made it so distinctive in later years. The Warden was given the princely salary of forty pounds per annum as against the miserable forty shillings granted to the Warden of Balliol. Further, six horses were at his service. Important visitors to the College were to be amply entertained out of a fund for the purpose. The Bishop forgot nothing.

The scholars who came up from Winchester were lads of about fifteen, who entered the Arts Course. For the first two years they were on probation; then, if satisfactory, they were admitted to full Fellowship. Even the youngest had a vote in the election of the Warden, but the real management of the Hall devolved on the Warden and a small group of the senior Fellows. At New College, for the first time at Oxford, if we except the slight beginning at Merton, there appeared the tutorial system of instruction. In this it followed Paris, where the Head was always a Regent Master. But here the older Fellows were the tutors, and the younger ones the recipients of their instruction. The tutors drew an additional allowance for their work, and thus a new institution had its beginning. These lectures were at first purely supplementary to the lectures in the public University Schools, but eventually the system of private tutorial instruction in the Colleges extinguished the University lectures, to a far greater extent than in Paris. The University became a fiction, an empty shell.

Ten of the seventy Fellows were to study Canon Law, ten to enter the lists of the Civil Law; and the remainder proceeded through Arts to the final goal of Theology. The Friars were meeting determined competition.

The students of New College obtained, in some unknown manner, a most curious privilege. They were admitted to University degrees without University examination; the examination of the resident Masters was deemed sufficient to prove the candidate's qualifications. It is quite possible that this home-grown examination was more rigorous than that of the University Regents, but in the course of time the inevitable happened. The New College requirements steadily degenerated into a farce; and the privilege was voluntarily surrendered in 1834.

Lincoln College was founded in 1429 by Richard Fleming, a follower of the Wycliffite heresy, whose recantation was rewarded with the Bishopric of Lincoln. Like all converted heretics, he outdid the regulars in his zeal for the cause. This College was established for the sole purpose of defending the Catholic faith from such damnable heresies as he himself had formerly held.

Magdalen was founded in 1448, near the end of the mediaeval period. The Renaissance had already come to Italy, and the waves of new thought were beginning to reach English

shores. Colet, Grocyn, and Erasmus were among the orna-
ments of Magdalen. The tutorial system was now an established
routine in the colleges, but Magdalen went further. Lecture-
ships were set up in Theology, Moral and Metaphysical
Philosophy, and Natural Philosophy. Latin Grammar, long
forgotten and left to elementary students, was again deemed
a worthy object of study. That meant a renewed acquaintance
with some of the classics, even though in mutilated form. The
Fellows were now able to start from scratch in the Arts course,
and continue through the professional Faculties, with their
whole curriculum self-contained within the College. The
public University lectures were henceforth unnecessary, and
gradually fell into desuetude, to the relief of the Regent
Masters.

Magdalene was a pioneer in another particular—the institution of Gentlemen Commoners. These were twenty young
sprigs of nobility, too proud to become Fellows, since the
faintest aroma of charity clung to the Fellowships, yet realizing
—or perhaps their noble fathers realized for them—that the
best accommodation and the best education were now to be
obtained within the College walls. The College salved their
vanity, and incidentally tapped a welcome source of income,
by permitting these twenty youths to pay their own way. In
time all the scholars of the University found domicile in the
Colleges, either as paying or as non-paying members, and the
wild, free life of an earlier age gave way to the discipline of
these pious institutions.

CHAPTER XXIII

The Oxford Curriculum

IN the beginning the course of studies at Oxford was but a bald imitation of that of Paris, from which most of its scholars and its forms of organization derived. The resemblance continued, but certain inevitable differences crept in. For example, in Arts less attention was paid to Dialectic as the be-all and end-all, and some time was actually devoted to the Quadrivium. Mathematics even had a certain prestige at Oxford, and rightly so, for some of her most glorious sons were thoroughly grounded in that austere science. Aristotle was a divinity, but no longer the effulgence who sat enthroned in Paris. It was possible even to question certain minor propositions of the great Authority without being forthwith flayed alive and boiled in oil.

At the instance of such notables as Grossetête, Roger Bacon, and others, there was some teaching of Greek and Hebrew during a limited period; and French, a *modern* language, was actually taught if desired. This would have been rank heresy in Paris.

Examinations for the various degrees seem to have been conspicuous for their nullity. For the Arts Licence, for instance, the candidate had only to swear that he had listened to the exposition of certain books, while ten Regent Masters testified of their own knowledge that he knew their contents, and five other Masters asserted that they believed that he knew them sufficiently. The superior Faculties did not seem to have made even this requirement.

Writers on the mediaeval Universities have held up their hands in horror at this state of affairs. What, no written examinations? What an impossible situation! But we may discount their disapproval, for most of them have themselves been professional teachers, thoroughly imbued with the sacred

Q

doctrine of the written examination as a test of knowledge. Modern methods, strangely enough, are tending to return to this mediaeval ideal. The capacity of a candidate may perhaps be better measured by the reactions of ten Masters who have lived with him during the period of his University career than by hastily written answers to certain specific questions.

More for the liveliness of its style, and for the malicious insight which it gives into the mediaeval methods, rather than for its objective value, I will quote from Vicesimus Knox on the examinations in vogue at Oxford during the eighteenth century. We are assured that the system had not changed substantially since the period in which we are particularly interested.

"The youth whose heart pants for the honour of a Bachelor of Arts degree," he says, "must wait patiently till near four years have revolved. . . . He is obliged during this period, once to oppose and once to respond. . . . This opposing and responding is termed, in the cant of the place, *doing generals*. Two boys or men, as they call themselves, agree to *do generals* together. The first step in this mighty work is to procure arguments. These are always handed down, from generation to generation, on long slips of paper, and consist of foolish syllogisms on foolish subjects, of the foundation or significance of which the respondent and opponent seldom know more than an infant in swaddling cloaths. . . . When the important day arrives, the two doughty disputants go into a large dusty room, full of dirt and cobwebs. . . . Here they sit in mean desks, opposite to each other from one o'clock till three. Not once in a hundred times does any officer enter; and, if he does, he hears a syllogism or two, and then makes a bow, and departs, as he came and remained, in solemn silence. The disputants then return to the amusement of cutting the desks, carving their names, or reading Sterne's Sentimental Journey, or some other edifying novel. When the exercise is duly performed by both parties, they have a right to the title and insignia of *Sophs*; but not before they have been formally *created* by one of the regent-masters, before whom they kneel, while he lays a volume of Aristotle's works on their heads, and puts on a hood, a piece of black crape, hanging from their necks, and down to their heels. . . . There remain only one or two trifling forms, and another disputation . . . called *answering under bachelor* previous to the awful examination. Every candidate is obliged to be examined in the whole circle of the sciences by three masters of arts *of his own choice*. . . . *Schemes*, as they are called, or little books containing forty or fifty questions on each science, are handed down from age to age, from one to another. The candidate employs three or four days in learning these by heart, and the examiners, having done the same before him, know what questions to ask, and so all goes on smoothly. When the candidate has displayed his universal knowledge of the sciences, he is to display his skill in philology. One of the masters therefore asks him to construe a passage in some Greek or Latin classic, which he does with no interruption, just as he pleases, and as well as he can. The statutes next require that he should translate familiar English phrases into Latin. And now is the time when the masters show their wit and jocularity. . . . This familiarity, however, only takes place when the examiners are pot-companions of the candidate, which indeed is usually the case; for it is reckoned good management to get acquainted with two or three jolly young masters of arts, and supply them well with port previously to the examination. If the vice-chancellor and proctors happen to enter the school, a very uncommon event, then a little solemnity is put on. . . . As neither the officer, nor anyone else, usually enters the room (for it is reckoned very *ungenteel*), the examiners and the candidates often converse on the last drinking bout, or on horses, or read the newspapers or a novel.''

The Faculties at Oxford were not as sharply distinct as those of Paris. The University itself, in the "Great" Congregation, legislated for all the Faculties, and the Arts Faculty, with its numerical predominance and the peculiar right of first discussion of proposed legislation in its own Congregation, maintained a degree of power unheard of even in Paris. The higher Faculties lost in prestige and in numbers, and none of them achieved anything like the degree of prominence enjoyed in the Continental Universities. Civil Law was especially weak. For this, however, there was a very good reason: England had never been in the main stream of the Roman Law. Her legal system, known as "Common" Law, derived rather from a potpourri of early Anglo-Saxon traditions and Norman customs, liberally interlarded with the feudal system. Roman Law, wherever found, was the final touch rather than a fundamental ingredient. This evolution of the English Common Law, devoid of any orderly system or carefully elaborated principles, subject in those early days to perpetual change, in accordance with the decisions of the judges of the realm, competent and learned, or incompetent and venal, never took root in the English Universities. It was not a fit study for their cloistered halls. It was more immediately practical; more related to the stuffy atmosphere of wrangling courtrooms and lawyers' offices; accordingly, young would-be lawyers preferred to live in London at the Inns, or apprentice themselves to active practitioners.

Canon Law, too, was a pale reflex of the full-bodied course at Bologna, and Medicine a scholastic exercise, with very few opportunities for practice such as were offered at Montpellier, and even the Theology course was a hasty shortening of the long Parisian curriculum. It was in the Colleges especially that Theology had its being; had it not been for the pious wishes of their Founders, the alleged "Queen of Sciences" would have been abandoned to its fate. Arts alone, the fundamental study, maintained its dignity at Oxford; the study which, save for Dialectics, was viewed with contempt in Paris.

Another cause of the degradation of the superior Faculties at Oxford was a pernicious series of dispensations, by which any requirement, whether of fundamental importance, such as an Arts degree for Theology, or some petty trifles in connection with an inconvenient Statute, could be abrogated. Everyone asked for some dispensation or other, and very few were refused. All that appeared to interest the Regent Masters was the conditions to be imposed for the granting of the favour. If the applicant was poor, he had to perform some senseless exercises, or act as substitute for their own lazy selves in delivering a sermon or a lecture. If, however, he was wealthy, it would cost him dearly. He might be required to repair certain broken windows in the schools, or disgorge a generous sum for the general fund; or, all pretence abolished, he would have to give a banquet to the Regents, or present them with fine new gowns, with vintage wine, or barrels of luscious oysters. In return for such magnificent presents the rich scholar could obtain almost any dispensation.

From this, however, the reader must not conclude that education had reached its lowest ebb at Oxford. Far from it. These exemptions were from purely University studies; the Colleges were strict in their requirements. It was simply the twilight of the public University system as opposed to the tutorial methods of the Colleges. The public Regents, as in Paris, either passed their necessary period in idleness, or, if they were more ambitious, and needed a regular income as against the precarious returns from pupils' fees, they entered the Colleges as salaried tutors.

Oxford had not the widespread influence of the proud University of Paris. The Church did not bow down in awe before the pronouncements of its Theological Doctors; foreign potentates did not express the hope that the local Universities which they were about to found would follow faithfully in the footsteps of the great Mother University; its decisions on points of Law had none of the binding force of Bologna; the King of England never dreamt of asking Oxford's opinion on affairs of State, nor did the University dare to volunteer it unasked; and its scholars were recruited almost exclusively from the British Isles. Hence it had not the cosmopolitan character of Paris. Even its Arts graduates, if they wished for higher education, were accustomed to finishing on the Continent.

This, in spite of the facts that it had achieved independence far greater than that of Paris, that its scholars were as numerous, and that almost the earliest of the great religious reform movements had its birth within the University confines, and was there fought to a hopeless finish.

This last may be the reason why the Papacy looked somewhat askance at Oxford; or it may have been because learning was a little less formal and less clerical than in Paris; so that the flame of intellect burned more clearly. It is Oxford's freedom from the theological smugness and intellectual rigidity that characterized most of the Continental Universities in their later stages that made her unique.

There were great scholars in England even before the existence of the University, and others, unconnected with it, in the days of its formation, so that Oxford was only the heir to an intellectual tradition already established.

There was Adalbert of Bath, for instance, a mathematician of note and a great traveller. He was well acquainted with the Arab civilization; he knew the startling fact that the earth was round, and that its centre of gravity reposed in the centre of the earth. (But then, so did Dante, writing his *Divine Comedy* not long after.—See "Hell," canto xxxiv. ll. 65-118.) Matter to him was indestructible, and he treated with deserved contempt the idiotic maxim that "Nature abhors a vacuum." Nor was he the lone prodigy of his age. Hugh of St. Victor had similar ideas, and Michael Scot, a little later, was not merely a notable astrologer, who acted officially as such at the Court of the great Frederick II, but an experimenter and scientist of more substantial attainments. He translated Aristotle's scientific works as well as those of the Arabs; and he was an acute observer. Yet in common with practically all of the great minds of the Middle Ages, he believed devoutly in the superstitious nonsense of the day. He prognosticated from the stars, from dreams, and from urine. He believed that sorceries might be wrought by the magical use of menstrual fluid, the semen of men, the hairs of an enemy's head, and footprints in the mud. There was Gilbert of England, the great physician of the early thirteenth century, who combined Aristotelian reasoning with the more adequate and sensible methods of diet, frequent bathing, plasters, ointments, and bleeding, advised by the Salernian School.

So that England, too, had her twelfth-century Renaissance, which laid more emphasis on science and mathematics than the great efflorescence of France. When Grossetête and Roger Bacon appeared on the scene they were not sports or sudden apparitions, but merely the culmination of what was already a venerable tradition.

Strangely enough, these great men were both of them Franciscans, as were many others of the Oxford School of philosophy. The Dominicans had reached England first, and established their particular brand of fanaticism more strongly at Oxford, but they were intellectually sterile. They followed slavishly in the footsteps of their great exponents on the Continent: Albert the Great and St. Thomas Aquinas. Their study was theology, and a particularly narrow theology at that. Partly because the rival order had appropriated Aristotle and adapted him to theology, and partly from a congenital leaning toward the Platonic-Augustinian development of ideas, the Franciscans shied away from the true mediaeval orthodoxy, and thus enabled their more radical members to possess a guilty knowledge of other fields, other sciences.

Robert Grossetête, who lived from 1175 to 1253, was one of the greatest of these. He entered the Order after achieving maturity, and was almost immediately requisitioned as the first lecturer in their Oxford School. He was also the first Chancellor of the young University, and afterwards became Bishop of Lincoln, in which office he died in the full odour of orthodoxy and sanctity. In spite of these impediments to true greatness, his was one of the most liberal and comprehensive intellects of the Middle Ages. His fame has been to a large extent overshadowed by Roger Bacon, yet it is a question which of the two was truly the greater man. Many of Bacon's ideas were derived from his master, and the debt gladly acknowledged.

Grossetête was a resolute and unyielding champion of liberty; he defied King and Pope impartially in defence of what he conceived to be right. Oxford never found a greater protector for her new-born liberties. Scholarship and the pursuit of truth were his gods, yet he somehow managed to reconcile them with his orthodoxy. He wrote extensively on a wide variety of subjects; he was equally at home in recondite mathematical theorems, in optics and physics, as in philosophy; he was interested in new methods of agriculture, he knew Greek and Hebrew, he wrote French verse of some distinction, and he dabbled in law and medicine. He was the complete mind of his day; what Lord Bacon aspired to be centuries later.

Grossetête taught and wrote of the formation of the universe in scientific, not in theological, terms; of the movements of planets and comets. He investigated the theory of colours, of the tides, of perspective, of the rainbow, of heat and light. He advocated a project for the reform of the insufficient Gregorian calendar; he applied geometry to the study of optics; and he believed that in mathematics alone lay the explanation of physical phenomena.

He was chiefly instrumental in introducing the new Aristotle to Oxford; yet, true to his background as a Franciscan, he favoured the Augustinian and neo-Platonic ideas to an unadulterated Aristotle. He was remarkably free from most of the superstitions of his time, and though a believer in astrology, did not carry it to the extravagant lengths to which even Roger Bacon, his disciple, was inclined to go. His is one of the less disheartening cases of mediaeval scholarship; the Church not only found no grounds for persecuting him, but actually advanced this scholar and scientist of humble birth to high office. But then, his life was unimpeachable, his philosophical and theological opinions fairly regular, and his scientific research, if noted at all, was not in manifest conflict with the priestly doctrines.

CHAPTER XXIV

Friar Roger Bacon

A MORE palpable and more tragic case was that of his beloved disciple, Roger Bacon, another Franciscan monk (approximately 1214 to 1292). Perhaps the greatest genius of the Middle Ages, Bacon was a strange mass of contradictions; a modern spirit with his feet firmly rooted in his own thirteenth century; a bold experimenter and inquirer into truth, who yet believed devoutly in every word of the Bible; a mathematician and scientist who outdid his age in obeisance to the quack "science" of astrology; a clear, penetrating thinker whose ideas were sometimes veiled in mysticism; a bitter anti-Scholastic who used the Scholastic forms with ease and elegance; a scorner of all but practical, workable truths, who had hardly any influence over his age; a lover of mankind and a savage assailant of his contemporaries; a dreamer of dreams and a despiser of visions; in short, a human being, compounded of many elements, warring with each other, yet somehow making up a totality.

We know that Bacon studied in Paris and received his Master of Arts degree about 1240. It is now considered doubtful whether he ever obtained a degree in Theology, as was once believed. About 1247 he entered the Order of the Franciscan Friars, and his troubles began. It may be wondered why such a man, imbued with the scientific spirit, an intellectual, an inquirer into moving causes, should have subjected himself to the physical and mental restrictions of a religious Order.

If we divest ourselves of our modern prejudices and preconceptions, the answer is comparatively simple. Bacon was after all a mediaeval man; he firmly believed in the divine inspiration of his religion, and that the Orders of the Mendicant Friars were praiseworthy organizations. It was then the natural thing for a scholar, an intellectual, to join one of the two great Orders. They were the foci of the intellectual activity of the time. The great scholastic Theologians gravitated to the Dominicans; the more liberal Philosophers, the neo-Platonists, to the Franciscans. Within the Orders one found assistance during the arduous years of scholarship, and the community of other great minds. There was hardly a man of note in the thirteenth century who had not joined either one or the other Order. The advantages were many: security and leisure to study and meditate, powerful protection against outside dangers, in an age when the single, unsupported man, not a member of any organization or guild, was little better than an outlaw. Albert the Great, Thomas Aquinas, Grossetête, and Adam Marsh found such membership of incalculable aid; the donning of the friar's habit meant no restriction of their genius. With Roger Bacon it was different. Yet it is a moot question even in his case whether the miseries and conflicts of his later years were the natural result of a fundamental clash of ideas, or merely a matter of personal enmities and resentments caused by his vitriolic remarks.

After joining the Franciscans, Bacon went back to Oxford, and sat as a disciple under the first lecturer of the Order in that Studium, Grossetête. From that great and noble spirit he imbibed enthusiasms that moulded the remainder of his life. Too little has been made of this influence of great teacher on great pupil; all through Bacon's work and ideas may be seen the thread of Grossetête's discourse; it is possible that his devotion to mathematics and physics was due to the impetus and guidance received from the master. Throughout his life, on every occasion, Bacon continued to speak admiringly of the Bishop of Lincoln, and many a theorem of Bacon's may be traced back to the writings of Grossetête.

Besides sitting at the master's feet, Bacon also lectured in the Schools of Oxford. Already his superiors in the Order sensed the essential boldness of the man, the intellectual audacity of some of his opinions. They seemed to have grown on him since his entry into the Order; there was no evidence of particular nonconformity before. Up till then he had been a normal scholastic, holding Dialectic and Aristotle in high repute, solving all problems by appeal to syllogisms, apparently following the crowd in reliance upon words rather than on the five senses. Even the question, "Whether it is possible that living beings can be generated by putrefaction" —surely a matter of experiment if ever there was one—was but another logical exercise. Then came the change to the second, the great period.

In 1267 he himself sets the dividing line: "During the last twenty years in which I have laboured, especially in the study of wisdom, after leaving the beaten track or abandoning the ordinary methods, I have spent more than 2000 pounds on secret books and various experiments, and languages and instruments and mathematical tables, etc. . . ."

Apart from the naïve boasting of this passage, and the almost incredible sum which he mentions therein, it is interesting in showing that the date when he ventured forth into the unknown was also the date when he became a "religious." This would seem to confirm the theory that Grossetête was responsible for the conversion, for the desertion of the beaten track.

In this second period of his life he bitterly denied the all-importance of Logic in the scheme of things. Because Scholasticism was essentially a matter of argumentation *in vacuo*, he ridiculed it in-season and out. And not content with attacks on the general structure of the philosophy of the time, he particularized and personalized. Almost every exponent of the scholastic method had a taste of his savage abuse. Thomas Aquinas, already deified in the imagination of the time, the Saint-to-be who had, so to speak, compelled Aristotle to make room for him, was the chief object of his wrath. He did not mince his words. Aquinas, said he, was the greatest corrupter of philosophy that had ever been among the Latins. Albert the Great, himself an experimenter and scientist of attainments, came in for an equal share of abuse. Albert was "a dumb ox"; Alexander of Hales, a fellow-Franciscan, wrote works that were "heavier than a horse"; Richard of Cornwall was "an absolute fool," and in general, all the Scholastics were full of "puerile vanity and voluminous superfluity."

H. L. Mencken, the *enfant terrible* of the twentieth century, does not wield the bludgeon on established reputations as fiercely as did this Friar of the thirteenth century, when authority sat on a pinnacle, and the men he so brutally criticized were held to be only a little lower than the angels. No wonder his superiors were aghast. It was not enough that he went after the Dominican intellectuals tooth and nail—that might be winked at, if not openly approved—but the madman lashed out indiscriminately and attacked his own brethren. That was serious. Resentment grew; the Dominicans meditated vengeance; the Franciscans, who ordinarily should have protected their own, were busy licking their own wounds. The storm was gathering, but it was years before it broke.

What made Bacon feel so strongly about the use of Logic? It was not that he was not aware of the value of deductive reasoning; it was merely that he was protesting against its excessive use. He himself used the scholastic forms; he appreciated Aristotle, Averrhoës, and Avicenna; he criticized the Thomist doctrine of "unity of form" in anticipation of Duns Scotus; he split matter into numerous forms, outside of and apart from the essence of God.

But more than all else, he saw clearly the vain sterility, the arguing in a circle, into which Scholasticism was already falling. The first fine intellectual vigour was over; the same things were now being said over and over again in different language; and very few thought to look at the world around them for a fresh take-off, a fresh view-point. Bacon did that very thing. He looked at Nature and noted its infinite variety; the idea of observation, the manipulation of factors in the natural order, under control and for definite purposes, which is called experimentation, aroused his ardour. He anticipated, as did many another, his namesake, Francis Bacon's, alleged discovery of the efficacy of inductive reasoning.

Mathematics and the study of languages were, he considered, the two principal doors of knowledge. In mathematics, with Grossetête, he saw the basis of the physical world. A great part of his writings was devoted to showing "the power of mathematics in sciences, and the things and occupations of this world."

The education of the time was the subject of his continual complaint. Bacon, indeed, was the great complainer, the Jeremiah of his day. For one thing, it was held that mathematics and the sciences were but poor things, unworthy of the student's attention.

"It is by knowledge of created things," he thundered against Aquinas, who completely disregarded the things of the visible world, "that we arrive at a knowledge of the Creator."

"Future generations," he dared to prophesy in an age when men deemed that all knowledge was already discovered and classified, "will know much of which we are ignorant, and a time will come when our successors will wonder that we were blind to things so obvious to them."

He delved into the mysteries of alchemy; that half-magical forerunner of the science of chemistry. His laboratory was a thing of awe and suspicion to the friars, his brethren. There were in it instruments of strange and unholy shapes; the stench that sometimes emanated, smacked of the devil himself. There were rumours as to mysterious experiments that grew into legends with the passing of the years, until in the later Middle Ages the very name of Friar Bacon became synonymous with magical practices and ungodly powers.

To such an opinion, no doubt, this famous passage from his work contributed:

"These have been made in my time as in ancient times, so I can speak with certainty of them—such as burning-glasses which operate at any distance we choose, so that anything hostile to the commonwealth may be burnt—a castle or army or city or anything; and the flying machine—and a navigating machine by which one man may guide a ship full of armed men at incredible speed; and scythe-bearing cars which, full of armed men, race along with wondrous machinery without animals to draw them."

Previsions of the aeroplane, steamship, and armoured car, it is true; yet obviously mere imaginative discourse, that found its counterpart as far back as the age that created the myth of Daedalus. It is noteworthy, too, that this Friar's mind ran to warlike things; to armed men, and burnings, and battles, and devastation. There may have been method in this, for he was trying to convince the Pope, and other monarchs, of the utilitarian value of scientific achievement; and for what has invention greater value than for war? We moderns need not feel superior; it is a well-established fact that the World War was chiefly responsible for the tremendous advance of the aeroplane within the short period of four years; and many another invention was geared to its greatest capacity because of its supposed efficiency in making war more devastating.

Then, too, it must be remembered that Roger Bacon was essentially a practical man, in spite of his bold dreaming. In-season and out, he insisted on the utilitarian value of knowledge; so that he advocated science, mathematics, and languages, and was scornful of logical abstractions and scholastic theology. Today, with a modern equipment and background he would doubtless have been an Edison, a Bell, a Marconi, rather than an Einstein, a Hertz, or an Euler. Always he was interested in the practical value of research; he was, indeed, the world's first commercial scientist. From his philosophy, if not from his actual discoveries, derived the amazing mastery of Nature which the developments of science have achieved in the last century and a half. The Greeks pondered on the subtle secrets of Nature, but made little effort to apply their knowledge; even Archimedes evolved his war-engines and burning-glasses as though reluctantly. The Romans had no science to speak of; the men of the Middle Ages were too concerned with the imminence of the other world to bother much about this one. Bacon was a lonely figure; a solitary voice crying that men could live better, fight better, die better, if they only used the tools which Nature indicated to the patient seeker. But this voice was unheard; the time was not ripe.

Nor could Bacon himself make use of his knowledge. If he did really discover the secret of the manufacture of gunpowder, he did not see how his invention could be applied, and let it lie fallow. If he knew of a certain arrangement of lenses which could make distant objects appear closer—in other words, the telescope—he either never thought of making a telescope, or, if he made one, he never dreamt of turning it on the stars overhead. Had he done so, he would have anticipated Galileo by centuries, and the discovery of the phases of Venus and the moons of Jupiter might have led to an earlier revolution in the intellectual history of the world.

It has been hinted that Bacon actually did these things; that he built the marvellous machines of which he speaks so eloquently—the aeroplane, the automobile, the telescope, etc. —but that he was fearful of the Church, and her accusations of heresy and magic; so that he concealed his actual accomplishments under the guise of vague predictions. One should be extremely sceptical of this theory. Bacon was exceedingly forthright in his statements; he did not hesitate to embroil himself with the Church, or with the most powerful individuals of the day. Further, he does not seem to have considered that such things were contrary to the teachings of the Church. As a matter of fact, he wrote of them in a direct appeal to the Papacy for support. Nor was he unfamiliar with the charge that he was guilty of working magic. He defended himself constantly and with vigour against such attacks on his alchemical experiments. It was not that he did not believe in true magic; but there were many impostors about, and he did not care to be classed with them. From the experience gained in his own experiments, he was able to expose the tricks of the charlatans. He describes them with great gusto in *De Secretis Operibus*—the dim lights, the ventriloquism, the sleight of hand, the table tippings, the accomplices, the balder-dash of awesome formulae and invocations of the spirits, which are the stock-in-trade of magicians, spiritualists, mediums, fakirs, or what not, of every age and clime. Most of the tricks which he describes have proved equally effective in the hands of Signora Palladino or Mme Blavatsky. No, the fact remains that Bacon was able to point out the path, but had neither the driving force, nor possibly the mechanical genius, to carry into effect his own suggestions.

Yet his scientific achievements, although they were without visible fruit, and were not rigorously worked out, included some startling anticipations. He knew more of optics and of optical laws than any other man of his time; he insisted that light is not an emanation of particles, but a movement propa-gated through successive parts of the medium (long before Huyghens). Further, he proclaimed that light is not simul-taneous in its action; it requires time for its passage from point to point. (This, remember, over four hundred years before Roemer.) He maintained the possibility of reaching India by sailing west across the Atlantic, in a passage which was incorporated without acknowledgment by one Peter d'Ailly in his *Imago Mundi*, and thus became known to Columbus. Thus it may be held that Bacon was the catalyst who precipitated the discovery of America.

Yet this bold and practical thinker was a devout believer in the influence of the stars on the most private affairs of mankind. So, however, was almost every other intellectual of the time. He was not alone in his folly. Frederick II, Aquinas, Albert, Grossetête, Michael Scot, Popes and kings and common people, all eagerly studied the intricate art of drawing horoscopes. Astrology had come from the Orient through the Arabs, and all Christian Europe believed in it, so that the statement that Bacon was finally condemned because of his absorption in astrology is evidently mythical.

The other great passion of Bacon's life, aside from the sciences, was the study of languages. In an age when Latin was considered the only language worth knowing, he advocated the study of Greek, Arabic, and Hebrew. We are living in an age of ignorance, he lamented. No one knows what Aristotle said and thought; no one is truly conversant with the Bible; men devour barbarous, pernicious translations and think they have achieved knowledge. There is only one way of cleaning out the swamps of ignorance. Learn the original languages in which these texts were written, and restore them to their pristine purity. Away with false translations and falser commentators, who conceal the very thought they are supposed to expound! The text of the Bible used at Paris was hopelessly corrupt. "I appeal to you," he writes to Clement IV, "against this corruption of the Text, for you alone can remedy the evil."

He does not hesitate to tilt against the famous *Sentences* of Peter the Lombard. Read the Bible itself, he demanded, and forget the commentators who have taken its place. He laboured on a Greek and a Hebrew grammar for the use of students, and it was possibly because of his efforts that the Council of Vienna, in 1312, decreed the establishment of chairs in Greek, Hebrew, and the Oriental languages at Paris, Oxford, and other Universities.

But the studies languished for lack of pupils. Not until the Renaissance were languages other than Latin to receive serious attention. Again, it must be noted that Bacon advocated the study of Greek and Hebrew, not because of the inherent value of the study of these languages, nor because of the literature embalmed therein, but for the eminently practical reason that Aristotle and the Fathers of the Church wrote in Greek, while the Scriptures were in Hebrew, so that it behooved philosophers and theologians to study the originals. Nor had he any ulterior motives in mind. He was no iconoclast, no heretic. He firmly believed in the tenets of the Christian faith; even in the absorption of Aristotle into Catholic dogma; he was

no Luther or Calvin, who quoted the Bible in order to overthrow existing forms.

In point of fact, his chief works were addressed to the Pope,
and his vision of the world was that of a gigantic theocratic
State.

In 1257 Roger Bacon had already earned the disapproval of
his superiors. Bonaventura, the mystical philosopher, who had
become General of the Franciscan Order the year before,
frowned on this most unorthodox Friar. Reports of his magical
practices were insistent; he was lacking in reverence for
persons and institutions; and perhaps, for the General himself.

Accordingly, he was ordered to Paris, where he would be
under the eye of headquarters, and there for ten years he
remained. There have been many disputes as to the meaning
of these ten years of residence. The older authorities, including
the greatest of all Baconian scholars, J. H. Bridges, insist that
it was tantamount to imprisonment, or at least, to close confinement and supervision, and that Bacon was strictly forbidden to write anything for publication. A. G. Little, however,
decries this theory. According to him, Bacon simply withdrew
himself from the publicity of Oxford to the retirement of
Paris because of ill-health. The older idea seems more reasonable. Paris could not by any means be considered a quiet health
resort; nor does the hypothesis agree with the facts of the case,
among which is the secrecy observed by the Pope himself in
obtaining the manuscripts of Bacon's works written during
this period.

For in 1266, while Bacon was suffering the tortures which
such a proud and embittered spirit must have suffered under
the supervision and open hostility of the Order to which he
had irrevocably bound himself, Pope Clement IV, himself a
man of learning and ardent curiosity, wrote in secrecy to the
badgered Friar. You are, he said in effect, to deliver to me a
fair copy of all your works, secretly and without delay, notwithstanding any constitution or prohibition of the Franciscan
Order to the contrary. This in itself is a sufficient refutation of

Little's thesis. The man *was* hobbled. Nor could the Pope, all-powerful though he was, dare openly and publicly to release Bacon from his vows and obligations to his Order.

It is easy to imagine the effect of this communication upon the despairing Friar, who had resigned himself to a life of continued obscurity. His courage revived; the Pope himself was taking an interest in him, not only as a man, but as a thinker. Grandiose visions stirred; he may well have seen himself the guiding hand of a Papacy risen to world dominion.

Then despair overcame him again. He could not speak in person to the Pope; for he was at Rome and Bacon in Paris. The Pontiff had demanded his written works. Alas, apart from a number of minor papers, he had none. He had taken the prohibition of the Order seriously. Yet he could not afford to miss this chance of remoulding the world to his heart's desire. He threw off his despair and set to work.

Alone, watched suspiciously day and night by his superiors, spied on by jealous brother Friars, compelled to work under cover and without avowing his plans, without money, without books, without the assistance of copyists, under the most adverse conditions, within eighteen months he had completed three huge volumes, works to which the formidable name of masterpieces may safely be applied. They were the *Opus Majus*, *Opus Minus*, and *Opus Tertium*.

These volumes, it must be remembered, were written for a specific purpose. They were not a well-rounded system of philosophy; they were not a calm, dispassionate mirror of the totality of Bacon's mind; they were bits of special pleading, hortatory and missionary in character; their sole purpose was to convince the Pope that learning was in a parlous state, that the Pope alone could originate a revival, and that the pursuit of science and the study of languages which he advocated would prove of immense benefit to the fabric of the Church. In short, that a change of curriculum and emphasis in the Universities would have a *utilitarian* value. For this reason, arguments based on a close and literal reading of these three works of Bacon's, which claim that they reveal the sum of his knowledge and his aims, may not be reliable.

The *Opus Majus* is a veritable encyclopaedia, in which Bacon treats of a great variety of topics for the one purpose of persuading the Pope. He deals with the four usual causes of error: authority, custom, the opinion of the mob, and the concealment of ignorance under the pretence of knowledge. Then he proceeds to the relation between philosophy and theology, in which he states significantly that all true wisdom is contained in the Scriptures. From this he goes on to the study of grammar and of languages, which lay nearest his heart. A translator, he said, must be thoroughly at home in both languages, and must be conversant with the subject-matter of the book itself. Good sound rules, which apply with equal force today. Then on to mathematics, with examples to show how it might be applied to natural problems and why it was an essential element in theological reasoning. Then to geography; the science of optics and perspective; mirrors and lenses; and the doctrine of the transmission of force by geometrical figures. And most important of all, the overthrow of mere logical arguments in the pursuit of knowledge, and the glorification of the experimental, inductive method.

The *Opus Minus* is an attempt at a summary of the greater work, perhaps because he felt that the pontifical attention might wander if confronted by the immensities of the first volume. Then came the *Opus Tertium*, acting as a sort of preamble to the other two, and supplementing them to some extent. All three, it must be remembered, were to Bacon no more than sketches, preliminary drafts of a much larger, more carefully elaborated work, to be written when the exigencies of the occasion were not so imperative. This work he never completed, and only a few fragments of it exist.

There was something else that he urged upon the Pope: an ideal, a vision, a synthesis of the world. Catholicism was to be the binding force, the Pope the all-wise sovereign. Nothing of good, nothing of spiritual or intellectual value evolved by other races, other religions through the centuries, was to be ignored. Within the very warp and woof of the Christian religion were to be incorporated the best and noblest elements of Judaism, Mahommedanism, and the ancient Greek Pantheon. Theology in its highest sense, a fusing of Mosaic and Christian tradition, interpenetrated by the Aristotelian philosophy, vitalized by the spirit of scientific research, was to provide and regulate the spiritual government of the world. A great Papacy, all-wise, all-pitiful, superhuman almost, was to be at the head of this world theocracy, and the vision would be accomplished—the lion and the lamb lying down together, the swords beaten into ploughshares; the world a synthesis of order, enlightenment, and progress, when philosophers would be popes, and the popes philosophers—in short, the millennium!

A noble and grandiose vision—and quite mad! Theocracy had been tried before, and found wanting, even as aristocracy had been, and tyranny, oligarchy, monarchy, and—before and since—democracy.

When Roger Bacon had finished his three manuscripts he sent them secretly to Rome in the charge of a youth who had been his pupil. It was a long and arduous journey to Rome, and Bacon waited impatiently, as the months passed, for a sign that the Pope had received, that the Pope had read, that the Pope had approved his ideas and his vision.

To this day it is not known exactly what happened in Rome. The Pope did receive the precious documents; but did he read them, hastily and cursorily, or carefully and with due regard to the genius that shone on every page, or did he lay them aside for a more propitious occasion? It is impossible now to say, but whether he read them or not, whether he approved or disapproved of them, the Pope made no sign. The Franciscan Friar, waiting impatiently in his narrow retreat, regardless of the curious and suspicious glances of his brethren, never knew. Within the year Clement IV, his protector, was dead, and his lips sealed for ever. A new Pope was elected, Gregory X, a Franciscan, and hence inimical to that errant Friar, Roger Bacon. The great opportunity was past, the manuscripts forgotten. The world was not to be saved by any scheme of Bacon's; the Universities continued their sterile curricula, theology was stifled by the accretions of the civil and canon law, as Bacon had prophesied; and the corruption of the Church increased.

Bacon returned to Oxford—thanks to a last kindly action of the dead Pope—a savage and embittered man. He wrote his *Compendium Studii Philosophiae*, a masterpiece of invective. He flagellated the age like an elder prophet; intellectually and morally the times were rotten and out of joint; the Church, which was to have led the world out of the slough, was now itself a sink of corruption, from the Pope down to the lowest parish priest. He sharpened his quill and tipped it with venom when he wrote of the great scholars, the celebrities of the day. They were pedants, ignoramuses, filled with a false conceit of wisdom, sterile, given to empty words and vain subtleties, knowing no Greek, taking the shell for the substance. Aristotle was a snare and a delusion in the barbarous translations in which he existed; better no Aristotle at all than such a distorted simulacrum. In short, he wielded a bludgeon, and many an honoured and respected head ached from the thwacks it received.

Once again Bacon was in trouble. The enemies whom he had aroused were numerous and powerful. For once the Dominicans and Franciscans agreed. In 1278 he was summoned before his Order to answer for "certain suspected novelties." He may have been charged with dark alchemical practices, with an overweening belief in Astrology, with heresies, as has been claimed, but if he was, these charges were so much camouflage. The real trouble was that he had called too many people numskulls, jackasses, and pompous fools. He was tried and duly convicted, and thrust into prison. For fourteen years he remained in jail. His life was over. When he was released, in 1292, it seems that he died almost at once. There was nothing more that he could say to his times.

To our modern eyes Roger Bacon stands forth as one of the greatest minds of the Middle Ages; perhaps the greatest, and certainly the mind most akin, in spite of its mediaeval peculiarities, to our own. In his own day he had little or no influence. The schools of philosophy continued their dialectic as though he had never existed. The plain man heard vaguely of the wonder-worker, the dark magician, the consorter with the Devil—Friar Bacon. The men of the Renaissance praised him as they would have praised anyone who fought the Scholastics; then once more he lapsed into comparative obscurity. In the nineteenth century, that century nearest akin to his own spirit, the pendulum swung upward again. The praise accorded him was so extravagant that now there is danger of a reaction. The truth seems to lie, as usual, somewhere between the two extremes.

CHAPTER XXV

Decline of Scholasticism

BESIDES Bacon, there were other scientists and mathematicians at Oxford. In fact, no other University of the thirteenth century could compete with it in the breadth and variety of its studies. Grossetête and Adam Marsh laboured there, and not in vain; John Holywood and John Peckham were two of the most eminent mathematicians of the age. Paris was outshone, as it deserved to be. The Scholastics, the special object of Bacon's onslaught, had little influence at Oxford; for the predominating Franciscans and the Seculars rather resented Aquinas and Albert the Great, and refused to bend the knee before the two great Dominicans.

But in the fourteenth century the tide turned. Philosophy wearied and grew faint in Paris, while it flourished and grew to astonishing proportions at Oxford. Now it was the English University to which the philosophers came as to a Mecca of learning.

Eminent among these philosophers was John Duns Scotus, who was born about 1270 and died in 1308, at a comparatively early age. He taught at Oxford; entered the Franciscan Order, as everyone of any intellectual pretensions seems to have done; took a degree in Theology in Paris, and taught also at Cologne. He wrote commentaries on Aristotle and on the *Sentences* (it was one of the passions of the Middle Ages to produce commentaries on commentaries on commentaries *ad infinitum*), and received the honorific appellation of the "Subtle Doctor." This was another mediaeval weakness—giving resounding names to its philosophers. Thus Bacon was the Miraculous Doctor, Aquinas the Angelic Doctor, Albert the Great the Universal Doctor, Alexander of Hales the Irrefragable Doctor, etc. etc.

Here again, in the case of Duns Scotus, we find extreme

divergencies of opinion. To the Humanists of the sixteenth century he was the *reductio ad absurdum* of Scholasticism. All their heavy artillery was used to blast him and his followers into nothingness. As a result, until quite recently, the judgment of the Humanists was accepted, so that the very name of John Duns Scotus became a synonym for stupidity. He was "Duns," and so through the ages every stupid, thick-witted dunderhead has been opprobriously called a "Dunce." Rashdall, ordinarily cautious in his estimates, followed the procession. To him Duns Scotus was the ultimate example of fine-spun Scholasticism with Realism at its wildest. All the popular characteristics of the Scholastic Philosophy, he says, are inherent in poor Duns—the splitting of hairs, the abuse of the syllogism, the multiplication of barbarous technicalities, and the use of unintelligible jargon.

It was almost inevitable that defenders would arise in this twentieth century. C. R. S. Harris, in his monumental volumes on Duns Scotus, has boxed the compass. It now appears that the Oxford philosopher, far from being the worst product of Scholasticism, was in fact its bitterest and most damaging critic. He brought to his task a technical equipment that Roger Bacon never possessed. He vigorously attacked the personalities and systems of most of his contemporaries and predecessors. Aquinas was his special bugbear. "Aquinas," it has been stated, "takes the *doctrines* which are to be proved, while Duns Scotus take the *proofs* of these doctrines, as the peculiar object of study."

If he did nothing else, he performed one worthy task. He showed the apparent harmony between philosophy and theology to be a sham and a delusion, and the two sacred dogmas of theology, to wit, the immortality of the soul and the existence of God, to be incapable of any rational proof.

Was he, then, an agnostic? Nothing of the sort. He had other fish to fry. The dogmas of Theology, he maintained, required no rational proof. Philosophy is but a lowly handmaid, and must be excluded from consideration of many of the doctrines of the Church. In fact, he was an anti-Scholastic. His object was to demolish the philosophical structure of Abélard and Aquinas, and the claim that reason was admissible into the sacred precincts of Theology, to test and examine, to affirm or deny. Now Scholasticism may have become sterile; it may have deteriorated from Abélard's day; in the hands of Aquinas and his mental inferiors reason may have become a weapon to affirm and strengthen, rather than to test and deny; but at least every Scholastic admitted the validity of an examination of the Christian dogmas in the light of reason. Duns Scotus sets the clock back to a crude and exaggerated form of Realism, back to the time of William of Champeaux. It seems that the Humanists must be considered more nearly right in their estimate of him than his present-day apologians.

Yet the first part of Duns Scotus' thesis—the impossibility of the rational proof of the two great dogmas—led to unexpected results. For a greater thinker arose, William of Ockham, who was born about 1300 and died in 1348. In most directions he reacted violently to his predecessor. He was the "prince of nominalists" as against the realism of Duns Scotus; but he, too, attacked Scholasticism and divorced Philosophy and Theology. He, too, declared that it was impossible to prove the existence of God; that it must be accepted by faith. Yet his claim to acceptance by faith was less belligerent than that of Duns Scotus. He held to the famous dictum that what might be true in Philosophy might be false in Theology, and vice versa. They were in separate, air-tight compartments. But he did not preclude Philosophy from a consideration of the same issues, and he seemed to take a delight in proving by Philosophy that a doctrine was false, and then in proclaiming its eternal verity as a Theological dogma.

In spite of his professed orthodoxy, he had decided leanings toward agnosticism and intellectual scepticism. And if he were to be followed, scientific research could safely proceed, for Theology would not interfere with it, no matter how heretical its findings. These could not affect religion; a most subtle and comforting doctrine. In fact, at Oxford, during the height of the controversy over the Wycliffite doctrines, a Master "strove to prove the opinion of Wyclif concerning the Sacrament of the Altar, and at length, when the Masters were congregated, he said in the presence of all that there is no idolatry like that of the Sacrament of the Altar. Yet the Chancellor said nothing to him but 'Now thou speakest as a philosopher.'" The lesson of Ockham had been well learned.

In one field, however, Ockham spoke out boldly. He was the leading anti-Papist of his day; he declared that the State was paramount to the Church in all political matters. Let the Papacy confine itself to its proper duties. In 1324 he was called from Oxford to Avignon to answer charges of heresy. There, for seventeen weeks, he was imprisoned, but he managed to escape, and became only more confirmed in his hostility to the Papacy. The following year, the Arts Faculty of Paris obediently prohibited his teachings as dangerous, and in 1346 the Pope made another determined effort to suppress his doctrines. The effect was seemingly to extend the influence of his teachings, and Nominalism in the fourteenth and fifteenth centuries became once more the leading doctrine.

But the spirit was fled; Scholasticism was dying of dry rot. Wyclif assailed the Church, and failed. The Church gripped the Universities with an iron hand, and efficiently crushed all independence of thought. The Schools could no longer be looked to for leadership in thought. Ideas were growing into maturity outside their learned halls. In Italy Petrarch, Boccaccio, and Marsilius of Padua were writing; and before long the Medici helped fan the coming Renaissance into flame. Oxford, Paris, and the German Universities were without vitality, absorbed in practical problems, and the Scholastic philosophy vegetated and spun itself out to interminable lengths until the Renaissance and the Reformation swept it out of the path of human progress for ever.

CHAPTER XXVI

Montpellier, Orléans, Angers, and Toulouse

THESE, then, were the three great Universities of the Middle Ages—Paris, Bologna, and Oxford. They towered above all the rest; yet the others cannot be ignored. Each was a centre of scholarship, of learning, a leavening influence in its immediate vicinity. Some, like Montpellier, Padua, Prague, and Salamanca, achieved international reputation. Others were of later origin, achieving fame only in our own day. As the nationalistic spirit awoke and grew at the expense of Empire and Papacy, more and more Universities were founded to keep the scholars at home, to feed the growing egotism and pride of the nations. In return, the Universities fed the fires of nationalism. Kings and cities were now their parents and direct progenitors; the Church stood more and more in the relation of a godmother only. Most of them were direct, deliberate creations; though a few, the older ones, had evolved even as Paris and Bologna and Oxford had done, and could boast of as lengthy and indeterminate an ancestry.

Montpellier was the most famous of the minor Universities. It was located in the South of France, a country as distinct from Northern France as though they had been alien territories. Montpellier, as old as Paris, or older, paid no heed to the growth of her mighty sister University; she looked rather to the South—to Italy, to Bologna, for her forms, customs, and governments. The Roman influence had always been strong in the South; clericalism did not possess the stranglehold which it had in the North. Law and Medicine were regarded more highly than Theology, and the classics did not yield so ignominiously to all-powerful Logic. Moreover, in the South there was a considerable population of Saracens and Jews, and these more civilized elements helped to evoke a certain distaste for the paradoxical mixture of crudity and subtlety which distinguished the North. Life was a little more pagan in the cloudless, sunburnt South; men were more preoccupied with the practical things of this world, and less with fantasies of the next.

From the eleventh century, and possibly before it, there was a Medical School at Montpellier. It grew in fame until it caught up with its older rival, Salerno, and then shot ahead, until it became the most famous Medical University of the Middle Ages. In the period of the Schools there seem to have been no requirements for teaching. All who would and could collect pupils taught freely without hindrance. This state of affairs could not last. Charlatans were bound to creep in, and with flashy arts entice away the pupils of the more learned and well-grounded Masters. The more responsible teachers got together, as in Paris, and organized for protection. At once the Bishop intervened, in pursuance of the settled policy of the Church northward of the Alps, and claimed authority over the incipient University of Medicine. He appointed a Chancellor whose jurisdiction was civil in character and considerably less than in Paris. For himself, the Bishop reserved all criminal jurisdiction over the assembled masters and scholars, and the right to confer the teaching Licence. This was a tyranny like that of Paris, but even worse; and the fight for independence began.

In 1309 Clement V limited the granting of the Licence to those cases in which two-thirds of the Masters concurred; later on, the same Pope decreed that a similar vote was necessary to confirm the appointment of a Chancellor. Thus the University of Medical Masters of Montpellier received its privileges later than Paris, but it received more of them. It began as a Master's University; but by 1340 the students, who had resentfully watched their fellows rise to power in the Law University, exacted a measure of government for themselves. Statutes relating to studies required their consent to be effective; they could discuss their grievances at the General

Assemblies of the entire Master and Student bodies. But that was the limit of their powers. Though a little more democratic than in Paris, they were far from achieving the liberties of Bologna. Freedom to complain was not coupled with any right to enforce their requests.

It was natural for the Medical School, subject as it was to Arabic and Jewish influences, to yield to the influx of the new ideas in medicine, and drift away from an exclusive preoccupation with the ancient Greeks. The curriculum was more liberal than at Salerno or Paris; anatomy was studied by means of an occasional dissection, yet there was no real progress. Even here budding doctors were advised to preface their treatment of patients with a visit from the priest to purge the soul; and the *Thesaurus pauperum* of Peter of Spain, who was later to become Pope Gregory X, was followed as diligently as elsewhere. This mediaeval textbook of medicine was filled with devout sayings and the grossest superstitions.

It advocated the use of the liver of a vulture and the warm gall of a dog for epilepsy; for a wide variety of diseases the genitals of animals were recommended as a panacea; the hair of a dog or a cabbage-root was to be hung round the neck to ward off ailments; if an aching tooth were touched with the tooth of a corpse all pain would flee; to fill a cavity in a tooth, the dung of a crow was the best material. The hellish brew of the witches in *Macbeth* was not more heterogeneous or more nauseating.

The Law University at Montpellier was considerably younger and less famous than its sister, the Medical University, yet because of its youth and its lack of tradition it was able to follow the Bolognese model so as to become a Student Society with considerable powers. It is noteworthy that most of the Law Universities were organized and run by the students, while the Universities of Arts and the other Faculties were mostly controlled by the Masters. It may have been that the Law students were more combative and assertive of their rights than the embryo doctors and theologians or the youthful Arts men, but the more probable explanation is that the whole process was one of pure imitation. Bologna, the parent of Law Schools, chanced by reason of certain local and peculiar conditions to become a student University. All subsequent Law Schools, therefore, obediently followed suit. In Arts and Theology it was Paris that set the fashion; in Medicine, Salerno to some extent, and Montpellier to a greater; and here the Masters were in the saddle.

It is claimed that the Montpellier Law School originated with the great Jurist, Placentius, driven from Bologna and Mantua by the fierce jealousy of his colleagues, to settle at Montpellier about 1160. At all events, by the end of the first quarter of the thirteenth century Montpellier boasted of a considerable number of teaching Masters and a great influx of pupils. Inasmuch as the pupils represented many nations, and the Masters had achieved a certain reputation, it began to be regarded as a *Studium Generale*. The Pope recognized this desirable status by conferring it formally by a Bull in 1289.

The Bishop sought to gain the same control over the legal School that had been yielded him by the Medical Masters, but the Law Students were less amenable. At Bologna the students had done thus and thus; why not at Montpellier? They promptly formed themselves into "Nations," which, in effect, were Student Universities, and elected student Rectors. The Masters, too, had formed their College, and made a bid for power. The result was a merry war, in which three bodies fought for control: the Church, in the person of the Bishop, the College of Masters, and the Student Nations, led by their Rectors. Cessations were declared by the Masters; the students, not to be outdone, seceded on their own account; there were riots in which the students, being younger and more numerous, gained bloody victories; the Bishop thundered his excommunications; the Masters appealed to Rome, as the Masters had always done, but so did the contumacious Students. And the Bishop sent envoys post-haste, crying a plague on both your houses.

The students got the better of the three-sided contest, and the beaten parties agreed to a compromise. The Law University of Montpellier became a Student University, based on the Bologna model, with certain modifications as a sop to the defeated but still powerful opponents. The Masters were admitted into the student organizations, and the Rector was a Master who was chosen by the outgoing Rector and the twelve Councillors. These Councillors were students elected by the Nations. The Bishop was placated by recognition of his ecclesiastical supremacy, and—which was of greater practical importance—of his right to limit cessations decreed by the Rector to eight days. The Masters, as at Bologna, were required to take an oath to obey the Statutes governing their lectures. Thus the Law University emerged as a tripartite organism in which the Students had managed to obtain the preponderance of power.

The Arts University was but a poor thing, as in most other Universities where the Law had attained a position of prominence. It was managed by the Masters; the students were youths who regarded the course as a necessary evil, preliminary to the study of Medicine or the Law. A Theological University was eventually founded by the Regulars, but this was an anaemic affair.

Law and Medicine were in control and, above all, it was Medicine, that lucrative profession which enabled its adept to own a fine house, fine horses, an elegant carriage, and dress his wife and himself in linens and silks, that made Montpellier a flourishing centre. Most of the great mediaeval physicians derived from Montpellier: Bernard de Gordon, Arnauld de Villeneuve, and Gui de Chauliac, who gave a scientific basis to surgery. Rabelais himself lectured at Montpellier when the Renaissance was in full swing.

Orléans, the ancient Studium in the North of France, dates

s

back almost to the ninth century. During the efflorescence of learning that marked the twelfth century, it was renowned far and wide as the home of the classics, of grammar and rhetoric. Together with Chartres, which somehow never achieved University rank, it flew the banner of humanism and culture when Paris was entangling herself in the logomachies of the dialecticians. Here the poets, the classical scholars, found their last retreat from the irresistible tide of Scholasticism, and here too, more unworthily, flourished the professional letter-writers and the professors of the imported *Ars dictaminis*. Even when Chartres was a backslider, Orléans stood proudly alone, well into the thirteenth century. Then it yielded to the temper of the age, as it must, if it wished to survive. It developed a School of Law.

It was in a particularly advantageous position for the creation of such a school. Paris had been forbidden the study of Civil Law, and Orléans was near enough to attract Parisian students who rebelled against this unwarrantable restriction. Even the Canonists of Paris were at a disadvantage, in that Civil Law was the practical basis of their own subject, and it was the general rule to graduate in both subjects simultaneously. So that Orléans, which conferred both degrees, soon evolved into a considerable School, and in a very short time far surpassed Paris and every other Law University in France. Only Bologna, and possibly Padua, exceeded Orléans in the fame of its Law School. The classics and the non-productive arts of Grammar and Rhetoric were contemptuously overlooked by the host of eager lawyers who flocked to make their fortunes in Church and State.

The Masters formed themselves into a University like their brethren in Paris—in fact, the early teachers seem to have migrated from Paris in the Dispersion of 1229—and tried to organize themselves along Parisian lines. The Bishop, here as elsewhere, claimed all power. After the inevitable conflict, the Masters obtained a good part of their demands, and even granted a certain degree of participation, largely nominal, to the students, in deference to the prevailing legal tradition. The Pope granted the Masters the right to elect a Rector, to make Statutes, and to regulate rents for the houses which they occupied. The Bishop exercised the usual powers of criminal jurisdiction.

It seems that the townsfolk of Orléans were exceptionally greedy, or else the University fixed excessively low rents, for the University privileges led to long years of trouble, rioting, and bloodshed. In 1312 Philip IV of France, who was violently anti-clerical, entered the fight on the side of the town. He suppressed University and Nations; he forbade the election of a Rector, or the calling of a University Assembly. More riots, more squabbles followed, with the result that in 1316 the angry Masters and scholars moved bag and baggage into Burgundian territory, where they settled in the town of Nevers. Now the Pope, John XXII, himself a graduate of Orléans, intervened, pouring oil on the troubled waters. Scholars accused of crimes were still exempt from lay tribunals, but the University could no longer require the fine and imprisonment of townsmen by their own Magistrates at the behest of a scholar who alleged that he had suffered injury. Thereupon the University returned; and there was no further trouble, except an occasional knifing, rape, or some such minor incident.

Angers was another great Law University, second in national prestige only to that of Orléans. It started as a Cathedral School, and developed into a University, like Paris, Montpellier, and Orléans, without Papal or Royal benediction. Like Orléans, it owed its prominence to the dispersions of Parisian students, and the prohibition affecting Civil Law. Civil Law was its specialty, and its lawyers were found everywhere. In the sixteenth century, even Orléans was left labouring behind.

Toulouse was the first University which was deliberately

founded by a Papal Bull. So far, all the Universities which we have considered were natural growths—guided, protected, or inhibited by clerical, municipal, and royal influences, but owing their foundation solely to congregations of students and teachers, and not to any particular act on the part of any individual or institution. Naples, it is true, had been a purely Imperial creation, but the Papacy had not yet discovered any reason for imitating its great mediaeval rival. But now it found such a reason, and a University was born by Papal decree.

There had been serious trouble in and around Toulouse. The ferment of the twelfth century took the form, in the South of France, of a great religious movement that harked back to a primitive Christianity, coloured by Orientalism and the ancient Manichaeism. Two sects were formed, the Albigenses and the Cathari, who preached the primitive heresies and the primitive communism and poverty of the Christians of the Catacombs. The world, they said, was dual in its nature: Good and Evil coexisted in almost equal proportions, and together they formed Man. Evil had made the body, and Good had formed the soul. Hence it was the duty of devout Christians to scourge the body, the home of Evil, and purify it by appropriate rites and austerities. The body being evil, it necessarily followed that sexual intercourse was an abomination, and the procreation of children a sin against the Holy Ghost. Within a generation, if these fanatics had their way, there would be no human race, or rather, no physical bodies attached to immortal souls, and Evil would lose its strongest hold on the world. Hence the Cathari forbade marriage, and for other good and valid reasons, the taking of oaths and war.

A curious doctrine, resembling the belief of the Pythagoreans, had crept into their philosophy. It was proclaimed by the leaders that the souls of some privileged few of this world were in fact fallen angels who had followed Evil in the first great rebellion, and were then condemned to be united to human bodies for a certain number of metempsychoses until their sin was thoroughly purged. Naturally, the leaders asserted that they were in fact the angels in question, and that their period of lustration was almost ended.

From such strange doctrines, which were offensive enough to the established Christian Church, they proceeded to even more subversive ones. The sects had renounced all earthly possessions as being instinct with Evil; the Church, swollen with riches and land and luxurious living, was naturally a creation of Evil, of Satan himself. Accordingly the movement became positive in its character; it was a mighty effort to throw off the yoke of Rome, if not to destroy the Catholic Church itself.

The movement spread rapidly. The masses of the South, ground down under an unconscionable burden of tithes and clerical taxes in every possible form, lorded over by an ignorant, lazy, sensual, vicious clergy, had found a new faith, a new enthusiasm. Nor was the heresy confined to the masses. The nobility, fired by a crusading urge, or having axes of their own to grind, flocked to the new standards. Toulouse was the very heart and centre of the Albigensian movement, and Raymond VI, Count of Toulouse, its chief defender and protector.

The Church saw the flame spread like fire over a tinder-dry prairie. The kindling heresies widened with alarming rapidity. A major crisis was at hand. The very existence of the hierarchy of the Church was threatened. Innocent III was Pope, and as always, he acted with despatch and decision. Excommunications, interdicts, all the weapons in the spiritual arsenal, were here useless. The embattled lords and peasants of the Albigenses and Cathari mocked at such vain fulminations. Innocent did not waste much time on such nonsense. Instead, he communicated with the King of France, and made certain representations. The King pondered the heinous spiritual crimes, and at the same time reflected that the territories of the outlawed Count of Toulouse were rich and fruitful, and would make a worthy addition to his own more northern lands. Whatever the deciding motive, he sent Simon de Montfort, his best general, and an army, to extirpate the pernicious heresy. Count Raymond, himself a good fighter, though sworn to a non-resisting creed, met force with force. After a series of bloody battles, Toulouse was defeated, and the heresy was crushed in a series of massacres, proscriptions, barbarous cruelties, Inquisitional questionings, burnings and gibbetings, that made the Albigensian Crusade infamous for all time.

The King of France, Louis IX, obtained what he wanted, the greater part of the lands of the Count of Toulouse, but that prince, as well as most of the nobility, escaped the full horrors that were so mercilessly visited upon the common people, their followers.

Innocent III installed the Inquisition in the South of France to root out the last vestiges of the damnable heresy, and the Dominican Friars were the Inquisitors *par excellence*. He had another brilliant idea: to erect a University in the heart of the conquered territory—Toulouse—whose prime function would be to defend the Catholic faith, to aid in the extirpation of heresy, and to act as a spiritual garrison in enemy country.

It was a good time for such a step; for this happened in 1229-30, when Paris had decreed one of her many Dispersions. Numbers of unemployed Masters were looking for profitable work, and many students were scattered about the land. But this was also the time when Averrhoistic tendencies and a spirit of bold speculation were especially rife in Paris, and it might have been fatal had such minor heresies been imported into the proposed stronghold of orthodoxy.

Innocent avoided this by picking only Friars from the Theological Faculty of Paris for his new Theological Faculty at Toulouse. They could be depended upon for their orthodoxy and their zeal in persecution of the heretics. This was the only occasion on which the Papacy deliberately encouraged the formation of a Faculty in Theology to compete with its

special favourite, the University of Paris. But the Papal
ambitions went further than this. Toulouse was to be a complete University, with every Faculty well represented: Canon
Law, Civil Law, Arts, and Grammar. Who knows the full
extent of Innocent's vision? A papal University to astound the
world, to gather to itself all learning, all knowledge, in the
service of the Church; the very citadel of orthodoxy, to
supersede or outshine Paris—for was not Paris ungrateful,
recreant to her trust?

Lectures were to start within a year. Count Raymond of
Toulouse, under the terms of the treaty of capitulation, was
to pay, for a period of ten years, salaries amounting to 400
marks per annum for fourteen Professors. By making the
Chairs salaried, the Pope hoped to attract Masters, and the
defeated heretic was compelled to pay for the further destruc-
tion of his heresies.

Among those chosen from the dispersed Masters of Paris to
help open the newly-founded University was John of Garland,
a notable Grammarian in an age when Grammar was the
despised outcast of Paris. But Innocent was shrewd enough to
realize that he must make the new University attractive to the
intellectuals of the South if it were to fulfil its functions
properly, and in the South Grammar was still a living subject.
The classics were still read, the troubadours had developed a
definite literary tradition, and Aristotle was not the Colossus
that he was in the North. So John of Garland went to help in
the shaping of the Arts Course. He was glad enough to go;
for one thing, his beloved Grammar was once more to come
into its rightful heritage; for another, he was to receive an
ample, dignified salary. The Pope, in his enthusiasm for this
creation of his, even permitted the newly-discovered scientific
books of Aristotle to be read and taught, though this was
expressly prohibited in Paris.

John of Garland, at the instigation of the Papal Legate, sat
down and wrote an advertisement for the new University,

entitled "Letter transmitted by the masters of Toulouse to all the Universities of the World."

In this he celebrated the glories of Toulouse, inviting all and sundry to desert their own Universities for the new Papal creation. Paetow, the editor of John of Garland's *Morale Scolarium*, gives his version of the prospectus:

"In the glowing colours of rhetoric this letter called upon masters and students everywhere to come south to rear the cedar of faith where heretical depravity had spread its forest of thorns. The Moses of this glorious enterprise, the Cardinal Legate of the Pope, would grant to those who came plenary indulgence for their sins. Here, in this promised land, which flows with milk and with honey, lectures and disputations would be conducted with more regularity and care than in the University of Paris. Those who should wish to penetrate into the very marrow and heart of Nature could here listen to lectures on the books of Nature, prohibited in Paris. Scholastic liberty was guaranteed. The liberality [*sic*] of the Count of Toulouse would pay the salaries of the masters and would protect all members of the University. Here wine and bread and meat and fish could all be had for very little." [1]

But in spite of the Garlandian eloquence and the benign favour of the Pope, the University was at first a failure. Not many Masters yielded to the blandishments of this promise of scholastic freedom combined with cheap fish and wine; earnest scholars everywhere suspected the Papal intentions, and were slightly horrified by the barbarities of the Albigensian Crusade. Those few carpet-bag Professors who did come found themselves in an embarrassing position. The intellectuals of the South, whom they were to attract to the blessings of orthodoxy, mocked at their vaunted learning—and remained away. The much-touted scholastic freedom resolved itself into suspicious smellings by the grim Dominican Inquisitors, who,

---

[1] Reproduced by special permission from John of Garland's *Morale Scolarium*, edited by L. J. Paetow, and published by the University of California Press, U.S.A., 1927. All further quotations from John of Garland are from the same volume.

thanks to long practice, were able to discover heresy even in a rule of grammar. All this did the new foundation harm, and so did the backsliding of the "liberal" Count of Toulouse, who, as soon as the pressure was removed, forgot to pay the stipulated salaries. Paris, in the meantime, had adjusted her troubles and reopened. The carpet-baggers, including a disillusioned John of Garland, were only too glad to return to the old precincts. After all, the precarious fees of pupils were better than unpaid salaries.

The University was dying before it had even made a good start. The Pope tried to resuscitate it. He granted the Masters and Students all the privileges of Paris; but to no avail. The city of Toulouse, at the instigation of its Count, rose and expelled the Dominicans. The Church, however, was not to be denied. Raymond was excommunicated and threatened with more material punishments. He saw the handwriting on the wall, and yielded. The Inquisition came back, more bloodthirsty than ever; terror roamed up and down the narrow streets, and over the wide countryside; the burnings and slayings were redoubled. This was the last effort of the persecuted sects. Raymond, still mysteriously unharmed, was compelled to pay the salaries he had withheld, and to adhere to the letter of the treaty. This was in 1239; and the Pope granted still another Charter to the moribund University, bestowing upon it the hard-won privileges which Paris had with difficulty managed to exact. This—and the fact that the salaries were now actually being paid—had the desired effect. There was an influx of Masters, and the University flourished.

It was chiefly as a School of Theology that the Pope had envisaged Toulouse. The Dominicans ran the School, and allowed no trace of intellectual ferment to enter its sacred confines. All through the Schism, when Paris and other French Universities had adopted the nationalist Gallican doctrines, the University of Toulouse was unshaken in its support of the Roman Papacy.

For such unwavering devotion there must be adequate rewards; and in 1360 Innocent VI, himself a graduate of Toulouse, showed his gratitude by authorizing Theological degrees with the *ius ubique docendi*, the right to teach everywhere, possessed hitherto only by Paris, Oxford, and Cambridge.

Ironically enough, Toulouse eventually prospered not as a School of Theology imported from the North, but as a Law School. The South demanded Law; a practical study, leading to safe and lucrative practice in the civil courts, or high office in the Church. Theology, with its barbarous terminology and speculative abstractions, was fit only for the cold and fogs of the North. And so Toulouse became for the South what Orléans and Angers were for the North—a great, practical School of Law.

Nor was Grammar completely forgotten, in spite of the discouraging experience of John of Garland. In 1229 there had been a provision for two Masters in that subject; in 1328, when Paris had forgotten that there ever was such a study, the Statutes of Toulouse mention Priscian, Eberhard, and other Grammarians. Even a certain amount of literature was read along with the rules. Degrees were given, and there was a distinct Faculty. In 1378 there were actually more students attending the courses in grammar than were studying logic —295 against 246.

As has already been noted, the University followed the Parisian model to a great extent, except that some concessions were made to the student body, especially in the Law University. Yet the tone of the institution was excessively ecclesiastical, which is but natural, considering its origin and its primal purpose. Bishop, Chancellor, and Papal Legates held extensive powers, and the Dominicans zealously fulfilled their Inquisitional office.

CHAPTER XXVII

The Lesser French Universities

THE other French Universities were of lesser importance. They were practically all creations of the king or the municipalities, who obtained for their protégés the all-important Papal Bull of Erection. Such a Bull constituted them Universities with the right to grant degrees which would be recognized for teaching purposes anywhere in the Christian world. The older Universities, those which arose during the twelfth and thirteenth centuries, like Paris, Montpellier, Orléans, and Angers, had achieved such general recognition without Papal aid, but even they eventually petitioned for, and obtained, the precious Bull to clinch and make binding their ancient privileges.

Some of these later created Universities need only be mentioned by name and dismissed as comparatively unimportant. Such were Cahors (1332), Grénoble (1339), Orange (1365), Aix (1409), Dole (1422), Valence (1459), Bourges (1464), and Besançon (1485).

Others were interesting not so much because of their intrinsic importance as for certain extraneous reasons. For example, there was Avignon, the seat of the Papacy during the so-called Babylonian Captivity. There was an early Law School here, and in 1298 Charles II, King of Naples and Count of Provence, took the scholars of Avignon under his especial protection, and ordained that Licences be granted to the students of Law by his Chancellor of Provence. This was a manifest attempt to imitate the Imperial foundation of Naples without Papal or Imperial blessing, but the degrees, if granted, could have had only a local validity. Recognizing his failure, in 1303 he applied to the Pope for the ultimate sanction, and the pontiff was complaisant enough to issue the necessary Bull of Erection. Avignon began as a Master University of Law

273

with the Bishop in almost complete control. Toward the end of the century the students, encouraged by a series of successful uprisings of their brethren in other Universities, demanded the right to elect a Rector and a share in the government. But the Papacy was already in Avignon, the Pope could not suffer rebels so close to his person, and the democratic revolt collapsed ignominiously.

Nevertheless, the University prospered; at least, during the days of the "Captivity." The practical scholars in Civil and Canon Law swallowed their pride and considered the very tangible advantages of studying in the Papal city. With a little pulling of strings, the ear of the Supreme Pontiff could be reached when the all-important matter of the distribution of benefices came up for attention. It was for the sake of these benefices, and the secured comfortable livings at the disposal of the Church, that a goodly number of seekers after knowledge had determined upon the Law as their profession, or, as in Paris, on the arduous pursuit of Theology.

Paris, in fact, had reduced the whole affair to a scientific system. Each year the Doctors of the Faculties made up a list of their graduates, which was sent by special messenger to the Pope for the preferential distribution of benefices. Avignon made up for its lesser prestige by its nearness to the Pope. When the Papacy returned to Rome, the chief reason for the University's existence was gone, and it naturally withered and decayed.

The most interesting feature of Avignon was the formation of a secret students' society, known as the Confraternity of S. Sebastian. When the students' revolt was crushed, this organization was their answer. It was the only one of its kind to enjoy a semi-official sanction in a Master University. In a way it corresponded to an American college fraternity, with its oaths and secret rituals, its ostensible furtherance of religious and social ends, its promotion of mutual harmony and its care of sick members. Joining it was supposed to be a voluntary act, but the members had ways of convincing a non-member that

it would be to his interest to belong to it. He would be ostra-
cized—a terrible procedure in mediaeval days—and if he still
proved stiffnecked, his books were "subtracted" from him.
Now books, being rare and costly, were the most precious
possessions of a student, and "subtraction," in plain words,
meant their forcible confiscation and their distribution among
the fraternity members. The Doctors imitated their students,
and formed their own "Confraternity," but just what benefits
they derived from it is not stated by the scanty records at our
disposal.

The next three Universities, Poitiers (1431), Caen (1437),
and Bordeaux (1441), were all products of the Hundred Years'
War, just as Toulouse owed its existence to the Albigensian
heresy. The value of propaganda and the employment of
intellectuals to further it was as clearly recognized in the
Middle Ages as in the recent World War. In 1431 the English
were in possession of Paris. We have already seen how they
managed to bend the University of Paris to their will. The
exiled King of France realized the importance of having
learned Doctors on his side, and Paris, now in the possession
of the enemy, was a centre of hostile propaganda. Accordingly,
he obtained a Papal Bull permitting the erection of a University
in his temporary and precarious capital of Poitiers. Its purpose
was frankly to draw students away from Paris, and so weaken
that former glory of his kingdom that further proclamations
by its Doctors would have but a shadow of their former
influence.

Caen was erected as a University for exactly similar reasons,
but by the English. The town was in English hands, and the
Regent, the Duke of Bedford, in 1432, with the consent of the
English king, took a leaf out of France's book. He organized
a purely legal University—to rival not Paris, which was
already under his thumb, but Orléans and Angers, the Law
Universities, from which issued an unending stream of legal

opinions to prove the inefficacy of the English claims. It was
to be a war of Universities as well as of men and munitions.
But he met with opposition from a surprising source. The
hitherto submissive Doctors of Paris, with whom the new
University did not pretend to meddle, suddenly found patriotic
tongue. They agitated and petitioned and fulminated against
this subversive School, and managed for a time to postpone
the necessary Papal Bull. When the intruders were driven out
of Paris in 1436, and the University became once more French,
then, and then only, were the English able, in 1437, to obtain
a Bull for their propaganda University.

Bordeaux was yet another example. It, too, was in English
hands. It received its Bull of Erection in 1441, on the petition
of the municipality, abetted and possibly coerced by the
Councillors of the English king, Henry VI. Its Statutes
contained some curious provisions. They admonished the
Examiners to treat candidates "with all tenderness and charity,
preferring pity and lenity to the rigour of the Law . . . to
increase the University rather than diminish it." At last
the dream of every nervous and diffident student was to
be realized—the University where no one ever failed.
Further, the Statutes openly and explicitly exempted all prelates, nobles, and sons of resident Doctors and Masters from
examination. The idea, of course, was to attract to this new
University, as speedily as possible, a large concourse of
students. But somehow the scheme failed to work. It was
obvious that a degree from an institution with such easy
requirements had little value.

The absence of *bona-fide* pupils caused the University of
Bordeaux to fall even lower. The Masters needed money, so
they instituted a regular traffic in the sale of bogus "absentee"
degrees. Anyone who could pay the price could obtain a
degree, flamboyantly enscrolled, from the University of
Bordeaux. Nor was Bordeaux alone in following this pernicious
practice. In the later Middle Ages, when Universities were in

low water, a surprising number eked out their incomes by accepting bribes during the course of examinations, and by the regular sale of degrees.

Nantes, founded in 1460, was ostensibly a modified form of student democracy; actually, only those students who were "dignitaries or Canons of important Churches" were permitted to vote in Congregation beside the Doctors, Masters, and Bachelors of Superior Faculties.

The earlier Middle Ages had been instinct with intellectual fire; learning was a vast republic in which the meanest student of peasant origin was for most purposes on a par with the scholar of noble birth and landed estates. But the early enthusiasm failed, and by the fifteenth century class distinctions had replaced intellectual distinctions. Some Universities of Masters permitted students of noble birth to vote in the Congregations, and the test of a scholar's patent of nobility was that he "lives like a noble"!

The French Universities generally were ecclesiastically controlled; the Bishop and his Chancellor having the right to license teachers and to intervene generally in the affairs of the University. In Paris, by decades of turbulent conflict, the Masters had achieved a considerable measure of independence, but the other Universities were not so fortunate. The division into Nations, or grouping of students and masters in accordance with their geographical origin, was almost universally imitated; yet, strangely enough, the pure Master form of Paris was not so closely followed. As a matter of fact, most of the French Universities were a mixture of Paris and Bologna in this respect, a compromise in which both masters and students had a voice in the government, ranging from the nominal participation by students at Avignon to the equally nominal participation by masters at Valence. To find complete and slavish imitations of the Parisian form, one must go to the German Universities.

The reason for the comparative independence of Paris to be observed in the other French Universities is that most of them were primarily Law Universities: whereas Paris was almost unique as a great theological centre. It was natural, therefore, for the infant Law Universities, looking about them for a plan of organization, to model themselves on the great Law School of the South, Bologna, and to adapt that student aristocracy to ecclesiastical needs.

CHAPTER XXVIII

The Italian Universities

IN Italy there had been a considerable number of early Schools of Grammar and of Law, some of which gradually developed into *Studia Generalia*; most of the Universities, however, resulted from one or more of the numerous migrations from Bologna; though others were special creations; and some represented a new phenomenon, being the offspring of the City-States of the Lombard plains.

In Northern Italy the Emperors of the vague Roman Empire had been definitely driven out; the Pope, all-powerful across the Alps, was given but scant attention in the busy commercial life of the era; kings and feudal lords there were none; the City-States, reminiscent of ancient Greece, ruled supreme. There were many of these, each a thriving centre of commerce; with the bourgeoisie—the artisans, the all-powerful guilds of weavers, tanners, butchers, jewellers, merchants—in control. The ancient and once powerful families of the nobility were submerged, with certain notable exceptions. These exceptions grew more numerous as the Middle Ages waned, until, on the advent of the Renaissance, the Medici, the Borgias, the Sforzas, the d'Estes, and others developed ruthless tyrannies—splendid in their artistic and aesthetic achievements, it is true—but tyrannies none the less.

To these pristine City-States, small, compact, self-governed, busy with the trade of the world, Law was a necessary function; the professors of the Civil Law fulfilled a need and occupied honoured positions in the community. The sons of the city folk were eager for learning. The inclusion of a University within the walls meant an influx of foreign students, which, to the thrifty citizens, meant money spent on food, clothing, and lodgings, as well as increasing size, importance, and prestige. Bologna had pointed the way—the city thrived and prospered, thanks to the international fame of her renowned School. The other cities were envious, and seized the first opportunity to follow her example.

The University of Naples stood outside this movement. It had been specially established by the great Frederick II in his own territories, to offset the influence of Bologna. He was preparing for his final struggle with the Lombard League, and this was one of his weapons. It was, apart from the doubtful case of Palencia, the first University to be specially created by fiat.

The mediaeval Empire, as an institution cutting across national lines, could grant the important right to teach everywhere under its Charter of Foundation. Only the Papacy was able to confer similar rights. In 1224 the University of Naples was born, and Frederick, to ensure its success, forbade his Neapolitan and Sicilian subjects to study elsewhere. But the collapse of his campaign against the Lombards made an end of his grandiose schemes, and the University of Naples was one of the casualties. It managed to drag out an intermittent existence, with the aid of various attempts at resuscitation, but it filled no real need; in spite of Imperial prohibitions, other and more vital Universities attracted the students who should have attended its Schools.

Its masters and students held no such privileges as those enjoyed in other mediaeval Universities. The Emperor was and remained in complete control. It was to be a centre for the dissemination of Imperial propaganda, and no chances were to be taken by granting it any independence of thought or action. The King's Chancellor supervised every detail of the University business; later on he delegated the task to the Grand Chaplain. Licences were issued in the King's name, and the scholars were under the criminal jurisdiction of the royal officers. But the far-seeing Emperor overreached himself, as is usual in such cases. He ensured the complete depend-ence of the University, but only by crushing all vestiges of spontaneous life.

Reggio possessed an old Law School, which for a time competed with Bologna, but by the fourteenth century it had definitely lost the race. Vicenza got its start from an early migration of the Bolognese (in 1204), but within six years it gave up the contest. Arezzo also began as a result of a secession from Bologna (in 1215), but this secession was strictly a private affair. A Bolognese Master, one Roffredus of Benevento, staged a one-man strike, and went to Arezzo. Evidently he was a man of parts, for students flocked about him, and a Law School was born. On his death, however, the nascent University seems to have petered out; but in 1338, when Bologna poured forth its scholars on account of the Interdict placed upon the University and the City, Arezzo gained a new lease of life, and received a Charter from the Emperor, Charles V; but to no avail. By 1373 it had ceased to be.

The greatest of all the Italian Universities, next to Bologna —and indeed, by the sixteenth century it had far outstripped its great rival—was Padua. Like most of the Italian Schools, it was a child of Bologna. In 1220 the Bolognese students had one of their perennial quarrels with the city authorities, and the whole body of them packed up in dudgeon, and walked out. This time, however, instead of scattering, they went in a compact group to Padua, and there set up their Schools. The Bolognese townsfolk soon learnt their lesson, and hastened to make peace; whereupon the students returned in triumph.

But many, for one reason or another, elected to remain in Padua; and with them remained a sufficiency of professors. If the students thought that Padua would be more complaisant than Bologna, they were soon disabused. In 1228 we hear of the rebel students of Padua entering into a solemn contract with the city of Vercelli, whereby the students agreed to rent over 500 of the better type of houses in Vercelli, to be used for the housing of the University and its scholars. Vercelli, in its eagerness to attract this famous body of students from its rivals of Padua and Bologna, yielded on almost every point.

The City Fathers agreed to lend the migrating scholars 10,000 *librae* at interest; to provide salaried Chairs for fourteen Doctors and teachers, thereby relieving the students of a considerable amount in fees; to permit the fixing of house-rents; to grant various immunities from taxation; to provide adequate supplies of provisions; and to recognize the civil jurisdiction of the Rector of the Students. In return for these generous privileges, the scholars bound themselves to remain at Vercelli as a Studium for at least eight years. This unusual contract is evidence of the peculiar prestige that surrounded a mediaeval University, and the lengths to which a community would go in order to secure such an institution. But once a community had acquired a University, it was rather in the position of a man holding an enraged lion by the tail—he dare not let go, yet he feels that he cannot hold on much longer.

Pursuant to the contract, a considerable number of the Paduan students shook the dust of the ungrateful city off their feet, and betook themselves to Vercelli. Yet there must have been many who remained, perhaps too lazy to move, or too insensitive to insult, for Padua continued to exist.

In the middle of the thirteenth century, when the Ezzelinos ruled the city, subjecting it to a ruthless tyranny, the University was at its nadir, and only another migration, in 1260, from that fount of all migrations, Bologna, revived its fortunes. This time it almost exactly imitated its parent, with the students in full control, and two Nations of Italians and non-Italians. Whenever the fortunes of Padua waned, Bologna came to the rescue with another migration.

In 1321, the Paduan authorities decided that the University was worth keeping, and the only way to keep it was to ensure that the malcontents from Bologna should not pursue their usual course of returning as soon as the fight was over. Extraordinary privileges were accordingly granted, including

the right of clerics to be tried by ecclesiastical judges; the
student Rectors to be permitted to bear arms; the teachers'
salaries to be paid by the city, and the famous Bologna
Statutes to apply as far as possible. To attract foreign professors it was even decreed that no native Master could hold
a salaried Chair. Election to these coveted posts was placed
solely in the hands of the students. This, it may be remembered,
was one of the chief causes of dissatisfaction at Bologna, where
the Professoriate tended to become a closed, native, hereditary
corporation.

In common with all the Italian Universities, Padua was
chiefly famous for its Law Schools, Canon and Civil. As
Bologna decayed because of its incessant quarrels and secessions, and the narrow-mindedness of its professors, Padua,
with its more liberal, and eventually wiser, city authorities,
forged ahead. Even when the city lost its political independence, first to the Dukes of Carrara, and then to the Venetians,
the University profited by the change, for the conquerors
behaved with great liberality. Indeed, the Venetians were so
proud of their subject University that they forbade Venetian
citizens and subjects to study anywhere except at Padua; and
it came to be well understood that a Paduan degree was a
necessary prerequisite to public and political life in Venice.

The Paduan Medical School, too, from an insignificant beginning, grew in prestige until the sick, the halt, and the lame
poured in from all parts of Europe to obtain treatment from
its learned doctors. It has yet another claim to fame; in an age
when the Jew was anathema, and already confined in North
Europe to his Ghetto, the Paduan School of Medicine was
tolerant enough to grant a Jew the coveted Medical Doctorate.

Siena followed what had become the general rule; that is, it
took advantage of trouble in Bologna, and thus obtained a
University. In 1246, while Bologna was on strike, the city of
Siena hired a number of Bolognese Doctors of Law, and sent
messengers post-haste in all directions, advertising the opening

of a Studium. For a good many years it flourished; then it decayed. In 1321 a Bolognese scholar was executed for rape, and inevitably the students again seceded. Siena profited by the secession, and the University was revived. In 1322 it was gone again, as peace was made with Bologna; but in 1338 there was more trouble in that tempestuous city, and again Siena had its higher culture. This comedy was played in most of the Italian cities. The scholars of Bologna had a quarrel with the city; at once a dozen other towns discovered that they had a Studium in their midst; Bologna composed its differences, and behold, a dozen Universities evaporated into thin air.

For some reason or other, possibly because of its lack of permanence, the School of Siena could not obtain the usual Foundation Bull raising it to the status of a *Studium Generale*, so in 1357 it appealed to the Emperor. He willingly obliged with a Charter, and fifty-one years later the then Pope relented and added his blessing. Thenceforth, fortified with such high credentials, the University prospered.

We may judge of the eagerness with which the various City-States of Italy competed for Universities by the fact that many of them deliberately founded their respective Studia and made application to Pope or Emperor for the Bull or Charter of Foundation. This latter, of course, was absolutely essential if the City was to attract any considerable concourse of students. Without it the graduation degree meant very little; no other University would recognize it, and the graduates would not be permitted to teach elsewhere; nor could they call themselves by the high-sounding title of Doctor. The Schools, which had originally been private affairs—each Master setting up his own, and collecting his own fees—gradually developed into City institutions, with permanent, salaried professors.

Piacenza was the first Italian city to apply on its own initiative for a Bull, which it obtained in 1248. Exactly 150 years later, the Studium having shown considerable weakness in the interim, it sought to mend its fortunes under the Imperial aegis. The change was beneficial for a while, but by 1412 there were no more students and no more lectures. The College of Doctors did not lose heart on that account. It carried on as though there had still been a University, and proceeded to sell degrees cheaply to all who had the wherewithal.

The city of Perugia advertised the ceremonial opening of its Studium in 1276, and by energy and discretion made a go of it. Perugia paid well, and was thus able to attract many famous teachers; and the Law School prospered. Both Pope and Emperor were its godfathers, though the latter was almost fifty years behind the pontiff.

Pisa, the offspring of yet another Bolognese migration (in 1338), received its Papal Bull in 1343. Within five years it seems to have perished as the result of a combination of adverse circumstances: to wit, war, famine, and the Black Death. It took Florence, who conquered the city in 1472, to rehabilitate the defunct University. So effectively did she do her work that Pisa, during the Renaissance, was almost as famous as Padua.

The action of Florence is rather strange, for in 1349 it had achieved its own University. But somehow, in spite of the fame of the city, in spite of money lavishly spent, and every effort to attract professors and students, the institution was a failure. In desperation, Florence forbade its citizens to go elsewhere, but to no avail. The famous city could not hold its professors; Petrarch, its own citizen, refused to return from Padua. Lorenzo the Magnificent solved the problem by abandoning the home University and concentrating on the captive, Pisa. It is hard to determine why Florence, the glory of the Renaissance, the home of scholars, poets, painters, sculptors, and next to Athens the most remarkable efflorescence of the human spirit in the history of the world, should have failed to support a University. The true explanation may lie in the fact that the mediaeval University, particularly at the dawn of the Renaissance, was a barren institution, absorbed in dry-as-dust studies that were completely outside the new currents of thought. Florence, fresh, and intellectually alive, made certain experiments: Boccaccio, for example, gave lectures on Poetry in general, and Dante in particular, at the University; while in 1360 there were actually lectures on Homer; but the mediaeval University was internally corrupt; it could not stand such heady stuff; and Florence had to do without such a centre of learning at the time of its greatest glory.

Pavia had been a law centre even before Bologna, but it wilted and died in the shadow of that mighty institution. In 1361 it was renewed by a Charter from the Emperor, duly supplemented, later on, by a Papal Bull; but it languished until the Milanese captured the city, and made the Studium in 1421 their official University. This was another example of the conquered conquering the conqueror.

Ferrara, founded in 1391, tried to obtain outside teachers and pupils, and succeeded in attracting a certain class by the sale of cheap degrees. The cost of a Doctor's degree in the Middle Ages was fairly high; remember, for example, the splendid ceremonies, the banquets, the fees, the gifts that were required of the student at Bologna; and if any city made it known that its University would deal gently with its candidates, it was sure to attract a host of poor fellows who could see no other way to obtain the coveted degree. Ferrara was disrespectfully known as the refuge of the destitute.

Other Italian Universities of little or no importance include Vercelli (1228), which could not keep the Paduan seceders after its eight-year contract had expired; the University of the Roman Court (1244-5), famous only for its peripatetic attendance on the Papal person wherever he went, and for the scandalous way in which its Doctorate was made to provide revenue for the Pope by granting dispensations from residence, or study, or both; Turin (1405) and Catania (1444).

In general, the Italian Universities followed a definite course of development, differing in important particulars from all other national Universities. Because of the unusual privileges accorded to native citizens of the City-States, the home-bred students had no need to organize. It was the foreigners who had to mass together for mutual protection. Accordingly, the Universities were entirely Universities of the alien students. Their aggressiveness made Masters and cities bow to their demands, and it was due to them that salaried Chairs were instituted, to be paid for out of municipal funds. But in this final victory the cause of student democracy really suffered a defeat. For with control of finances came control of more fundamental matters. Gradually the City-States interfered more and more in University affairs, until the old student government retained but a shadow of its former glory.

In their almost complete independence of ecclesiastical control, the Italian Universities differed considerably from the French; Theology, moreover, was almost an unknown study in those busy and practical centres of Law and commerce. But with the exception of Paris, Toulouse, and one or two other Universities, the same condition existed across the Alps. In spite of our usual preconceptions, the mediaeval period was *not* an age of mysticism and metaphysical wool-gathering; it was essentially a practical, pragmatic era, somewhat fearful of the future, it is true, but casting an appreciative eye upon the sensuous and sensual delights of the present.

CHAPTER XXIX

Cambridge, Salamanca, and Coimbra

THE Spanish Peninsula started early in the race for knowledge, at least, as regards the establishment of formal institutions. The Spanish Universities were primarily royal creations, artificial affairs erected by ambitious kings, actuated either by an ingrown love of learning, by envy of the rising glories of Italy and France, or by consideration of the increased prosperity and the revenues to be derived from the influx of foreign students and the keeping of native talent at home.

The earliest of these Universities, and possibly the first to be created artificially anywhere, was Palencia, founded between 1212 and 1214 by Alfonso VIII of Castile. But it had no formal charter, nor could it grant any but locally recognized degrees to its graduates. The precious *jus ubique docendi* required the intervention of Pope or Emperor. Apart from its claim to priority, Palencia possessed no other title to distinction, and was gone by 1263.

The case of Salamanca, founded about the year 1220, was different. It became one of the great Universities of Europe; in the years of the later Renaissance only Padua could compete with it as an international centre of thought and learning.

Alfonso IX of Leon founded it as a purely local institution, with small success. Ferdinand of Castile did what he could for it in 1242, with much the same result. It was Alfonso the Wise who was responsible for its final prosperity. Apart from Frederick II, no other mediaeval monarch could boast of his intellectual brilliance. He was equally famous as a philosopher, an astronomer, an alchemist, and a poet. It was he who, studying the structure of the heavens in the infinitely complicated Ptolemaic version, remarked that if God had but called upon him for advice, he could have constructed a much simpler universe for Him.

In 1254 he granted a definitive Charter of privileges to the youthful University of Salamanca, modelling it as far as possible upon Bologna. It is a curious fact that the autocratic Kings of Spain followed the student democracies of Bologna rather than the more conservative Master University of Paris. There may be several reasons for this. For one thing, Italy was nearer, and more closely akin in temperament; for another, they may not have relished the thought of the active ecclesiastical influence that seemed inseparable from a Master University.

Alfonso the Wise granted the power to imprison scholars to the Bishop and the Magister Scholarium (Chancellor) alone, and the taxation of rents for student lodgings to the Dean of Salamanca and a fellow-ecclesiast. It is noteworthy that in this instance the unfortunate townsfolk had absolutely nothing to say about the renting of their own premises.

By a later Code, Alfonso recognized the Masters and Scholars together as forming the University, with joint power to elect a Rector. To the Masters he granted privileges and exemptions surpassing those of any foreign University. The Doctors of Civil Law had perpetual entrée to the King's private chamber; when one of these proud individuals entered a Court of Law, it was the duty of the Judge to rise in token of respect and invite him to a seat beside him on the bench. After twenty years of teaching, the Doctor achieved a patent of nobility, the title of a Count of the realm.

Alfonso patriotically tried to dispense with the intervention of the Pope. He insisted that he, as King of the realm, could effectually found a *Studium Generale*; but, unfortunately, the jurists of the day did not agree with him, nor did the other Universities, when the Spanish graduates applied for teaching privileges.

However, as far as Salamanca was concerned, Alexander IV had already, in 1255, given it a Foundation Bull, which gave its graduates the right to teach everywhere except in Paris and Bologna. This irksome restriction was finally removed in 1333. He also granted to scholars the right to obtain absolution from the Master of the Schools for assaults upon fellow-clerks. Ordinarily this heinous offence required special absolution from the Pope; no inferior ecclesiastic could save the guilty party from the future torments of hell. He also gave priests and clergy, excepting only the Regulars, the right to study Civil Law: which was forbidden them in Paris and elsewhere.

Salamanca was chiefly a University of Canon and Civil Law, and in this respect it followed in the footsteps of all the southern Universities. But it was susceptible to more liberal influences as well. It assisted its true founder, Alfonso the Wise, to prepare his famous astronomical tables. When Christopher Columbus sought wearily through the Courts of Europe to obtain backing for his scheme of reaching India by sailing westward across the uncharted terrors of the Atlantic, it was in the cloistered halls of Salamanca that he found faith and encouragement. In the sixteenth century, while Galileo was still proscribed, Salamanca, remembering the impatient disgust of its founder, Alfonso the Wise, was the only University in all Europe to teach the Copernican system. It followed the leadership of Paris in taking an active part in the religious dissensions of the time, and pronounced vigorously for the Avignon Popes in the days of the Schism. In Medicine, too, it was famous, following the Arabic rather than the classical Greek school. Its title of "Queen of the Spanish Universities" was well earned.

Lerida was founded by James II of Aragon in 1300, in opposition to the Castilian Universities, which were draining students from the Aragonese kingdom. To ensure its success he forbade the teaching of Law, Medicine, and Philosophy anywhere else in his kingdom. It was a strict Student University, almost slavishly copying the Statutes of Bologna, with a student Rector and student control over its Professors, and the rights of foreign students were carefully protected.

The other Spanish Universities were comparatively unimportant during the Middle Ages: among these were Valladolid, dating from the middle of the thirteenth century, with salaried chairs to which the occupants were elected by the student body; and Perpignan and Huesca, which was endowed in a novel way. A tax was placed upon the meat sold in the public market of the town, the proceeds of which went to the payment of the Professors. The indignant citizens thereupon went to the Moorish quarter for untaxed and cheaper meat. The king countered this move by extending the tax to the market of the Moors, and by levying a heavy contribution upon the Saracen and Jewish communities for the support of his most Christian University. In spite of his pious efforts, the University languished, and eked out a miserable existence until it died in the sixteenth century.

Ferdinand and Isabella did much the same in 1482 in the case of Avila, endowing it with the confiscated property of the Jews whom they were driving out of their kingdoms; with like results.

Other mediaeval Universities were Barcelona (1450), Saragossa (1474), Palma on the Island of Majorca (1483), Sigüenza (1489), Alcalá (1499), and Valencia (1500).

Portugal had only one University to its credit: the combined and peripatetic institution of Lisbon and Coimbra. It was founded in Lisbon in 1290, but owing to the unrelenting hatred of the townsfolk for the intellectuals in their midst, about 1308 the University, in fear of its life, migrated to Coimbra. But this town, though peaceful enough, was too small and unimportant to attract students and teachers, and accordingly the University went back to Lisbon. The citizens of Lisbon had not forgotten their old enmity, and the scholars devoted more time to riots and calls to arms than to the pursuit of learning. By 1355 they were forced to return to Coimbra.

There the Studium languished in vacuous quietude, to pass peacefully away by 1377. A group of students who had managed to resist the general lassitude revived the University in hostile Lisbon; this time successfully. It survived until 1537, when a final migration occurred to its old place of refuge, and there it remained.

In England a remarkable situation existed. Whereas in other European countries the number of mediaeval Universities ranged from a dozen to twenty or more, that flourishing kingdom possessed only two. One of these, Oxford, was of world-wide importance, ranking only after Paris and Bologna in the intellectual history of the age. The other, Cambridge, now its equal in importance, was singularly insignificant throughout the Middle Ages, being completely overshadowed by its greater rival.

The reason for this paucity of educational institutions is perhaps explicable. It was not that the English had no tradition of learning. Even in the Dark Ages the Schools of England and her scholars had won wide renown. Not even in Paris was there gathered such an array of intellectual giants as walked the narrow streets of Oxford in Grossetête's and Bacon's time. The English scholars were numerous in every great Continental University; in Paris they were especially active and influential. The explanation may be found in the comparative smallness of the kingdom, the fixed determination of the Crown to permit no other Universities after several migrations had proved rebellious to the Royal person; and above all, in the opposition of all-powerful Oxford to the remote possibility of any new rival.

Even Cambridge might never have achieved maturity, had it not grown from an almost equally early beginning, when Oxford was too small and too weak to oppose it effectually.

There had been religious houses which had gathered students into Schools during the twelfth century at Cambridge, but they did not rise into any prominence as a Studium until in 1209 troubles at Oxford sent a swarm of seceding scholars to the Cam. In 1229 Henry II, in his seductive letter to the discontented scholars of Paris, offered them Cambridge as a refuge. By 1231 the Studium had grown to such proportions that there were the usual complaints of excessive rents and profiteering in foods, and friction with the townsfolk had already risen to formidable proportions.

Henry III's remarks to the townsfolk of Cambridge were sharp and to the point:

"It is well known to you," he wrote, "that a multitude of scholars flow together to our City of Cambridge for the sake of study from various places at home and abroad; which We hold right pleasing and acceptable for that from thence no small profit comes to our kingdom, and honour to Ourself; and above all you, amongst whom the students have their daily life, should rejoice and be glad, but We have heard that in letting your lodgings you are so heavy and burdensome to the scholars dwelling amongst you, that unless you behave yourselves more measurably and modestly towards them in this matter of your exactions they must leave our city, and having abandoned the University, depart from our land, which We in no respect desire. And therefore We command you firmly enjoining you that, concerning the letting of aforesaid lodgings, and keeping yourselves in measure according to the custom of the University, you shall estimate the aforesaid lodgings by two masters and two good legal men of your town, and according to their estimate shall permit them to be hired. Thus bearing yourselves in this matter ye may be held safe, for if that any complaint should arrive to Us We should put our hand to the matter."

The history of Cambridge follows that of Oxford so closely that the two might almost be considered interchangeable. Yet Oxford led the way; Cambridge followed at a slower pace, achieving its successive privileges and immunities years after its great exemplar, and remaining, throughout the Middle Ages, something of a Cinderella. Not until the close of the fifteenth century, at the beginning of the Renaissance, when Oxford had fallen into disrepute on account of the Wyclif movement, did Cambridge begin to bask in the royal and ecclesiastical favour as a stronghold of orthodoxy, and attract the sons of the conservative nobility.

Cambridge also had its Chancellor, and won its final independence from Bishop and other ecclesiastical powers. Cambridge, like Oxford, had its riots with the townsfolk, and its troubles over rents and food, and was victorious over the citizens, but it never obtained the peculiar domination over the town that distinguished Oxford.

There were points of difference, of course. For example, at Cambridge the individual Master could try cases in which his students were defendants instead of having them haled before the Chancellor's Court. The Proctors of the Faculties were known as Rectors, and there seems to have been no Black Congregation, and no Proctorial vetoes. Dispensations from the statutory requirements for degrees required the consent of the Chancellor and two Doctors of the superior Faculties. In the courses of study also there were modifications of the Oxford model. The course in Theology was shorter and less gruelling; Mathematics and the sciences seem to have received earlier attention than at Oxford. To this day, Cambridge has a reputation for scientific and mathematical learning as against the classical heritage of Oxford.

But these differences are comparatively unimportant; in the main, Cambridge was a smaller edition of Oxford. Even the College system followed Oxford slavishly. Peterhouse, the first of the foundations, and subsidized by the Bishop of Ely in 1284, was modelled on Merton at Oxford. It is significant of the relative standing of the two Universities that the Peterhouse Charter provided that two or three scholars might be licensed to proceed with their studies at the rival institution of Oxford.

The King's Hall, erected before 1316, gave the King's bounty to twelve members of the Choir of the Chapel Royal.

Michaelhouse (1324) required all students to be "Priests or at least in holy orders," and prescribed the study of Theology. Then followed University Hall, and Pembroke (1347), which gave the preference to scholars of French parentage. This exception to the general insularity of the English Colleges was due to its patroness, the Countess of Pembroke, herself of French birth.

Gonville, Trinity Hall, and Corpus Christi followed in rapid succession. God's House was unique in that it was devoted entirely to the training of Grammar School Masters. King's College (1441) was the royal retort to the heretical state of affairs at Oxford. Henry VI had determined to make Cambridge the superior of the defiant former favourite, and he lavished magnificent buildings and ample endowments on his College. Lacking in originality, he carefully copied Oxford's New College in almost every detail; the Statutes themselves were a direct transcript. In one particular he went further. He obtained from the Pope a special exemption for his College from all ecclesiastical jurisdiction, and even immunity from the decrees of the Chancellor of the University. The protest against this last, however, grew to such proportions that the privilege was modified by voluntary relinquishments.

Queen's College, founded by his queen, had a similar object in view; and the last of the mediaeval College foundations were St. Catherine's, and Jesus (1497).

U

CHAPTER XXX

Prague

CENTRAL Europe possessed no Universities until the middle of the fourteenth century. Not that scholarship was unknown, but the early rise of the great institutions in Paris and Bologna drew great numbers of Germanic students to those teeming centres, where the intellectual life was freer and more generously patronized by Royalty and the Church than at home. Germany, though ostensibly the seat of the Roman Empire, was in fact an aggregation of practically independent feudal lords, rude in hand and in thought, given to mutual hostilities and the robbing of travellers, secure in their eyries and strongholds, contemptuous of priests and shavelings and the written word. It was little wonder that those Germans who thirsted for learning found no comfort in their native land.

Prague, the capital of Bohemia, was the first in the field. There had already been a Studium in the city, but Wenceslaus I had failed in his endeavours to raise it to the dignity of a *Studium Generale*. In 1347 Charles IV, King of the Romans and of Bohemia, achieved what the earlier king had failed to accomplish. Although by virtue of his Imperial position he could have proclaimed Prague a *Studium Generale*, he was shrewd enough to realize that practically no Imperial foundation had succeeded without a concomitant Papal Bull. Accordingly he petitioned for, and received, the precious Bull of Erection from Clement VI. To this he added his own Charter in the following year.

Charles was determined to make a success of his home University. He had studied in the University of Paris, and was an ardent admirer of that great institution. What was more natural than that he should model his godchild upon this pattern? Accordingly, the right of Licence was vested in the Archbishop of Prague; there were four Faculties, united under a single Rector, whose Court possessed almost unlimited jurisdiction over causes to which a scholar was a party. Only in 1372 did the Law students obtain their own University and their own Rector.

Paris had its four Nations, though these no longer possessed their original significance. Nevertheless Prague, starting *de novo*, must also have its four Nations. Therefore four Nations were arbitrarily created: namely, Bohemia, Poland, Bavaria, and Saxony. In 1397 Boniface IX granted the University a total exemption from all ecclesiastical jurisdiction, so that Prague was on a par with Oxford, Cambridge, and Bologna, and possessed of greater privileges than Paris itself.

The University, of course, was a Master University, apart from the later concession to the students of the Law School. From the first, Charles aided the Professors with an endowment out of which salaries were paid. He preferred not to rely upon the fees of pupils, which might or might not be sufficient to attract to his University teachers of the calibre he desired. The Royal Exchequer bore the expense at first, but later it was shifted to the revenues of the monasteries and chapters of the kingdom, to their great discontent. Colleges were established, but on a different plan from that of the foundations of Paris. Nor did they resemble those of Oxford. They were primarily endowed residences for teachers rather than for students, and possessed no such corporate independence as in the other institutions. Accordingly they never played any great part in the life of the University or in the shaping of its policies.

Prague, as the first University of Central Europe, became a model for all future Universities in that region. All the Germanic Universities followed in its footsteps, becoming Master Universities, with Nations, and a College system.

From the very beginning, Prague was as successful as Charles could have wished. There were many who thirsted after knowledge in the Germanic countries but could not afford the arduous and expensive journey to Paris or England or the South. Most of those who did go so far afield were rich and well born, or were priests with rich benefices that worked for them *in absentia*. Prague was a godsend to the sons of the middle classes, to the artisans and tradesmen and the ambitious offspring of the poor. By the end of the fourteenth century there were some 4000 students on its rolls, of whom at least half came from outside Bohemia. These foreigners were mostly German. Bohemia itself was at this time possessed of a flourishing civilization and culture, and the University of Prague made its own contribution to the Renaissance.

But the University's most important contribution, and one which had international repercussions, was its cradling of a great nationalist and religious movement. Even more than Oxford, where the doctrines of Wyclif were taught, or Paris, which accepted the comparatively minor heresies of the Averrhoists, did Prague become the heart and centre of political and religious nonconformity. All Europe resounded with the heat and dust of the conflict. History was being shaped and changed in the confines of the University.

Prague itself was soon rent by internal dissensions. Paris, its model, by its division into Nations, had assured equal representation to all foreign students; there could be no predominance on the part of the natives. Bologna was entirely a University of foreigners. This was true cosmopolitanism. At Prague, however, which had blindly followed the Parisian system of Nations, an anomalous situation arose. Of the four Nations, two, the Bavarian and the Saxon, were altogether German, and even the Polish Nation was chiefly German. Accordingly, the Bohemians, the indigenous students, with their one Nation, though in numbers they constituted at least half the University, were completely outvoted by the three Germanic units. Now at this time there was bitter enmity between Germany and Bohemia. There had been wars between them, and there was a tendency on the part of the

Germans to regard the kingdom of Bohemia as a fief of the Roman Empire. Nationalist resentment was strong.

In 1384 the disaffection in the University came to a head. The Colleges were the ostensible source of irritation. They had been consistently filled with teachers of Germanic origin, and the native Bohemians found themselves unable to avail themselves of their valuable privileges. The Bohemian Nation petitioned the King and the Archbishop against such unjust discrimination, and the Archbishop promptly responded by veering to the opposite extreme. He decreed that only Bohemians should be admitted to the Colleges, as long as they could produce duly qualified candidates. The Germanic Nations angrily appealed to the Pope. But inasmuch as the appeal would take some considerable time, the Rector of the University, who was naturally a German, ordered a suspension of lectures until the wrong could be righted. The Bohemians refused to obey this partisan decree. At once the University became an armed camp, and the opposing factions rioted and pursued each other through the streets. The Rector was seized and soundly beaten, barely escaping with his life. At length the dispute was somewhat adjusted by a grudging concession to the Germans, but the underlying bitterness grew stronger than ever.

When it broke out again, the matters involved were no longer of minor or purely local importance. They were issues of a far-reaching character, involving Europe in a series of political and religious disputes that did not cease until the Reformation.

It was the time of the Great Schism, of the strange and undignified spectacle of two Popes, each claiming to be the only duly anointed successor to St. Peter, fulminating against each other in most unapostolic language and with a fury of vituperation almost unexampled in the history of a most vituperative age. The whole ecclesiastical system was tottering. Graft, corruption, bribery, nepotism, sloth, and indifference were undermining the whole edifice of the Church. The lay powers, princes and kings and emperors, seized the golden opportunity to fish in the troubled waters. Within the Church there was dissension—and blind conservatism. The older religious Orders, the Benedictines and others, had never betrayed the slightest desire for reform, and did not propose to begin now. The Mendicant Orders—the Dominicans, Franciscans, and so forth—more missionary and aggressive, were bound heart and soul to the Papal monarchy, and could be counted on to fight tooth and nail in its behalf. The Canon Lawyers were interested in one thing, and one thing only: in securing for themselves the most lucrative positions within the power of the Church to bestow. They were not interested in the reform of abuses; for they battened on them.

The common people, the ordinary everyday folk who paid the tithes and Peter's Pence, and built the vast cathedrals in the sweat of their brow, and furnished the oil that greased the ways of the mighty machine which the Church had erected during the ages, were beginning to grow somewhat sceptical of the imposing edifice, and to question the purity and holiness of the clerical orders, from the lowest curé up to the Pope himself. Their resentment was gathering, but they were scattered, they were bewildered by subtle theological arguments, they were liable to be distracted by red herrings, and they were intimidated by excommunications and threats of hell-fire. They needed leadership.

That leadership could come only from the Theologians, and they were in the Universities. All other classes of clerics had a stake in the old order. They alone were comparatively aloof, with habits of thought and scholarship that led them to consider fundamentals. They alone could detect and refute the supersubtle arguments of the proponents of things as they were.

Yet the Theologians, too, were human, and susceptible to worldly considerations. In Italy and Spain they were chiefly Mendicants, and as such immune from the virus of discontent. In France, where the Theological Faculty had managed to emancipate itself from the control of the Mendicants, there was a vigorous demand for the retirement of both Popes, and the suppression of certain abuses. But the roots of the matter were not in them. Oxford had had its Wyclif movement. Wyclif was thorough-going enough; he had struck deep and hard; and Oxford had supported him to its own grievous peril. But the theologians and philosophers who defied king and archbishop in his behalf were more concerned for the protection of their ancient University rights than inspired with a fiery zeal for reform. They had been thrust into an awkward position, from which there was no retreat save at the cost of diminished independence.

At Prague, however, the spark struck by the English Wyclif burst into flame. Whereas at Oxford the movement had resolved itself into a question of academic integrity, the Prague theologians seized upon the gist of the matter, hailed Wyclif as a master, and proceeded with zealous enthusiasm to improve upon him.

The theologians of the University were already in sympathy with the popular discontent, and were canalizing the demands of the laity for religious reform. The Doctors preached in their native Czech to students and townsfolk at great public meetings, exposing the abuses of the Roman hierarchy. Popular emotion was roused to fever pitch.

Only the Bohemians in the University were involved. The whole question was complicated by nationalistic feeling. The Germans at the University were Nominalists—the old controversy had flared up again at the beginning of the fifteenth century—so, with the logic of all good haters, the Bohemians promptly espoused Realism. This, of course, served to widen the breach between the two factions, and kept the Germans not only aloof, but actively opposed to the reform movement.

At the turn of the century the proscribed works of Wyclif began to circulate among the disaffected at Prague. Bohemian

students were well represented at English Oxford, and ideas
moved freely from one University to the other.

John Hus, a Prague theologian, and Rector of the University in 1403, took up the gage of battle. In season and out
he preached the Wycliffian doctrines; more, he augmented
them and elaborated on the text. His fiery oratory and uncompromising zeal roused the University and the people in town
and country to uncontrollable enthusiasm. The Bohemian
Masters followed his leadership. The Germanic Nations cried
heresy. Faction fights broke out with redoubled violence. To
the former nationalistic hatred between Teuton and Czech,
and the philosophical opposition between Nominalist and
Realist, was added the fury of religious controversy.

In 1403 the Congregation of the University, where the Germans were in control, condemned forty-six articles of Wyclif's
works as heretical. But the Bohemians defiantly continued to
read and teach the condemned doctrines in the Schools, and
Hus, as their Rector, openly encouraged their disobedience.

In 1408 a second Congregation again condemned the offending articles, but added that this condemnation applied only to
teaching them "in their false and heretical sense." This was a
victory for the Hussites, but it was shortlived. For in the same
year the Bohemian Synod placed the ban on all the works of
Wyclif, and demanded that the University scholars and
Masters should surrender their precious volumes to the
ecclesiastical authorities. The Masters claimed their privileges,
and five of the students appealed to Rome.

Meanwhile the political and ecclesiastical pot was boiling
merrily. Wenceslaus, the Bohemian King, was opposing
Rupert, the Count Palatine of the Rhine, as a candidate for
the Imperial Crown. The Pope favoured Rupert. Wenceslaus,
in retaliation, called upon his realm to refuse further obedience
to Rome. The clergy sided with Rome. In the University,
however, the Bohemian Nation upheld their king, and the
Germans, out of sheer contrariness, violently opposed him.
But the Germans with their triple vote ruled the University.

Hus seized upon the occasion to break the power of the Germans. He petitioned the king in the name of the Bohemian Nation to secure a majority in the University to the Bohemians. The king complied. In 1409 he decreed that thereafter the Bohemian Nation was to have three votes, while the other three Nations were to have a single vote between them!

The Germans at once took an oath to secede if the decree were not immediately withdrawn. This was the old, hitherto effective threat of secession, but the times had changed. This was the fifteenth, not the thirteenth century; nationalism and royalty were both much stronger; outside political and religious passions were involved. The threat fell flat. The king held his ground, and ordered the German Rector to surrender his office to a Bohemian whom the king had appointed.

True to their oath, the Germans, to the number of 5000, migrated from Prague. Masters and scholars went to Heidelberg, to Cologne, to Leipzig, sowing in German soil the seeds of scholarship. They never returned to Prague. Theirs was the greatest cessation in the history of the Universities.

It was more than an academic cessation; it was a confession that the old cosmopolitanism of the Universities was no more; that no longer could alien students meet together in joyful scholarship unmindful of the fact that their several countries were at war. Nationalism and religious prejudice had destroyed the old republic of letters. Thereafter the Universities tended to become more and more local institutions, faithfully reflecting the policies of their country.

The effects of this migration were incalculable. All over Germany were sown the bitter seeds of resentment and hostility—to the Czechs as a race, to Hus and his followers as religious reformers. At the Council of Constance the German exiles led the pack in yelping for the blood of Hus. He was condemned by them before he was heard. The repercussions of that old University quarrel are felt even today between Czech and German.

The Germans having gone, Hus redoubled his efforts for

complete reform. He now openly defied the ecclesiastical authorities, and in so doing alarmed the more elderly and conservative among the University theologians. They began to edge discreetly away from him, but the younger theologians, and the University as a whole, stuck by him to the bitter end.

When Hus went to Constance, relying on the treacherous safe-conduct of the Emperor, when his opinions were solemnly condemned, when he refused to retract, and went to the stake as a martyr, the victim of religious intolerance and nationalistic passion, the remnants of the University yielded not an inch. Hus was their leader, and in Hus they believed.

An enraged Council suspended their privileges in 1417, but could not break the spirit of the University. This was the last stand of a cause already dead. There was no one to take Hus's place; and the bitter reaction set in—Catholic, hierarchical, anti-national. Bohemia was crushed.

The University, too, was broken by its gallant stand. After 1419 the Faculties of Law, Theology, and Medicine were all but extinct. Even the Faculty of Arts conferred no degrees for ten years. The University was avoided like the plague by all who sought ecclesiastical preferment, by those to whom scholarship meant definite material rewards. In the terrible Hussite Wars, through the years of siege and countersiege, the University was a pale shadow of itself. The Emperor Sigismund confiscated its property; and it lay beaten and quiescent until after the Reformation.

When the Reformation did come, it was the Germans, the bitterest opponents of Hus and all his works, who were the standard-bearers; and it was Martin Luther, within the precincts of a German University, who issued the famous theses that shook the Church to its very foundations. Had the Germans listened to Hus as they did to Luther, the history of the world might have been different.

CHAPTER XXXI

The Universities of Germany and Scotland

THE second Germanic University to be founded was Vienna, chartered by Duke Rudolph IV in 1365, and afterwards promoted to the dignity of a *Studium Generale* by a Papal Bull. The Duke had his own notions of history; he granted the nascent University privileges "according to the ordinances and customs observed first at Athens, then at Rome, and after that at Paris." Paris, naturally, was the actual model. As at Prague, Royalty swallowed everything Parisian without regard to fitness or necessity. Once again the strange division into four Nations made its appearance. Inasmuch as geographical names were inevitable, they were called Austria, Saxony, Bohemia, and Hungary. Together the four Nations of the Arts Faculty elected the Rector. In accordance with custom, it was a University of Masters, which granted certain privileges to the students; and notably, inclusion in the Nations. Rudolph, with the example of Paris before him, even provided for a School of Theology, but this the Pope peremptorily forbade. Paris must be unique. Here, of course, there was inconsistency. Oxford and Cambridge, without the Papal sanction, had their Schools of Theology; Toulouse was the deliberate foundation of the Papacy, and Prague had been granted the precious privilege.

Rudolph, in his anxiety to attract scholars, gave them special privileges. Serious crimes committed by masters and students were to be tried by the Chancellor; all other civil and criminal cases by the Rector. No assailant of a scholar could claim benefit of sanctuary; if a scholar was robbed, and the booty never recovered, the Duke was to compensate him for his loss. An outrage on a scholar might lead to confiscation of the aggressor's property, to be divided equally between the University and the injured party.

The Duke went even further. He set aside a special and most desirable quarter of Vienna for the use of the students, who had the right to choose any house therein for their residence; the rent to be fixed by the usual arbitration board. Further, for the protection of the scholars against outbreaks of violence among the townsfolk, the Quarter was guarded by a special wall, behind which the students could retire in case of need.

Rudolph died before he could establish the endowments which he had intended for his University, and civil wars followed. The institution languished until 1384, when it underwent resuscitation. This time the Pope relented and granted permission for a Theological Faculty. In most respects, in its government and its courses of study, Vienna followed Paris.

When Prague went down in ruin, Vienna became the most prominent of the Central European Universities, and held its position for a considerable period.

In most Universities married students were absolutely barred from attendance; this, of course, in accordance with the theory that they were clerics. Even today, following the ancient custom, a good many Universities will expel a student who enters into wedlock. But Vienna was more tolerant. A student might get married if he wished, *but*—and this is how the University registers describe such a strange anomaly. An entry for 1397 reads: "Baccalarius Johannes de Bertholzdorf, primus qui duxit uxorem" (Bachelor John of Bertholzdorf, the first to take a wife). And more eloquently: "uxorem duxit versus in dementiam" (he took a wife in a fit of insanity).

Germany had been late in entering the University movement, but she made up for her delay by the number of them, and the rapidity with which the country ripened into intellectual maturity.

Erfurt, the University of Martin Luther's early youth, was established in 1379. In 1385 Heidelberg, famed in song and romance, was founded by Rupert I, and received the customary

Papal Bull. The Roman Popes were now quite willing to scatter Universities broadcast over Europe. Paris, their darling, had turned traitor, and was espousing the Avignon schismatics.

Cologne was created by the municipality in 1388; Würzburg followed in 1402, and Leipzig was given a good start in 1409, by the accession of forty Masters and four hundred Bachelors and students who had taken part in the great migration from Prague. The provincial Universities—Rostock, Louvain, Treves, Greifswald, Freiburg-im-Breisgau, Bâle, Ingolstadt, Mainz, Tübingen—were springing up like mushrooms.

The Germanic Universities were all based on the Parisian model, with certain slight exceptions. For example, the Law students of Prague had their own University, somewhat like that of Bologna; Vienna permitted her students to enter the Nations; but otherwise the Masters were in control. The Rectors declined to purely honorary importance, and were students only when there was a princeling or a youthful noble of high degree to be so honoured.

The teaching staff, the Professoriate as we know it today, by reason of the special endowment of the Colleges, became the governing power. The inclusion of non-teaching graduates in the Congregations was gradually abandoned.

In Poland, Cracow was the first University to be founded. Casimir the Great provided the Charter in 1364, and Urban VI the Papal Bull. Law was the principal Faculty, and therefore the privileges of the students were based upon the great Law models, Bologna and Padua. Both Rector and Professors were elected by the students. Unfortunately, the democratic University had only a brief career, and when it was resuscitated in 1397 the Masters had managed to gain control. The Rector was almost always a Master, though he was still elected by the students.

Fünfkirchen, the first Hungarian University, came into existence in 1367. Buda was next; then Pressburg, renowned for the astrological prowess of its Masters. Upsala, in 1477, was Sweden's contribution, and Copenhagen followed in 1478 in the land of the Danes.

In Scotland the end of the Middle Ages witnessed the birth of three Universities. The Scotch were great travellers, and their students, in the early days of the University movement, were scattered all over Europe. Oxford and Cambridge were avoided for nationalistic reasons.

As the Continental Universities became more and more provincial, the Scotch were compelled to fall back on their own resources. St. Andrews was founded in 1413, and modelled itself on Orléans and Angers, with their mixture of the Paris and Bologna systems. Masters and students together were formed into four Nations: Fife, Lothian, Angus, and Britain. They elected a Rector, who was a graduate and in holy orders; but custom required further that he should be a Professor of Divinity or a Principal. The real power devolved into the hands of the Faculty.

Glasgow, founded in 1450, with the privileges of Bologna, maintained no more than a mean existence during the expiring Middle Ages. The Arts Faculty was practically the entire University. The students were mere boys, and were treated as such. In no other University were scholars so hardly dealt with. A student not in bed on the ringing of curfew, a student who "rashly or temerariously" met Rector, Dean, or Master in the street without holding his hands in front of his face, or running away from the basilisk glare, was publicly to be whipped. Ball-playing, that most innocuous of sports, was a penal offence, and bathing—that invention of the Devil—was visited not only with whipping, but with expulsion. The dour Presbyterian temperament of the Scot was already well to the fore.

Aberdeen completed the tale of the mediaeval Universities by its foundation in 1494. Here and there the breath of modern times was already stirring.

Strangely enough, it is in these late mediaeval Scottish Universities, almost outside the main current of their days, that the old mediaeval customs have been best preserved. At Aberdeen and Glasgow the students are still divided into Nations and still elect their Rector. The Rector today, however, is usually an absentee. Lord Balfour and Rudyard Kipling have both borne the honorary title.

CHAPTER XXXII

Student Life and Customs

THE tale of the Universities has been completed. From earliest Salerno, Paris, and Bologna, to the latest regional Germanic and Scottish University, the growth and evolution of this distinctive mediaeval institution has been traced. Incidental mention has been made of the students, the youngsters and adults without whom there would have been no reason for the complicated social, political, religious, and economic conglomeration called a University. But such mention has been purely in passing, to elucidate some phase in the growth of the institution itself. Now we have to consider the student himself, as a living, breathing human being, with appetites, desires, enthusiasms, phobias, and routines—rich man, poor man, beggarman, thief—in short, the everyday life of a mediaeval student at a typical University such as Paris or Oxford.

A good number of the students were desperately poor and of lowly origin. The Middle Ages were a period when class lines were rigidly and sharply defined; when the lord of the manor gave birth to the ensuing lord of the manor, when sons grew up to follow naturally and unquestioningly the trade of their fathers and grandfathers; when it was understood that the son of a peasant would continue to till the soil and share his produce with his feudal lord and the Church. The mediaeval man had his niche in the scheme of things, here on earth and in Heaven.

There was only one exception to this unalterable law of Nature. In reckoning up the tale of the mediaeval Church this one thing must for ever stand on the positive side of the ledger —that its hierarchy in some respects cut directly across the rigid class divisions of feudalism; that the son of the lowliest peasant, the poorest labourer, could lift up his eyes to the hills and aspire to priesthood, to deaneries and bishoprics, even on occasion to the Papal Throne itself. Not, of course, that such apotheosis was common; even today in our own democracies the doors of wealth and privilege do not readily swing open to the poor; but at least there was no absolute bar.

Small wonder, then, that every bright and ambitious lad, every youngster with dreams and visions, yearned for the ecclesiastical life, where, as in the case of Napoleon's soldiers, the marshal's baton was implicit in every knapsack. But theoretically for the lower orders of priesthood, and actually for the higher orders, learning, the knowledge of Latin, the ability to read and write, was a *sine qua non*. That meant the University!

So Jean Corbin, son of a peasant, who had exhausted the slender knowledge of the parish priest, took the few coins that his toil-worn parents had scraped together, added to them a few more that the priest had managed to find for his brightest pupil, borrowed a little from relations, and with all his belongings on his back, was ready to start on the long, weary journey to Paris, the Mecca of all scholars, the *gloria mundi*.

But first it was necessary to have the crown of his head shaven in a neat circle—in other words, to take the tonsure. Thereby he established his clericality, which was his by virtue of the fact that he was a scholar; and thereby he became *ipso facto* entitled to the many privileges accruing to members of the ecclesiastical order, and on enrolment in the University, to the even greater immunities of that particular institution. Too often it was the village barber, and not the proper ecclesiastical authority, who made a holy man where only common clay had existed before; the tonsure was the sign manual of clericism, to be taken usually at face, or shall we say, head, value. Suspicious people might further require a knowledge of reading to prove *bona fides*, but that test would often leave honest clerics out in the cold, and enable rogues to avail themselves of benefit of clergy.

x

However, Jean Corbin had come by his tonsure honestly.
For several weeks he trudged the dusty, tortuous highways to
Paris. His poor and mean appearance was protection enough
against the bands of robbers and the unemployed soldiers,
worse than bandits, who infested the country. His visible
clericality exempted him from the customary exactions and
tolls with which the lay traveller was burdened. Indeed, it did
more than that; for after the first few days, when his initial
stock of bread and cheese had become exhausted, the scholar's
privilege gave him the unquestioned right to beg his bread
from hamlet to hamlet, from door to door. What little money
he had could not be spent on food; he required every penny
for lodgings and masters' fees in Paris.

Thus arose the famous institution of the begging or
"wandering" scholar, the Goliard, the scholar who sought alms
on all the roads while travelling to and from the University,
or wandering from University to University, or drifting
about in idle, riotous vagabondage, while pretending to be
en route.

But Jean Corbin was no Goliard. He arrived eventually in
Paris, a young lad of fourteen, after weeks of arduous, footsore
travel, alone, bewildered, without friends or relations, a boy
who, from never having left the confines of his village, was
now hundreds of miles from home, pitchforked into the roaring, odorous, fascinating city of Paris.

About the same time there may have passed through the city
gates a company of respectable wayfarers, footsore and weary.
Among them was Pierre Bonheur, the son of a substantial
burgher of Besançon. His knapsack was well stuffed with
worldly possessions; perhaps he had even hired a donkey to
carry them. Having more reason to fear outrage on the road,
he accordingly joined a group of travellers who were well
armed and prepared to defend themselves.

Barely had Pierre passed through when there was a clatter
of horses, and a cavalcade came dashing up, spattering the
liquid mud on the bystanders. This was Robert of Tours, the

young scion of a famous house, likewise on his way to imbibe of the learning of Lutetia. With him were his armed retainers, and much gear and baggage, as was meet for a most noble lord.

Three scholars from mutually exclusive strata of society— yet once within the University precincts, subject to the same rules and regulations, endowed with the same privileges and immunities; with the odds, perhaps, in favour of Jean Corbin, the son of the peasant, for a brilliant career in the Rue du Fouarre.

If this were the early thirteenth century, the youngster of fourteen came to Paris without commitments, at liberty to select lodgings for himself and to pick and choose among the masters under whom he was to study.

He could lodge at an inn, or in the house of a citizen, or in a wretched garret if he had but little money; or, as was most usual for the middle-class student, he might join a Hall. This was a group of scholars under the tutelage of a Principal, usually a Master, who took over a house, and made of it a self-sufficing community. The poorest student, as we have seen, lived in a garret; in Paris he was called a "martinet" and in Oxford a "chamberdekyn." At first these were honourable terms, but gradually every cut-throat, cut-purse, pimp, and roisterer adopted the names to give themselves the semblance and protective coloration of scholarity, until finally they became the worst terms of insult that one could hurl at one's enemy. In the end, with the rise of the Colleges and regularly organized Halls, the University Statutes abolished these classes, compelling all students to live within the Halls and Colleges.

The rich scholar and the noble preferred to live alone, in luxurious private quarters, with servants and retainers to take care of his material wants while their lord studied philosophy, logic, and the law.

In the beginning the townsmen profiteered on the rents which they charged, but after a few riots and a secession or two, they saw reason, aided by certain reminders contained in royal decrees and Papal Bulls. The rents for lodgings were determined and fixed by a committee on which Town and University had equal representation.

Jean Corbin, not knowing anyone in Paris, let his wandering footsteps carry him to the nearest inn—*La Cloche Perse*, for example. Hardly had he laid his tattered bundle on the floor, and spent a precious sou on wine to wash the dust out of his throat, than he was fairly besieged. This was the golden age of the free-lance Master—duly licensed, of course, but entirely on his own—dependent for his livelihood on the number of pupils whom he could attract to his lectures and the amount of the fees he could extort.

The Masters hung about the inns, lying in wait for newly-arrived scholars, or, if too dignified for that, they hired "chasers" to enlist pupils for them. Poor Jean was surrounded by a clamouring horde of Masters and "chasers," each vaunting his own wares, decrying the others, bidding against each other for his patronage. Free lectures for limited periods, commissions, discounts, were some of the undignified methods employed. Robert de Sorbon complained that any Master who promised prebends or new robes to his pupils lectured to throngs of scholars, while other and better, but more modest Masters, had scarcely an auditor. In 1290 Paris definitely forbade the practice, but no doubt it was continued, with a little more secrecy, until the rise of the Colleges with their salaried teachers practically eliminated the free-lance Regent.

After obtaining lodgings to suit his purse, and arranging with the Master or Masters under whom he was to sit, the next step was to appear before the Rector of the University and enrol himself as a student. The entrance requirements were absurdly simple. If the applicant could apply to the Rector in person in fluent Latin, not halting or interjecting words of the vulgar tongue, he was deemed sufficiently well grounded in fundamentals to attend the University lectures.

He then took the oath of obedience to the Rector and the Statutes of the University, paid the matriculation fees, and was a full-fledged scholar, entitled to all the privileges and immunities and the protection of the powerful University.

But his fellow-students were not satisfied. He was a freshman, a *Bejaunus*, a yellow-bill, a fledgling, who had to be trimmed and pared and hazed with rude and sometimes savage horse-play before he was admitted into their fellowship. The modern American hazing of freshmen, the "Greek letter fraternity" initiations, may be traced back to the violent and brutal mediaeval treatment of a *Bejaunus*.

The following account of such a ceremony is taken from the interesting little *Manuale Scholarium*, which appeared in 1481—its authorship unknown—and which presents certain aspects of student life at Heidelberg in the later Middle Ages. But the practice was universal.

The *Bejaunus*, or freshman, is visited in his room by a committee of students. They pretend that he is a stinking goat, with an unbearable, unmentionable smell; then that he is a horned monster like a devil, seeking whom to rend and devour. After the rude wit of the scholars is exhausted in ringing the changes on this sprightly horse-play, they command him to stand still for inspection.

One of his tormentors pretends to have pity on the unfortunate freshman, to recognize him as a fellow-countryman, and offers him "wine" to drink to stave off faintness. This "wine," in a good number of instances, seems to have been plain urine. On the victim's refusal to drink, the pity changes to rage, and the nauseous liquid is forced down his protesting gullet.

Then the vituperation begins afresh, until someone suggests that a physician be called in to pluck and shave the terrible monster, so as to make him presentable for student society.

One of the hazers, dressed ludicrously in the guise of a doctor, appears with the instruments of his trade. He pretends to draw the tusks of the monster, to cut off the too long ears

and the hideous nose; a sport accompanied by much torment-
ing and mauling of the unfortunate wight. Then, in good
earnest, hair is pulled from his nose and head, and his face is
scraped with a wooden razor.

He is then forced to swallow pills compounded of
"melampus flowers," known to the modern pharmacopoeia as
hellebore, a violent cathartic. Not content with this, "Greek
White" was thrust down the victim's throat. The Manual
states baldly that this was a compound of the excreta of
hyaenas and other carnivora; its actual ingredients may safely
be left to the imagination. Then an ointment was applied
to the nose and mouth, indescribably filthy in origin;
"herbs" from a garden manured from cesspits, steeped in
water, and used as a shaving compound on the outstretched
initiate.

By this time the victim is faint in good earnest; his tormentors pretend that he is dying, and call for a priest. The
pretended priest confesses him in roaring burlesque. It is
solemnly averred that he is a thief, a ravisher of virgins, an
adulterer, and a resister of student customs, and the penance
decreed for absolution is that he immediately feast and dine
the student body.

This was the consummation to which all the filth and rough
handling had been gradually leading. The initiate was now
rid of personal and physical indignities, but his purse was
about to be subjected to a severe strain.

The initiation banquet was one to which both masters and
students were invited. It was usually held at a neighbouring
inn, and the feasters waxed merry at the expense of the
initiates.

The University authorities did their best to abolish the
custom of hazing, but in vain. A typical Statute is that of
Leipzig, enacted in 1495:

"Each and every one attached to this University is forbidden
to offend with insult, torment, harass, drench with water or
urine, besprinkle or defile with dust or any filth, mock by

whistling, accost with a terrifying voice, or dare to molest in any way whatsoever . . . any who are called *beani*. . . ."

Restrictions as futile as any modern prohibition of ragging or hazing. The excessive cost of the initiation banquet was another source of constant complaint, and attempts were made to control it. Numerous Statutes sought to limit the amount of the exaction. In the early days, an unfortunate student might find that the money with which he had hoped to defray a whole year's expenses, perhaps the life-savings of his hard-working parents, was squandered on one banquet. At Cornouaille the new-comer had to pay according to his means; at Dainville and Cambray, all the initiation cost him was a quart of "good" wine. In 1342 the University of Paris enacted that only a freshman's *socii*, or housemates, might exact a money contribution, and even this was supposed to be a free-will offering. But in spite of Statutes, and in spite of total prohibitions, the evil continued.

The most famous street in the mediaeval world was a narrow, tortuous, dirty thoroughfare; noisome with mal-odorous mud in rainy weather, with dust and slops in dry; clamorous with the comings and goings of thousands of scholars from many lands. This was the Rue du Fouarre, "Straw Street," where the Schools of the Masters of the University of Paris were situated. Houses were rented from the bourgeoisie by individual teachers to accommodate their pupils; later on they were leased by the Nations and parcelled out among their Masters; finally they were owned in fee by the Nations.

These Schools were not the nobly proportioned buildings, ornately furnished, and subdivided into the offices, class-rooms, laboratories, et cetera, that today are deemed in-dispensable adjuncts to the pursuit of learning. They were ramshackle frame-houses, always leaking and always damp; overrun with vermin, draughty, icy cold in winter and stifling hot in summer. Here each Master found accommodation; the larger rooms being apportioned to the more famous teachers, and the smaller to the Regents but recently incepted, who lectured to echoing walls.

It is early on a winter morning: 5 A.M., to be exact. A famous Master is lecturing on the intricacies of the syllogism; his room is crowded. It is dark and bitterly cold; some four smoky candles, guttering and flaring, shed a dim illumination over the School. There is no central heating system, no stove, not even a fireplace. The sooty windows are rimed with frost; the breath of the attentive pupils ascends in clouds of steam.

The rich and well-born are enveloped in furs; the poor and the lowly draw their tattered cloaks about them; their lips are blue and pinched, their limbs almost numb with cold.

One and all, they squat on the straw-strewn floor (whence the name, "Straw Street"), their legs crossed beneath them like any Turk, none higher or lower than his fellow. There are no benches, no comfortable chairs. A democracy of straw! Yet such is the magic of the Master that all discomforts are forgotten; blue fingers laboriously note the gist and substance of his speech; the more conscientious take it down verbatim.

The Master is a man of dignity and substance; he and he alone is seated. A rough pulpit is before him; a hard chair his throne. Sometimes a Bachelor, an assistant, is seated by his side.

This is the only concession to comfort in a draughty, ill-ventilated room. For centuries this Spartan custom prevailed. When benches finally came into fashion, the Papal Legate decreed their immediate abolition on the ground that such luxury was bound to have an enervating effect on body and mind. It was not until 1452 that the benches came to stay, and then only despite the fulminations of Cardinal d'Estouteville.

The Master, a famous and brilliant logician, disdained to read his lecture from a prepared manuscript, or worse still, to sit in state while his assistant, the Bachelor, read it slowly to the squatting scholars. Such easy-going methods were for the lazy and ill-informed, and were deprecated in a succession of Statutes.

He preferred to let the golden words drip extempore from his mouth, inspiring his scholars with an enthusiasm not to be obtained in any other fashion. The Statutes went so far as to prescribe the exact pace at which the words were to flow from the Master's lips. He was to lecture not "drawlingly" but "rapidly"; that is, "bringing out the words as rapidly as if nobody had been writing before him."

Therein was the root of the matter. Books were few and far between; the toil of laborious copying on parchment made their cost almost prohibitive to the average scholar. Hence the lectures of the University Masters constituted practically the only means of obtaining knowledge. The Masters lived on the fees of their scholars, and the University being a Master University, it is understandable why it legislated against lecturing so deliberately that the scholars could take down the lectures verbatim. Such literal transcriptions could be copied and hawked about, without payment of royalties to the author.

Students are an ingenious clan. Shorthand, as we know it, had not yet been invented, but the scholar without a book managed somehow. For example, in noting down the line of Virgil, quoted by an Arts lecturer: "Tityre tu patulae recubana sub tegmine fagi," the student would write: "Tityre t p r s t f."

The students were not always meek recipients of the pearls of wisdom. If the Master's logic was impeachable, if his conclusions erred, the pupils might show their disapproval by "shouting, hissing, groaning, or the throwing of stones, by themselves or their servants or confederates."

The average number of lectures was three per diem; one in the early morning, one about noon, and one during the "long session" of the afternoon. Each lasted from one to three hours. Lest it should be thought that the mediaeval

scholar's life was an easy one, glance at the following programme of daily events in the average College of the day : [1]

4 A.M.	Rising.
5-6 A.M.	1st lesson.
6 A.M.	Breakfast, consisting only of a small piece of dry bread. Rest then, but no recreation.
8-10 A.M.	Principal forenoon lesson.
10-11 A.M.	Discussion and argument on the preceding lecture.
11 A.M.	Dinner, accompanied by reading of the Bible or the lighter passages in the Lives of the Saints. The Chaplain intoned prayers, and the Principal of the College admonished, praised, blamed, and announced the punishments for the day.
12-2 P.M.	Interrogation on the morning lessons.
2-3 P.M.	Rest period, so-called, while someone read aloud from a Latin poet or orator.
3-5 P.M.	The principal afternoon lecture.
5-6 P.M.	More discussion and more argument on the theme.
6 P.M.	Supper.
6.30 P.M.	General questions on all the day's lectures.
7.30 P.M.	*Compline* and Benediction.
8 P.M.	And so to bed, in winter; in summer—9 P.M.

When, may one ask, was there time for sports, for recrea-
tion, for plain day-dreaming and lounging? Well, on Tuesday
and Thursday afternoons, a little free time was permitted for
strolling in the Près-aux-clercs, where the scholars were
supposed to walk in seemly fashion, two by two, their thumbs
in their belts.

Sings Villon:

"Chaperons auront enformez,
Et les poulces sur la sainture."

(They will wear their hoods well over their eyes, and thumbs in the
belt.)

It is not to be wondered at that such modest promenades,
which must have left youthful bodies aching for action, some-

---

[1] The general scheme is taken from Frère Azarias.

times ended in bloody riots between the Nations, or against the townsfolk, or with the clerics and armed retainers of the Abbey which claimed jurisdiction. A word, a jeer, a taunting look, was sufficient to cause an explosion.

This rigid programme was, of course, that of later years, when the Colleges had made an end of the wild, free life of the "martinet," the "Goliard," and the rich noble living in chambers with his servants.

CHAPTER XXXIII

Books and Disputations

THE lectures were the backbone of the University course, but what the scholars enjoyed the most, what the Masters chiefly prided themselves upon, achieving fame and a following thereby, were the *Disputations*. Mediaeval Scholasticism derived more from these battles of wits than from any other institution. It was by disputation that Abélard overthrew William of Champeaux; it was in disputation that every candidate for the Master's degree tussled with his fellows.

The mode of an Inception Disputation was fairly well fixed.

The Bachelor Candidate announces the theses which he intends to defend well in advance, and sends out invitations to all and sundry. The larger the audience, the greater the glory for his neatly turned syllogisms. The great day arrives. The Master seats himself on the platform; the candidate stands facing his partisans; perhaps there are enemies present. The first thesis is announced, and the Bachelor immediately divides it into headings, explaining each in turn. An opponent, prepared for the occasion, rises and picks flaws in the thesis. All is expressed in the form of syllogisms: major premise, minor premise, conclusion. The disputation has the effect of a stately dance, of formal point and counterpoint.

The Inceptor retorts with answering syllogisms. His opponent counters. The tempo increases. The debate takes on colour and warmth. The dance of argument and counter-argument loses its stately grace; it begins to follow broken rhythms. This is what the listeners have been waiting for. They are on their feet, like "fans" at a prize-fight. Suddenly the candidate is impaled on the horns of a dilemma. His enemies yell triumphantly. His friends are dumbfounded. He shakes his head as if under the impact of the blow, thinks for a moment, wriggles out of the difficulty with neat phrases, and in turn catches his opponent. His friends shout in glee. The opponent is discomfited, and sinks back into his seat. The candidate struts a little, but he is not safe yet. A fresh and unwearied opponent rises who has found a flaw hitherto unnoted.

And so it goes on, and on, for hours, days, and even weeks, "amid loud clamour on the part of the audience, and on the part of the combatants, great shaking of the head and stamping of the feet, and extending of the fingers, and waving of the hands, and contortions of the body as though they were crazed."

This was what the mediaeval audience loved; this was the cause of their almost unintelligible mania for Dialectic as against the humanistic Arts. The disputations were battles, literally battles of words, just as the jousts and tournaments were battles of physical strength. Both satisfied a deep-seated spiritual and physical need.

Considered from another angle, the disputation, the vigorous matching of subtle wits, was a safety-valve for thoughts otherwise repressed. Aristotle and the Bible were twin deities, the Fathers of the Church archangels; Gratian, Peter Lombard, and the other commentators, principalities and powers. All knowledge was formalized, sealed with the seal of authority; the Church stood on vigilant guard against all suspicions of heresy; there was nothing new to be sought out.

Repressed and circumscribed, these lusty scholars, with keen and agile minds, were forced to turn them inwards. Propositions were set before them with all the awful majesty of authority; what could they do but analyse them, play with them, dissect them, turn them inside out, probe them, pick them to pieces, read fantastic meanings into them? It was a game; a game that had all the fascination of an intellectual crusade. It gave them some measure of liberty of thought, and a pretext for sharpening their intellectual tools. The game grew into a passion, a mania, until there was no end to disputations. Says Vives, in *De causis corruptarem artium* (1531):

"They dispute before dinner; they dispute during dinner; they dispute after dinner; they dispute in private and in public, at all times and in every place. . . . Their self-esteem compelled them to propose questions on the simplest propositions. On the mere words, *Scribe mihi,* they discussed questions of grammar, physics, and metaphysics. They gave their adversary no time to explain himself. If he ventured upon any developments, they cried, 'To the point! to the point! reply categorically!' They had no concern for truth, but sought merely to defend their opinions. Is a man too hard-pressed? He eludes the objection by dint of obstinacy; he denies insolently; he blindly strikes down all opposition in despite of evidence. To the most convincing objections, which drive him to the most absurd consequences, he contents himself with replying: 'I admit it, because it results from my thesis.' . . . Provided he can defend himself logically, he passes for a man of ability. . . . Men shout until they are hoarse; they make use of insulting speeches and threats. They even come to blows, bites, and buffetings. Discussions degenerate into quarrels, and quarrels into fights."

One may almost fancy himself in the very thick of a twentieth-century political campaign wherein great issues are being argued for the edification of the voters!

Latin, of course, was the universal language of the day; not a dead, meaningless matter of irregular verbs and syntax, but a live, vigorous, growing tongue. Every educated man wrote and spoke it with the same facility as his native language; the Universal Church recognized no other means of communication; all legal and all medical knowledge, all charters and political documents were written in stately Latin periods.

It is a fascinating subject, this of the mediaeval reliance upon a common, elder language. A flexible Latin style was the mark of an educated man; he was equally at home in England, in

France, in Italy, in Northern Scandinavia, on the plains of Hungary. Nowhere was he an alien; everywhere he found fellow-citizens of the great republic of Latinity.

The Universities made exclusive use of Latin. The vulgar tongues were rigorously forbidden. Not only the formal lectures and disputations, but the ordinary, everyday conversation of the students was to be in Latin. Manuals of common words and phrases were prepared for the halting speaker, but the rule was fixed and unalterable. Latin, and only Latin, was to be used for all purposes; in hiring a servant, in the discussion of philosophy with one's fellows, in play, in quarrelling, in making love.

Such a hard-and-fast rule naturally met with difficulties. Not every novice knew as much Latin as he pretended to in his fluent, carefully memorized speech to the Rector. The vigorous expression of one's likes and dislikes, reference to sexual matters, and vituperation called for the racy idiom of the vernacular rather than the formal epithets of the classics. There were infractions of the rules.

To detect and punish these, the University authorities instituted a despicable system of espionage. Certain students were set to spy upon their fellows, to listen to their private conversation, and report upon their use of forbidden tongues. Such spies were known as *lupi*, or "wolves." A first offence cost so much; a second more, and so on.

But the universal Latin of the Middle Ages was not the stately, classical Latin of Cicero, Virgil, Horace, and Tacitus, or of even St. Augustine.

It is true that in the first Renaissance of the late eleventh and twelfth centuries, the Latin spoken and written was comparatively pure. Abélard wrote and no doubt spoke a good, vigorous, classical Latin; John of Salisbury was the finest Latin scholar of the age; Bernard of Chartres and others were not far behind.

But in the closing years of the twelfth century, and with accelerating pace during the thirteenth, the Latin tongue degenerated, or underwent development according to one's point of view. For one thing, the reading of the great classics had gone out of fashion; for another, Scholasticism with its new terminologies in Logic, Philosophy, and Theology, had added innumerable words and turns of expression to the language; and for another, inasmuch as Latin was a living, universally used language, it was inevitable that it should change, and take on colour from the surrounding tongues, and evolve as all spoken languages do.

Consequently, the Latin of the fourteenth and fifteenth centuries would hardly be recognizable by Horace. For that matter, it is doubtful whether he could have understood much of the Latin of the fifth or sixth century. The scholars complain bitterly of this degeneration in the later Middle Ages, but such complaints are purely pedantic. A language, if generally spoken, and kept burnished by constant usage, *must* change and evolve.

So that the University student had for his daily use an easy, flowing, colloquial, salty Latin, a sort of *lingua franca*, a vigorous, practical tongue, which Rabelais satirizes as a barbarous jargon in the scene between Pantagruel and the Limousin scholar:

"He asked him thus: 'My friend, from whence comest thou?' The Scholar answer'd him: 'From the alme, inclyte, and celebrate Acadamie, which is vocitated Lutetia (Paris).'

"'Thou comest from Paris then' (said Pantagruel), 'and how do you spend your time there, you my Masters the Students of Paris?' The Scholar answer'd, 'We transfretate the Sequane at the dilicul and crepuscul; we deambulate by the compites and quadrives of the Urb; we despumate the Latial Verbocination; and like verisimilarie amorabons, we captat the Benevolence of the omnijugal, omniform, and omnigenal Foeminine Sexe.'"

Books were rare and valuable possessions in the Middle Ages. Each manuscript had to be copied laboriously on expensive parchment. The process was long and tedious, the number of copies limited, and the finished product costly.

The poor student could not afford a book; the average scholar could acquire only a few; and none but the wealthy could hope to possess every book requisite for or incidental to his course of study. The Statutes of Paris required every student of Theology to bring a copy of the Bible or of the *Sentences* of Peter Lombard to class with him; and in a good many Colleges the students of Logic and Philosophy had to provide themselves with texts.

To satisfy the demand, there grew up around the University a permanent colony of tradesmen—"Librarii" or booksellers, who sold books to or for private individuals, taking a fixed commission, and "Stationarii," who employed a permanent staff of copyists to make fair copies of texts for the use of the University. These were sold to those who could afford them, or, more often, lent on hire to the poorer students, a deposit being made as security for the safe return, in good condition, of the precious copy.

The University controlled this trade in books. The "Librarii" and "Stationarii," as clients of the University, were possessed of certain University privileges. In return, the University imposed all sorts of restrictions and precautionary measures. No book could be sold or rented until the accuracy of the copy had been attested, and the price fixed, by a Board of four Masters and four booksellers. No book was to be offered for sale to a stranger until the University had been notified, and given the first option.

The earliest Paris tariff (the date is about 1286) lists copies of 138 different works for hire. In 1323 there were twenty-eight booksellers operating under the aegis of the University, besides the small bookstalls which sold books of little value to the students.

The sale of parchment also became a University monopoly. At an early date the Rector had succeeded in establishing a prior claim to the supply of parchment needed by the University for the coming year. Until his mark had been stamped on the skins which he required, the merchants were unable to dispose of the balance of their stock.

This notable event usually took place at the fair accompanying the *Landit*, the nine-day June pilgrimage of the people of Paris to the plain of St. Denis, there to venerate the relics of the patron saint. The Rector attended the fair, which developed into a ritual holiday. He rode in state to Ste. Geneviève, accompanied by the whole student body. From this point a formal procession started, marching with banners and singing to the fair grounds.

There the Rector and his students saw and venerated the relics; the Rector partook of a stoup of wine proffered him by the monks, and proceeded to the business of purchasing parchment, while the students roamed the fair grounds, mingled with the chattering holiday crowds, patronized the stalls where meat and drink were sold, stuffed and gorged themselves, succumbed to the lures of the women of the town, became heated, drank more wine to cool their thirst, raised their voices, took umbrage at a look, and by eventide there were broken heads and widespread rioting.

To cope with the scarcity of books, some of the Colleges established libraries, consisting at first of only a few books, and never, of course, approaching in size or catholicity our modern University libraries.

The greatest library in Paris was that of the Sorbonne, which was divided into two parts: *Magna Libraria*, containing the works most in general use, which were chained to the wall, and were for reference purposes only; and *Parva Libraria*, consisting of duplicate copies or volumes of lesser value. These were loaned on payment of a deposit. But in spite of this precaution, books were stolen, lost, or never returned.

In 1322 the library of the Sorbonne contained 1017 volumes; by 1338 there were 1700. About 1480 the number of volumes had so increased that an imposing new building was erected, in which the gallery of the main reading-room was forty feet by twelve. The books were chained, as formerly, to the wall—student morals had not appreciably bettered—and the five-foot chains just permitted the reader to lay the book on one of the twenty-eight desks or tables.

The rules established for the Sorbonne library are interesting:

I. No member of the house may enter the library unless he be wearing cap and gown.

II. Children and unlettered persons are to be excluded.

III. If any worthy and learned persons desire to enter, one of the *socii* (members of the College) must introduce them, but their servants must remain outside.

IV. Each *socius* shall carefully keep the key, and shall lend it to no one.

V. At no time shall fire or light be taken into the building.

VI. No book may be removed from the library without consent of the house.

VII. Before placing a volume on a desk to read it the dust should be removed; after reading it should be replaced, closed.

VIII. It is forbidden to write on the volumes, to make any erasure, or to tear out the leaves.

IX. Whether a person is writing or reading, he shall not disturb others either by talking or walking about.

X. As far as possible silence shall reign in the library, just as in a holy place.

XI. Books whose doctrines are condemned and writings of a dangerous nature shall be given to no one but a professor of theology; moreover, he must swear that the requirements of an argumentation or a controversy force him to have recourse to it.

XII. The professor himself must not read them out of pure curiosity, lest their poison penetrate his own mind.

XIII. If anyone does so he shall be punished with a reprimand.

The paucity of books and their costliness made, of course, for the lecture system of instruction. The Master orated, the student listened and took notes. The power of use and wont is nowhere better illustrated than in the survival of the lecture method in our modern age, when books are cheap and plentiful; when the student can obtain fuller and more thorough knowledge from texts and original documents, without being hurried from thought to thought so quickly that he cannot consider and question what he has just heard.

CHAPTER XXXIV

Poverty and Hardships

MANY mediaeval students were poverty-stricken; youths whose parents were of limited means, or none; who counted every sou before paying their Masters' fees. Only too many had little left for food, clothing, and shelter. Books were out of the question for such.

Of course, there were also substantial and wealthy students, and priests whose benefices kept them in Paris or at other Universities, where they spent long years in the study of Canon and Civil Law and perhaps Theology.

With the advent of the Colleges there was less and less dire, grinding poverty. The impecunious student, if he could gain admission, was assured of food and clothing and shelter; enough, at all events, to keep body and soul together.

But in the early days the destitute scholar was something of a problem, to himself, to the University, and to the authorities of Church and State. The wilder individuals—the Goliards—roamed the highways and frequented the taverns and brothels. The more conscientious starved and shivered in their fireless, barren garrets, and begged their bread from the charitable.

Hearken to the tragic lament of the poverty-stricken scholar, nobly born:

"... Would to God I had been born a peasant, that I might not be a laughing-stock. They call me noble, point me out as I go by, and I go with my head down and my eyes on the ground, for my beggary devours me. And to make matters worse, my fellow-students are *parvenus*, the sons of nobodies, who go everywhere, entertain everybody, and live in the best chambers while I sit up in my garret, or go out in my coat with the fur worn bare, and so poor that I cannot even buy my fill of bread. I cannot write home to my people for more, for there's my brother to be knighted, and my sisters to be married, and no end to the daily expenses that cannot be avoided. And so I come to you as to my other God, asking you to dip your little finger in the fountain of your liberality, and touch your wretched nephew's tongue."

Or John of Garland's mournful picture of the student of his day:

"The poor scholar is overcome by study, not deprived of virtue; moreover, the rich man, who does not study and who lives in his tall houses, scoffs at poor scholars, and even strikes them. I eat sparingly in my little room, not high up in a castle; I have no silver money, nor do the Fates give me estates. Beets, beans, and peas are here looked upon as fine dishes, and we joke about meat, which is not on our menu for a very good reason. The size of the bottle of wine on the table depends on the purse which is never fat."

Or of the worthy teacher who still clung to the Arts in an age that had more respect for the lucrative professions:

"Lean and hungry, I overwork myself by heaping up verses instead of gold. With one poor servant and with meagre fare I console myself. May I not suffer shameful need, may I have the necessities of old age, a bed of my own, and clothes on my back!"

Envy and resentment are felt by the poor scholar:

"These (learned men) must walk on foot, but such priests ride high on their palfries and often have unlawful intercourse with women."

Matthew Paris pictures a young clerk in the year 1250, coming from a French village, "bearing water in a little vessel with its sprinkler, and the crusts of bread given to him for sprinkling holy water." He encounters a Papal agent who demands a tenth of his benefice, to meet which demand, and to prolong a starved existence, the poor clerk sells his books and "keeps school for many days."

For the poor scholar, begging was the accepted and indeed the official means of keeping body and soul together. The Chancellor of Oxford, in 1461, licensed two begging students, giving them the right to cry for alms from door to door. In the fifteenth century such begging became a regular business, especially in Germany. Young men, often accompanied by mere boys, roamed from town to town, claiming to be scholars, begging and stealing and ravishing. Even in Bologna, the University to which the mature and wealthy students flocked, there was the obverse side of the picture. Boncompagno gives a pathetic picture of the poor student of Bologna:

"I ought to spend my time in following the courses and studying, but want compels me to go begging to the doors of churchmen. I am reduced to crying twenty times in succession: 'Charity, my good signor!'—usually to hear the response: 'God be with you!' I betake myself to the houses of laymen, where I am rudely repulsed; and if, perchance, one says to me, 'Wait a moment,' I receive a scrap of mouldy bread which the dogs would not eat. Beggars by trade, oftener than I, get the stale vegetables, the uneatable skin and gristle, the discarded offal, the sour wine. At night I roam about the city, stick in one hand and wallet and flask in the other; the stick to protect me against the dogs, the wallet to collect the leavings of fish, bread, and vegetables, and the flask for water. Often it happens that I fall into the mire, that mire of Bologna which smells like a corpse, and thus besmirched I return home to satisfy a growling stomach with the leavings that have been thrown to me."

Then there is the famous, if possibly apocryphal story of the three students so poor that they had but one *cappa* (cloak) between them, which they wore in turns in order to attend their lectures.

At Vienna there were Halls of the Poor (*Domus Pauperum*) whose residents went out regularly to beg, dropping the alms received into the common chest for equal sharing.

It is true that some of these accounts are rather highly coloured, to give them literary value and the cathartic quality of tragedy, but in the main they are desperately sincere, and have the truth within them. Not for these poor scholars the riotous, wine-swilling life of their fellows; the roasts, the spits, the joyous recourse to the taverns. The whine of the scholar, cap in hand, humbly begging his bread from door to door, was one of the most characteristic street cries of Paris, and if the truth were known, of most University towns.

The wretched garrets of the poor, and the chambers of the rich, with their student companions and servitors, chaplain, and tutor, were gradually replaced by the Halls and Colleges. Originally—at least in Paris—pious foundations, charitable institutions for the aid of the poor scholar, the Colleges came to be the home of all students, rich and poor alike; those able to pay bearing their just burdens, and those unable to do so living on the endowments. In the more aristocratic Oxford and Cambridge, some of the Colleges made the recipients of charity work for their keep by waiting at table, or acting as the personal servants of the more lordly Fellows.

There was a wide disparity between the various Colleges; some were notably well endowed, and liberal in the comforts which they afforded their inmates; others were insufficiently endowed, to the detriment of the students; and in others the most rigorous discipline and asceticism were the rule.

Rarely were fires permitted in College chambers, even in the bitterest winters. Wooden shutters through which the keen winds blew; unplastered ceilings; cold floors of clay or tiles, bare or strewn with straw; a straw pallet for bed, a bench for study; these were the amenities of the average College.

Ingenious students found many pretexts to visit the kitchens, where the fires gave forth a grateful warmth, though the Statutes expressly forbade such evasions of a Spartan existence. No wonder that at every opportunity the scholars forgathered in the well-lit, well-warmed taverns, to luxuriate in the comfort denied them in College or Hall.

Lighting, too, was a problem. In the winter months the darkness fell, long before the end of the last lecture. Studying and reading were possible only by candlelight. But since candles were expensive, the average student was compelled to do without them; the Colleges gave no allowances for such luxuries. On the cold, dark evenings there was nothing to do but go to bed and shiver under insufficient coverings, or join in a disputation in the College hall, in the dim light of a single candle.

The well-endowed English Colleges had better quarters, and even fires. So had the Sorbonne. But the Sorbonne was the wealthiest endowment in Paris; it even possessed fifteen silver forks and spoons!

What food the students ate depended, of course, even as today, on a wide variety of circumstances. In the days of external lodgings the scholar's means and his appetite decided the issue.

Peter Comester, Chancellor of Notre Dame, preached feelingly of the gluttony of the students.

"In eating and drinking," he thundered, "there are not their equals; they are devourers at table, but not devout at mass. At their work they yawn; at their feasts they stand in awe of no one. They abhor meditation upon the divine books, but they love to see the wine sparkling in their glasses, and they gulp it down valiantly."

With the rise of the Colleges, however, all students conformed more or less with the general fare provided in the College dining-room. Those with long purses could visit the tavern from time to time, and partake of delicacies which their less fortunate brethren were compelled to do without.

As to the fare provided in the Colleges, there is plenty of evidence, most of it bitterly critical. There is the letter of a Brother Maurice, a student in the convent of the Friars Preachers in Paris, who writes that he has been afflicted all the winter with one sickness after another, but now he is able to partake of eggs "more corrupted and fewer in numbers than those of the *Eifel* which are supplied to our brethren in Cologne." He longs for "the fleshpots of his native village —fresh eggs and potherbs." In fact, the regulation diet of the age, for monastery and college alike, seems to have been a handful of dried beans, peas, and cabbage.

Montaigu, notorious for its harsh discipline and asceticism, compelled its unfortunate students to stand in line daily at the adjacent Carthusian monastery for a breakfast of dry bread. The bread-line was evidently an ancient institution. Montaigu, incidentally, was the College excoriated by Erasmus, who insisted that the inhuman treatment which he there received, and the putrid, unwholesome food, shattered his constitution while he was still a student, and left him enfeebled for life. Rabelais also struck a blow at the infamous Montaigu. Ponocrates remarks of the College: "Criminals and condemned murderers are better treated."

The junior students received for their daily portion a little stale bread, half an ounce of butter, a plate of sodden vegetables, half a herring, and one egg, of which the less said the better. The older and more indulgently treated scholars received a whole herring *or* two eggs, a small piece of cheese, and some fruit. Meat was unknown as far as the inmates of Montaigu were concerned.

Montaigu was the worst of all the Colleges; others were far more liberal. At Harcourt, for example, the wine was so plentiful that it was impossible to hold a chapter meeting after meal-time, the students being too full of the juice that is red to pay strict attention to the proceedings. This was the opposite extreme—for Paris, at any rate. Between these extremes were the moderate Colleges, with an average allowance of fifty sous a week per scholar for food, which was normal middle-class fare. This permitted of two meals a day; no breakfast, even though the scholar rose at five or six o'clock; dinner at 10 A.M., and supper at 5 P.M. On fast days, and these were many, one meal at noon had to satisfy healthy appetites. Meat was a rarity; the food was of the plainest; the pious founders did not wish to pamper their charges.

Many of the martinets and chamberdekyns lived on bread and porridge all the week, with a little wine and meat on Sundays and holidays. At Oxford the food in the later Middle Ages was notoriously poor. "Oxford fare" was a synonym for bad food. Sir Thomas More wrote: "My counsel is, that we fall not to the lowest fare first; we will not therefore descend to Oxford fare, nor to the fare of New Inn, but we will begin with Lincoln's Inn diet."

And this is what Lever, the Master of St. John's College, Cambridge, has to say of the food provided for scholars of his College: Their dinner consists only of a "penye pece of byefe amongst iiii, hauying a few porage made of the brothe of the same byefe wyth salte and otemell"; supper is "not much better." For lack of fire, the students were forced "to walk or runne up and down halfe an houre, to get a heate on their feet" before scrambling into their icy beds.

But the wealthier foundations of Oxford treated their Fellows right royally; the food was good and abundant, and they were given poorer scholars for servants. These poor beneficiaries had much to complain of. In return for menial work, they were graciously permitted to partake of the broken meats, the leavings, the stale bread.

The dress of the scholars was subject to strict regulation. Yet it was clerical rather than distinctively academic. In the Northern Universities every scholar was *ipso facto* a tonsured cleric. The most important item of the clerical garb was the long outer garment, closed in front. The ordinary robe was called the *tabard*, a still longer one the *toga*, and the more distinctive *cappa* or cope was confined to formal occasions. At first exclusively worn by Masters, it became, with sleeves attached, the garb of the Bachelors also, and was even worn surreptitiously by undergraduates. It was in the *cappa* that the mediaeval love of colour and display found full expression. Each College had a distinctive colour. Navarre chose sombre black; Beauvais, blue or violet; Queen's, at Oxford, blood-red; the Doctors of the Superior Faculties were resplendent in red and purple; while in Paris the Rectors wore violet or purple, and the Masters scarlet, with tippets and hoods of fur. The fur was not merely for ostentation; it helped to keep the Master from freezing in "Straw Street" during the winter.

For undergarments, heavy, thick woollens kept out the chill and damp; worn all day, they were slept in at night, and were changed when the wearer thought fit, provided he had others in his wardrobe. The Statutes inveighed with such constant repetition against the vain fashions of the laity as to lead to the belief that they were honoured more in the breach than in the observance. "Indecent," "unhonest," "dissolute," or merely "secular" attire was the burden of their discourse. "Trunk-hose," for instance, puffed sleeves, pointed shoes, fantastically curved red or green boots—these were the extravagances to which the scholars were addicted, in spite of Statutes to the contrary.

The students and Masters of the Northern Universities, being clerics, were forbidden to marry. This, indeed, seems to have been the only price which they had to pay for the valuable privileges of clericality. Ostensibly the prohibition required celibacy, but the Middle Ages winked at sexual lapses on the part of its clerics, provided they did not lead to the holy and respectable bonds of matrimony.

Even to this rule there were exceptions. We have seen that in Paris the Doctors of Medicine were finally absolved from compliance, and Vienna was not inflexible.

In Southern France, where the Church had to cope with violent heretical outbursts, the rule was not quite so strict. At Aix, if any Master or scholar desired to marry, the University did not stand in his way, but merely required that he should pay a fixed charge for the privilege. If, however, the bride was a widow, the charge was doubled. Perhaps widows were in great demand. If the bridegroom refused to pay, the whole University proceeded to his house, armed with frying-pans, pots, bassoons, and horns, and serenaded him on his wedding night. Such vigorous measures were usually effective. If he still proved stubborn, the accumulated garbage and filth of the town was placed upon his doorstep every feast day as a gentle reminder.

CHAPTER XXXV

Riots and Bloodshed

THE most spectacular features of the student life of the Middle Ages were the bloody affrays, the pitched battles, the mayhems, rapes, and homicides, which fill the records of the times with monotonous regularity. Indeed, by the frequency of riots one may trace the rise of the University to power and privilege. The more frequent the rioting, the greater the bloodshed, the more powerful the University when it emerged from the struggle.

It seemed to be a maxim of University practice that the scholar or the Master, no matter what his offence, was always in the right. Any retribution visited upon his sacred head led to an immediate demand for redress, and if it was not forthcoming, to cessation. The Pope and the dignitaries of the Church backed up their children, and so, for that matter, did the Throne and the forces of the State.

The immunities conferred account very largely for the unremitting hatred felt by the townsfolk for the students in their midst, and also for the turbulence of the scholars, their swaggerings and readiness with cuff and blow, and their tendency to ride roughshod over the lesser rights and privileges of the townsmen. The lay courts had no jurisdiction over scholars, and the University or ecclesiastical courts were a farce. For the gravest crime the penalty was a penance, a small fine, the mumbling of a few prayers.

Consider that a University meant a great concourse of men and boys, far from their homes, freed from all parental restrictions, introduced perhaps for the first time to the delights of the tavern and the brothel; add to this the fact that in the Middle Ages violence and bloodshed were almost normal, so that the slitting of a throat was not regarded even by the Church as the worst of mortal sins; and we need no other explanation of the turbulence and tumult of University life.

An old French monk remarked: "In Paris they seek liberal arts, at Orléans authors, at Salerno gallipots, at Toledo demons, and in no place decent manners."

Roger Bacon went further: "Whenever clerks are met together, as in Paris and Oxford, they shock the world with their feuds, their contentions or their vices."

And Philippe Auguste, King of France, himself a contributor to the privileges of Paris, said of the scholars in his kindgom:

"They are hardier than knights. Knights, covered with their armour, hesitate to engage in battle. These clerics, who have neither hauberk nor helmet, but a tonsured head, playfully fall upon one another with daggers; most foolish behaviour, and very dangerous."

The Universities did nothing to exact discipline from their scholars; morality was a private affair, and so were their comings and goings provided they did not interfere with the University itself. Nor did the Masters disapprove of riotous courses. As a matter of fact, the Arts Masters, themselves not much older than their pupils, only too often joined in the affrays and carousings, the ravishments and bludgeonings. An injury to one was an injury to all.

Nation sometimes fought with Nation, scholar with scholar, in private feud, but if the townsfolk, or the guard, or any outside force took a hand, their enmities were forgotten in opposing the common foe. The Provost Guard of Paris led a dog's life as far as the students were concerned. They dared not exact summary punishment for the escapades of the students; their various attempts to do so had led to the most serious consequences; reports to the University and the ecclesiastical authorities were worse than useless, evoking no more than vague promises and indulgent smiles.

The scholars, knowing this, would mock the raging Guard with cries of: "Allez au clos Bruneau, vouz trouverez à qui parler!" In other words—take your complaints to the University authorities!

Students roamed the narrow, brawling streets of Paris until curfew, and then repaired to the nearest tavern, to spend half the night in carousing. The taverns of Paris were many, and almost all of them appear in the records of the English-German Nation as having been frequented by that turbulent body for the purpose of legitimate feasts. *Le Coq et la Poule*, *L'Image Notre Dame*, *L'Etoile*, *La Trousse-Vache*, were some of the picturesquely-named places in which the students foregathered. Sometimes the thirsty scholar had no need to leave the house in which he was lodging; the same building might shelter him and find room for a brothel or tavern. No social pressure was brought to bear upon the vagabond scholar; the spirit of the age was free and easy, despite the frown of Church and priest.

It was some time before the University bestirred itself to exact a slightly higher degree of morality and discipline from its students; namely, in 1338, when the Colleges had already begun to take strict measures in respect of their inmates. The famous Rue du Fouarre was barred at either end with gates and watchmen, who permitted the entry only of *bona-fide* students within the sacred precincts, excluding disreputable characters, thieves, and prostitutes. One fears, however, that even such precautions failed of their purpose.

Many were the complaints of the period against the scholars of Paris, or for that matter, the scholars of Oxford, of Prague, of Vienna, of Salamanca. The trouble was not local; wherever students were gathered together, their behaviour was much the same.

Respectable citizens and their wives complained of taunts and insults, of the throwing of filth on their sober finery, the slicing of noses in drunken pranks, the picking of pockets in jest or in earnest, the ravishment of wives and daughters, the irruption into houses in the dead of night, burglaries, and what not.

And as for the preachers of the time, they literally raged at

the sinful excesses of the scholars. According to them the
typical student was a drunkard, a frequenter of taverns, a
gambler, addicted to roaming the streets in gangs, shouting,
singing, quarrelling, throwing stones, breaking down doors,
and smashing heads, ready with his dagger, and given to playing practical jokes of the most brutal kind. The scholars
infested the streets of the Latin Quarter, raping and burning,
quarrelling among themselves over dogs and women, or for
no reason at all, wounding and slashing and fighting in groups.
They played on tambourines and guitars, they sang bawdy
songs, they hissed and clapped and shouted, they passed
scurrilous remarks over a lady's false hair, they delighted in
throwing itching powder down the necks of the passers-by
(*vide* Rabelais), they stuck out their tongues and made faces.

Nor were they more respectful of the things of the Church.
Deserting Theology for the more lucrative and practical
pursuits of Canon Law and Medicine, they cared nothing for
the sermons of the aggrieved preachers. The holy days were
to them no more than occasions for idleness and drinking;
they liked their masses short and their disputations long;
confession was neglected; instead of cleansing their minds
with the scouring of religion, they sought the laundresses of
Paris for the laundering of their vain apparel. As a rhyme of
the period had it:

> "Vox in choro, mens in foro
> Vel in mensa vel in thoro."

They were familiar with the name and the charms of every
prostitute in Paris; they threw dice even on the altars of the
churches, and the infuriated preachers did not even stop at
accusations of pederastic practices.

Nor were the Masters immune from commination. Jacques
de Vitry, the most eloquent of preachers, accused them of
beginning to teach before they themselves had studied; of
securing pupils by personal solicitation, by the use of runners,
and even by papering the house—*i.e.* by hiring students to

z

attend their lectures in order to give a false impression of their popularity.

According to Jacques de Vitry, these Masters prided themselves only on the number of their pupils, and in order to fill their classrooms they would preach strange and novel doctrines, with more than a hint of heresy about them, and, provided they were paid for it, they were willing to lecture even on Sundays and holy days. Others did their best—or worst—to make life easy for the students who lived with them, allowing them to sleep late of a morning, and even conniving at and participating in their vices.

The preachers set up the ideal of the meek, studious, and prayerful student, who scorned the temptations of Paris, sat long over his books, and never missed mass or confession; but it would seem, from their anguished outcries, that no such student existed.

Of course, the complaints of the preachers must be taken with a grain of salt. In modern times the purple vices of the Colleges and Universities are a favourite theme with sensation-seeking pulpit pounders, and the breed has not changed during the centuries. But that beneath much exaggeration there was a considerable basis of truth, in so far as certain elements of the student bodies were concerned, we have plenty of independent evidence.

A proclamation of 1269 denounces those scholars or pretended scholars of Paris who "by day and night atrociously wound and slay many, carry off women, ravish virgins, and break into houses," and who commit "over and over again robberies and many other enormities hateful to God."

At Oxford, an examination of the records of the Coroner's Inquests reveals entry after entry to the effect that So-and-so, clerk of Oxford, killed such and such a citizen or brother clerk, and thereupon incontinently fled. There is hardly ever any mention of seizure, conviction, or punishment; but occasionally the fact is recorded that the accused was obliged to seek sanctuary, and more rarely, that he was banished from the realm. In this case the homicidal scholar departed for Paris, and there continued with his interrupted studies.

The annals of every mediaeval University are replete with records of violence and of crime. There was the case of the student of the College of Boissi who made it a practice to leave the College confines at any hour of the day and night without permission. When he returned in the dead of night, accompanied by boon companions picked up in the tavern, the gates were locked. Thereupon the worthy scholars hacked and pounded them with their great swords, and banged them with heavy stones, to the discomfiture of more law-abiding students.

For these practices he was reprimanded, but not otherwise penalized. When, however, he atrociously assaulted a fellow-scholar, he was excommunicated. Being a contumacious sort of fellow, he refused to seek easy absolution, and boldly entered the Chapel. When he was forcibly ejected for this sacrilege, he set fire to the bed in his chamber in an attempt to burn the offending College to the ground. Further reprimands followed.

Growing bolder, he stationed himself on the roofs of the lecture and dining halls, and pounded them with great stones, so that lectures could not be heard, nor food eaten for the dust that fell in the dishes. For this and other high crimes he was summoned to appear before the Rector. Thereupon he stationed his brother and ten armed men in front of the Rector's dwelling, who prevented that dignitary from attending the Rectorial Court. Still nothing happened. But a later examination of his scholarship disclosed that the offender was "of rude intellect, not fitted or apt for acquiring proficiency." He was then deprived of his Bursar's place in the College, though still permitted all other University privileges. If he had passed the examination, no doubt all would have been forgiven.

Naturally, with discipline of this sort, even within the College walls, one might expect a little wildness in the scholars. Not until the fifteenth century did Paris—the University, as distinguished from its constituent Colleges—make a serious attempt to suppress the almost daily fights and battles. The Rector and Proctors were empowered to enter both College and Hall to seize an offender, and to deprive any conniving Master of his Regency, which meant the loss of his livelihood.

At Oxford, poaching in the King's forests was a popular sport among the scholars; and on all the roads leading into the city were to be found bands of expelled scholars, turned highwaymen, who took purses from incoming students, not overlooking those of ordinary citizens.

Nor were riots and outrages lacking which involved the Universities themselves. Some such incidents have already been discussed, in connection with their effect upon the growth of University privileges.   There were others.

Notable among such disturbances in Paris were the constant quarrels with the Abbey of St. Germain, just outside the city walls, to the west of the students' quarters. The bone of contention was the use of a great field, the famous Pré-aux-clercs, where the scholars were accustomed to walk and play in their leisure hours. The University claimed the ownership of this field, and so did the monks. Clashes were frequent.

In 1278 the field was crowded with scholars at their accustomed pleasures, unarmed for once. Suddenly the Abbey bell sounded. A plan of attack had been devised by the monks, to rid the field once and for all of obstreperous scholars. Armed men took possession of the three gates leading back to Paris, to cut off the retreat of the surprised students. From the Convent itself, led by the Provost, and to the sound of horns and trumpets and shouts of "Death to the clerks," a band of armed retainers issued on the run. They fell upon the defenceless scholars and Masters with clubs and swords, bows and arrows, and iron-tipped staves. Thereupon ensued a great slaughter. Caught between cross-fires, the scholars were cut down and maimed as they fled, and many, grievously wounded, were dragged into the Convent dungeons.

The University bestirred itself, and complained to King and Papal Legate, threatening cessation if justice were not done. The Abbot and his Provost were deprived of their offices, though the Abbot was given sufficient revenues to take the sting out of this humiliation, and the monks were required to found and endow two chaplaincies, to be in the perpetual gift of the University, and to say masses for the dead scholars.

In 1404, while the University was peacefully walking in procession to the Church of St. Catherine, a party of horsemen in the service of Charles de Savoisy, the King's Chamberlain, rode roughshod through the marching University. Immediately the procession was broken up, many were trampled down, and the indignant scholars seized stones and other weapons.

Savoisy's men, seeing themselves outnumbered, made off, but returned with reinforcements, and again the battle raged, with many casualties on either side. The Rector proceeded at once to the King and demanded redress, threatening a cessation. The King, however, was reluctant to discipline his Chamberlain, a great seigneur in his own right. True to his word, the Rector decreed the suspension of lectures and sermons throughout Paris for the term of six weeks.

The matter having become serious, the King yielded. The Master of the Chamberlain's household, held responsible for his men, was fined 1000 *livres* for the benefit of the scholar victims, and forced to pay 1000 *livres* to the University; he was also required to endow five chaplaincies of the annual value of 100 *livres*, to be in the gift of the University. Nor was this all. Savoisy himself was dismissed from his posts, and banished from the Court. It was decreed that his hotel was to be razed to the ground, and the scholars, "promptly and almost before the decree was pronounced," proceeded to execute the sentence. Three of the offending retainers, clad only in their shirts, and carrying lighted tapers, went to three churches in public procession, and were publicly flogged, to the great satisfaction of the scholars.

There are many such instances. At Toulouse, in 1332, there were five noble brothers, all students of Law. One was an Archdeacon, one a Provost of a monastery, one an Archpriest, one a Canon, and one was a bastard son of their father, and squire to his brother, the Canon.

On Easter Day the bastard Peter, with others, including a friend, Aimery, had dined and drunk too well. In an excess of jollity, they repaired, with certain light women, to the house of the reverend brothers, before which they danced and shouted and beat upon iron pots, making a hideous noise in the public street. The noble ecclesiastics sat at the window, watching with smiles of amusement the antics of their illegitimate brother.

But the other inhabitants of the neighbourhood were not so sympathetic. A Capitoul appeared on the scene with his guard, saw that the revellers were carrying prohibited weapons, and demanded their surrender. The scholars refused, whereupon the Capitoul attempted to arrest the offending parties. He should have known better. The scholars fell upon the guard with sword and poignard; Aimery sliced off a portion of the Capitoul's nose, taking with it part of his chin and lips, and breaking eleven teeth. Another member of the guard was killed by Peter, and then they fled.

That night, secure in the consciousness of the immunities of scholars and clerics, Peter slept openly in his brother's house. A posse of citizens, led by other Capitouls, swooped down upon the household, took it unawares, dragged its members off to prison, and proceeded to loot the premises.

The Archbishop intervened and demanded the immediate surrender of the ecclesiastics. The five brothers, including Peter the bastard, were thereupon released, but Aimery was dressed in lay garments and was wearing a long beard. It was therefore claimed he was not a cleric, though the chroniclers maintain that the signs of his tonsure were plainly visible until an ingenious Capitoul had his whole head shaven in order to obliterate the marks.

Aimery was put to the torture, and he confessed his crime. His offending hand was cut off, and he was dragged by horses to the gibbet, and there he was hanged.

The Archbishop's Official at once excommunicated the Capitouls, and the University, likewise intervening, complained to the Parlement of Paris on the ground that Aimery was the servant of a University scholar. The result was that the Capitouls were imprisoned, fined heavily for the benefit of Aimery's family, and required to erect a chapel for the salvation of his immortal soul. The city itself was mulcted of all its former privileges, and the body of Aimery, which had been hanging, dried and blackened, on the gibbet, during the three years of the hue and cry and the final judgment, was cut down and given a solemn and proper funeral, with four Capitouls as pall-bearers, and all the fathers of families of the city walking in slow procession. On reaching the University, the citizens begged forgiveness of the assembled scholars, who thereupon, to the number of some 3000, joined the procession. It ultimately cost the city 15,000 *livres tournois* to recover its civic privileges.

All this because a servant, who happened to serve a scholar, but whose clerical quality was doubtful, had been punished by the secular arm for his admitted crimes. More than any other incident, this shows the overwhelming influence of the mediaeval University.

In the year 1387 one Jean Rion, a citizen of Orléans, for private reasons, hired two thugs to waylay Guillaume Entrant, a Bachelor of Civil Law of the University. They bungled their first attempt, but the second was more satisfactory. Poor Guillaume was left for dead, a finger slashed off, an eye gouged out, and an arm hanging by a thread. For this atrocious crime Rion was summoned before the Parlement of Paris, where he pleaded in his defence that the wounded scholar had seduced his wife. This was not denied, yet, in an age when an injured husband had rights almost of life and death over a guilty wife and her lover, Rion was condemned to pay 300 *livres tournois* to his victim, and a further fine of 100 *livres*, and to implore pardon on his knees, clad only in his shirt. In short, when the seducer was a scholar, the unwritten law did not apply.

This sentence led to great indignation amongst the other citizens of Orléans, who were naturally apprehensive in respect of their own good wives. A mob gathered, and went hunting for scholars. One was beaten almost to death, others were wounded, and many were dragged off to the city jail. The scholars, unable to cope with the enraged citizens, fled the city, and the University was for the moment extinct.

But once more the long arm of the law intervened on behalf of the scholars. The royal officers who had led the riot, and the participating citizens, were all heavily fined, condemned to ample penance, and compelled to make the inevitable and humiliating apologies.

And here are some instances of another kind from Leipzig, as set forth with great detail in the *Acta Rectorum* for the year 1545:

On Holy Innocent's Day a Bachelor was murdered by a skinner in a street brawl, and the murderer escaped, though he was seen by respectable citizens, who, however, refused to identify him. A student, on the other hand, who had killed a man, was punished, after trial by the University, with imprisonment for life in the Bishop's Prison. And again, a Bachelor, going quietly about his business outside the city, was killed by two rustics. Though their names were known, the city authorities refused to take any action.

Evidently the hatred between University and Town had reached fever heat, and this time it was the University which was careful to give no offence. Nevertheless, the outrages continued, and the University appealed to Prince Maurice of Saxony, who promised protection. Edicts were published, only to be followed by another outrage. A skinner (always a skinner) named Hans von Buntzell, wounded the son of a

Doctor of Medicine with a sword, and promptly sought refuge in the house of yet another skinner. This time the Prince compelled the City authorities to act. They offered three alternative punishments to the aggrieved University: should Hans lose a hand? should he be publicly whipped and banished for ten years? should he be branded in the hand and then banished? The University declined to make any choice, and the City authorities reluctantly prepared a scaffold in the public market-place, preparatory to cutting off the offender's hand. The whole populace of the town gathered to plead for mercy, and a deputation of skinners waited on the Rector to beg for a commutation of the penalty. They offered to beat Hans with greater ferocity than the public executioner himself, if only the banishment were lifted. Banishment in those days meant a lifetime of wandering in strange and therefore terrifying places. Again the University was adamant, and Hans was duly branded and banished from the town.

CHAPTER XXXVI

Regulations, Feasts, and Student Letters

APART from serious homicides and riots, the students, like any normal lads, loved noise and disorder for their own sakes. Half the night would be spent in gaming and dancing, and playing on instruments in their rooms, to the confusion of all good people who went soberly to bed at sundown. Dicing was a passion with them, and many a poor scholar lost his year's tuition money on the wrong turns of the spotted cubes.

Not all the students were the eager enthusiasts for knowledge that the hardships which they endured would seem to indicate. Some attended lectures but once or twice a week, spending the rest of their days in idleness and gaming. Others preferred the courses in Canon Law, which began late, giving them ample time for sleep after a night's debauch. In the classrooms life was made miserable for the Master by stamping and whistling and the throwing of stones. Many students were satisfied with the mere name and immunities of the scholar, and drifted from Master to Master, from University to University; vagabonds, tramps, and even worse.

This, of course, is the dark side of the picture of University life. For every scholar involved in felonious offences, there were tens and twenties whose annals are unknown, for the very good reason that they never got into trouble. The annals of the virtuous, like the annals of a happy people, are short and barren. They studied conscientiously, attended all lectures and disputations, worked hard, ate frugally, drank their modest stoup of wine, and had no time for the delights of tavern or brothel.

The Colleges, too, modified the life of the scholars considerably. The stricter houses imposed the strictest discipline on their charges, and forbade them even the simplest pleasures. For one thing, they mapped out regular programmes, which

352

began with rising at dawn, and apportioned every minute of the student's time until curfew at night. Very little time was allowed for any of the normal amusements that we now associate with youth. Only on holidays was some measure of licence granted. It is little wonder that the scholars kicked over the traces when they had the chance, and indulged in the darker and more violent forms of amusement. But the Colleges were not all equally strict; and the mere existence of Statutes did not always mean that they were faithfully observed. And those Halls which still continued to exist were much more lenient in their attitude toward their boarders.

The College Statutes, however, were strict enough, at least on paper. Curfew rang early in mediaeval days, and in the English Universities the Proctors, with pole-axes on their shoulders, and accompanied by an armed guard, patrolled the streets nightly to round up scholastic stragglers.

At Leipzig the College gates shut promptly at 9 P.M. in winter and 10 P.M. in summer. This was liberal, for in Paris and Oxford 9 P.M. was the general rule, and the gates of Narbonne were closed at sunset. But there a small fine would open the gate for entrance or exit, so that its early closure did not unduly inconvenience the student on pleasure bent. And if a drunken scholar chose to break down the gate, he had only to pay the cost of repairs plus a fine of half a mark.

Ball-playing was forbidden at Narbonne as an "insolent game"; jousts and hawking were prohibited almost everywhere, as unclerkly and costly, and chess was frowned upon as in some way immoral. Cornouaille forbade attendance at the performances of jesters, mountebanks, and the drama. Gambling was usually severely censured, and in some cases wholly prohibited. But total prohibitions led only to wilder excesses, so that the Statutes, on the whole, preferred regulation; limiting the stakes, or permitting play only on Feast days, and at Narbonne "rarely for a pint or quart of wine or fruit and without great noise or expenditure of time."

Peterhouse forbade dogs or falcons, dice or chess, engaging in trade [*sic*], the frequenting of taverns, attending the drama or even conversing with actors; and musical instruments were anathema. New College decried throwing stones in Chapel, dancing and jumping in the Halls, and games of every description. Then there were rules against lateness, idleness, scurrilous language, sleeping out of College, carrying arms, talking in Hall or Chapel, and throwing water out of the upper windows. Scholars were forbidden to remain in the Halls after meals for fear of scandal, idle conversation, and quarrels. Only on Feast days could they sit by the fire and sing holy songs and hearken to the reading of sober chronicles.

Conversations at all times were to be exclusively in Latin, and the infamous *lupi* reported infractions of this rule. At Peterhouse, however, French might occasionally be spoken, if just and reasonable cause arose; at Queen's College it was freely permitted; at Jesus, Greek, Latin, and Hebrew were all proper tongues, and New College was broad-minded enough to permit English in addressing a layman.

Every minute infraction of a rule carried its separate penalty. But these penalties were usually small, and were devised rather for the gratification of the vinous appetites of the supervising Masters and senior Fellows than for their prohibitory effect. And the gravest offences, regarded from our modern standpoint, were usually visited with the slightest penalties.

In the English Colleges the most serious punishment was expulsion, and this was reserved for high crimes and misdemeanours. Ordinarily the punishment was a fine, or the withholding of the scholar's allowance for a stated period. Flogging was rare, and inflicted only in the later Middle Ages. One of the Statutes imposed flogging "for making odious comparisons."

Bringing women into College quarters was adjudged a penal offence; at Cornouaille the first offence was visited with fifteen days' confinement to the chamber, on a diet of bread and water, to cool the heated blood; the second offence was punished with thirty days' meditation; and the third proved the offender incorrigible and liable to expulsion.

The German Universities had prisons that were as well equipped with the refinements of life as the Colleges themselves. The convicted student was politely requested to betake himself into jail; if he refused, he was regretfully subjected to expulsion. Very serious crimes might be punished by expulsion, temporary or permanent banishment from the University town, or by postponement of the degree. Lesser crimes were punished by small fines.

For example, attacks on Masters with stones were carefully differentiated at Leipzig. The mere picking up of a stone with intent to throw cost ten *groschen*; actually throwing and missing increased the price to eight *florins*; hitting the Master cost still more.

But the most popular method of punishing infringements of the Statutes was by "sconcing," a term used even today at Oxford and Cambridge for fines that accrue to the benefit of the Masters and the offender's fellow-scholars. At Sorbonne a Fellow who assaulted or beat a servant was "sconced" one quart of good wine for the benefit of his brother Fellows' dusty throats. The poor beaten servant was not considered. The same punishment was imposed for talking in the vulgar tongue and for excessive hilarity at table. A head cook was fined for "badly preparing the meat for supper" and not putting salt in the soup. This was a noble precedent. Every little misdemeanour called for a "sconce": leaving the chapel door open, refusing to go to bed when ordered, lateness at table, everything!

And every scholar was eager, nay, anxious, to inform against his offending comrades. For the punishment meant more wine for all, at someone else's expense. An indignant clerk who declared that the Fellows were in the habit of finding excuses to sconce one another was threatened with expulsion for his temerarious veracity.

As the Middle Ages waned, the regulations became more

and more severe and petty in their minuteness, until the old wild freedom of the mediaeval scholar was completely quenched by the most personal restrictions. The new discipline extended to the Halls, so that the poor scholar, if one is to believe the Statutes, had no part in the frailties of this world.

In France the younger students were confined to their Halls, and were not permitted to walk outside, except with a Master, walking two by two, with decent mien and lowered eyes. Oxford, between 1431 and 1453, for the first time legislated as a University for the Halls, imposing burdensome restrictions. The poor scholars were not permitted to swear, to gamble, to walk out alone, or to keep late hours, and were forbidden to indulge in "dishonest garrulity," or to make "odious comparison of country with country, nobility with commonalty, Faculty with Faculty." Mass was to be attended daily, and attendance was required at all University sermons and the necessary lectures. The golden age was definitely over.

Yet, as we have seen, the records of the times do not justify the belief that these Statutes were very strictly enforced, nor do the penalties for disobedience seem to have been very burdensome to scholars who felt the urge to break loose.

The ideal, law-abiding student must have led a colourless life for the greater part of the year. Only the great Festival days broke the monotonous round of early rising, lectures, meals, studies, disputations, responses, Bible reading, cold, chilblains, et cetera. Fortunately the Festivals were many and colourful, and were celebrated by the Universities with great exuberance. Almost every Feast day had its procession, when scholars and Masters alike, arrayed in their best, marched, with much waving of banners, between the ranks of the admiring townsfolk.

In Paris there was the great celebration of mass in the cloisters of the Mathurins. On four stated days during the year all members of the University, with their retainers and clients, were compelled to attend, and no one ever evaded this duty. At eight in the morning the brilliant procession set forth on its way to the convent. The Masters had National Vespers and National Mass once a week; and for scholars and Masters both there were frequent masses, sermons, and processions. The Nations in particular, those social clubs, were greatly addicted to feasting and processions and festivals. They had their own vespers and masses, and a banquet on the days of their respective patron saints.

The English-German Nation had an annual business meeting and banquet; another banquet on the Feast of St. Matthew, and a gala feast on the day of St. Edmund, their patron saint. Then there were frequent bouts in the taverns after the election of officers, the initiation of new members, et cetera.

Any pretext served the University for a holiday and an occasion of riotous enjoyment; national victories in the field especially. When the news came of the victory of Bouvines in 1214, the University feasted and danced without stopping for a whole week. Then there was Christmas Day, St. Nicholas' Day, and greatest of all, the Feast of Fools, which came between Christmas and Twelfth Night.

On this characteristic occasion, a sub-deacon was made into a bishop, and carried in triumph to the sanctuary, where he read a burlesque mass, giving the lections in a farcical, rollicking fashion, while his pseudo-religious flock sang obscene songs, burlesquing the words of the Church ritual, and in some instances danced with great indecency, and ate sausages at the altar, or played at dice or cards.

It is no wonder that the Church did its utmost to put a stop to the rites of the Feast of Fools, but the tradition, which went back almost to pagan days, was too strong for them. The Feast persists to this day under a variety of Carnival disguises.

Apart from such occasions, holidays were short. It was decreed by Gregory IX in 1261 that the "long" vacation of summer must not exceed one month. It fell in September, the month of the grape harvest, and was therefore known as "les vendanges." During this period the rich students rode back to their distant homes, and the poor trudged wearily along the highways; or, if they were too poor to take a holiday, or if their homes were too distant, they remained disconsolately in Paris, watching with envious eyes the pleasures of their more fortunate brethren, or resolutely thrusting their noses into their books. By the end of the fourteenth century the vacation had lengthened, until in Arts it lasted from June 28th until August 25th, and in Theology and Canon Law from June 28th until September 15th.

A fruitful source of information concerning the manners and mentality of the student is found in such letters of the medi-aeval scholars as have managed to survive the wear and tear of time. However, despite their value, they must be accepted with a good deal of caution.

Letter-writing was not a widespread, casual art in those days. Even among the students, there were not many who had the faculty of penning long, rambling letters to their friends and relatives, replete with the little everyday occur-rences, the hopes, fears, ambitions and thoughts that we associate with a letter today. The common man, of course, was totally at a loss, and did not even feel the need to write except on the most urgent occasions.

For him, and for such occasions, there were the profes-sional scribes and notaries, who, for a consideration, under-took to compose a letter to suit their client's needs. Even they, however, did not play quite fair. There were formularies, compendiums of letters for every occasion, forms which they kept beside them and copied; in most instances changing only the names and such details as were necessitated by the matter in hand.

As we have seen, the art of writing letters was considered so important that courses were given in that subject as a branch of Rhetoric, and many professors of the noble art, called *dictatores*, went from place to place, making a lucrative living by their calling. The composition of letters, says the rhetorician, Albert of Samaria, is "often and exceedingly necessary for the clergy, for monks suitable, and for laymen honourable."

But most correspondents, University students included, found the pangs of original composition too arduous, and followed the example of the scribes in laboriously copying out examples from the formularies—bad Latin and all—and despatching them to their relatives as their own original utterance.

For this reason, and because the average student's letter home would have little chance of survival, there are hardly any spontaneous compositions at our disposal. The great majority of the letters that have come down to us are frankly formal in style, following models prepared by professors of the art for normal and habitual use.

Nevertheless, while lacking in spontaneity, these letters have considerable value. Even their formalism proves their universality; that the matters they discussed were near and dear to the heart of the average student.

The professors of Rhetoric, of *Dictaminis*, advertised their wares like the purveyors of modern business courses. They offered a short, practical course of instruction, with no nonsense about culture or the broadening of the mind. They taught a man to write practical letters for every occasion, guaranteed to bring results. (How did the impression get around that the Middle Ages were devoted to metaphysics and fine-spun, arid distinctions?) Special attention was paid to the student's letters to his parents, and the best methods of extracting money from the parental purse. "Let us take as our theme today," says one professor, "that a poor and diligent student at Paris is to write his mother for necessary expenses."

And by far the greater number of the letters extant are appeals for money, giving innumerable and ingenious reasons for the additional demands. How modern sounds the plaint of a father in an Italian collection!

"A student's first song is a demand for money," he says

bitterly, "and there will never be a letter which does not ask for cash."

An Oxford student, about the year 1220, writes home in particularly atrocious Latin:

"B. to his venerable master A., greeting. This is to inform you that I am studying at Oxford with the greatest diligence, but the matter of money stands greatly in the way of my promotion, as it is now two months since I spent the last of what you sent me. The city is expensive and makes many demands; I have to rent lodgings, buy necessaries, and provide for many other things which I cannot now specify. Wherefore I respectfully beg your paternity that by the promptings of divine pity you may assist me, so that I may be able to complete what I have well begun. For you must know that without Ceres and Bacchus Apollo grows cold."

Note the fine classical flourish at the end.

A student of Paris, fearing the parental refusal if he wrote direct, asks a friend of his to explain, "since the simplicity of the lay mind does not understand such things, how at length after much study nothing but lack of money for the inception banquet stands in the way of his graduation."

From Bologna we hear of the terrible mud which the poor youth must wade through, begging his way from door to door, all for lack of funds; a Viennese student who has written that he has spent his all on books and other implements of scholarship obtains a welcome response, receiving "by this present messenger ten Rhenish gulden, seven ells of cloth for a cloak, and one pair of stockings."

The list of things demanded is varied: clothes, linen, bedding, books, parchment, chalk, their father's top-boots, lambskin for winter wear, and money—money—money! The excuses are as varied: the cost of living in town, unlucky personal encounters with enemies and consequent fines, the robbing of messengers, or disaster on the road. One scholar writes from an Austrian prison that the bread is hard and mouldy, the drinking-water mixed with his tears, the darkness dense enough to feel; another lies on straw with no covering, goes without shoes or shirt, and eats he will not say what—a skilful tale addressed to a soft-hearted sister, and guaranteed to bring in return a hundred sous *tournois*, two pair of sheets, and ten ells of fine cloth, all without her husband's knowledge. Still another wants to take his degree and return home. But he has attended few lectures and his chance of passing the examinations is poor. A judicious distribution of gifts to the examiners might help, so he writes home for money—enough to give a feast to the professors and provide for incidental gifts. He receives the money, gives the feast, distributes the presents, and obtains his degree with flying colours.

The *dictatores* are practical men. The students pay for model letters to their parents, but what of the parents themselves, who naturally have more money than their impecunious sons, and are less able to fend for themselves in meeting cleverly-worded demands for cash? The *dictatores* come to the rescue: here is a new field for their efforts.

Having told the students how to demand money, they now teach the parents how to evade compliance with their unworthy sons' requests.

Send in return, the formularies say, giving chapter and verse, a letter complaining of a hard winter, of the failure of crops, of the fact that a sister has to be married and provided with a substantial dowry, or that a brother is about to be knighted; or, in more brutal fashion, reprove the applicant vehemently with some such letter as this:

"To his son G. residing at Orléans, P. of Besançon sends greetings with paternal zeal. It is written, 'He also that is slothful in his work is brother to him that is a great waster.' I have recently discovered that you live dissolutely and sloth-fully, preferring licence to restraint, and play to work, and strumming a guitar to studying like the others, whence it happens that you have read but one volume of law while your more industrious companions have read several. Wherefore I have decided to exhort you herewith to repent utterly of your dissolute and careless ways, that you may no longer be called a wastrel and your shame may be turned to good repute."

Then the ever-obliging professors turn their coats, and behold, the berated student is armed with a reply wherein he feigns indignation and imputes the ill reports to the calumnies of his enemies.

From Orléans a scholar begs for money because, having quarrelled with another, as the devil would have it, he struck him on the head with a stick, wherefore he is now in prison and must pay fifty *livres* for his release.

The formularies disclose the fact that many scholars were most reluctant to quit the academic life. Boncompagno gives the example of a student who spent twenty-eight years in study, and the model letters are full of requests for permission to prolong the student's life at the University. War, deaths, births, marriages, mean nothing to the earnest scholar. There is the case of a student of Siena, whose parents wish him to marry a certain lady, who is possessed of many attractions. He replies that it is foolish to desert the cause of learning for the sake of a woman, "for one may always get a wife, but science once lost can never be recovered." It is a touching sentiment!

Then there is the clever letter written by a woman to her husband who has been absent from her, studying in the Schools, longer than he had promised. She is certain that he is studying in some other Code than that prescribed by the Faculty of Law; and she proposes to do a little such studying on her own account!

CHAPTER XXXVII

The Goliards

INTIMATELY connected with the Universities, or rather, with the life of the mediaeval scholar, are the Goliards. In an age when the hand of the Universal Church lay heavily on the common, everyday life of mankind—when organization and regimentation were the rule—the Goliards, with their songs, their loves, their laughter, and their sheer, irresponsible vagabondage, strike a fresh, lyric note that seems wholly out of tune with the rigid spirit of mediaevalism.

Yet if we discard all preconceptions, it is easy to see how intimately the Goliards enter into the very fabric of the life of the times. Their beginnings are dimly seen. Some time in the twelfth century, or even earlier, when the yeast of the new Renaissance was fermenting, when the first great teachers, like Abélard, and Bernard of Chartres, and John of Salisbury, were surrounded by companies of eager scholars, when the cleansing wind of intellectual curiosity was blowing away the fog of centuries—men, young men, everywhere caught the contagion. They hastened from teacher to teacher, from School to School, until the open road became a habit, and the *Wanderlust* an imperious passion.

Clerics they were, naturally, being scholars, and they wore the privileged tonsure. They were therefore under the protection of the Church; but their outlook on life, their philosophy, harked back to pagan days, to a time when bright-eyed gods and goddesses peeped from every bush, when wine and laughter were the be-all and end-all of life, when there was no hereafter with eternal rewards and punishments.

Gradually the wandering scholars became a familiar sight in Europe, begging their way from village to town, content with a crust of bread if only it were moistened with wine, seeking the Schools and the great Masters, flitting like bees from the honeyed lips of one to the other, lingering only until their restless blood and the voice of the spring set them wandering farther. Over Northern France, through Germany, across the Alps into Italy, they wandered back and forth, forgetting the pursuit of knowledge in the more pagan delights of the moment, remembering their clericality only when the arm of the secular law threatened to descend upon them.

Everywhere their tattered, threadbare garments and their jaunty gait were familiar; every tavern knew their faces and echoed to their songs and carousings; many a maid thought wistfully or bitterly of the adventuring scholar who loved and wandered on.

A strange class, clerical only in name, ostensibly devoted to celibacy and other-worldliness, more pagan than the pagans, more disreputable than the vagabonds, light of heart and purse; notorious wine-bibbers, with cut-throats, thieves, and scamps among them, who nevertheless brought men a fresh, keen vision of the world and its delights, who sang in tender phrases or mocking ribald accents of love and life and laughter; such songs as the world had not heard since pagan days.

The jongleurs, the troubadours of the South, laymen all, had already risen and flourished, using the vulgar tongues as their medium; but their songs of love and life were courtly and conventional, poured into an unyielding mould that had little or no relation to the world of things as they are, and they were not definitely estranged from the Church in their principles or ideals.

The Goliards, on the other hand, though clerics, who wrote and sang in Latin, the language of the Church, were as far removed from the spirit of Christianity as any mortals might be. Their supreme delight in the life of the senses, in the joys of wine and pretty women and good roast meats, was so frank, so fresh and miraculous, that to this day there has hardly been any other movement to compare to this great outburst of pagan lyricism.

Even as the class itself was vague and indeterminate, so is

the origin of the name, "Goliard." The name itself was used by the Goliardic authors, who call themselves Golias, or disciples of Golias. And Golias is probably Goliath, the Philistine, described in the later Dark Ages as the Devil, the leader of all the evil-livers of the earth. As early as the tenth century a decree ascribed to Archbishop Walter of Sens denounces "the family of Golias." [1]

The wandering clerics, with their ribald irreverence, their wastrel lives, may well have seemed to the eyes of an outraged hierarchy the veritable sons of the Devil, or of Golias. Nevertheless, the anathematized class very cheerfully adopted the designation, attributing their origin to one Bishop Golias, a sort of spiritual father, an arch-poet.

Most of the Goliardic poets and songsters were anonymous, content to compose and sing their lyrics without thought of fame or posterity, but two there were who stand out from the nameless mass. Yet even they are shadows, of whose lives very little is known, and only one of them bears a name for us.

They are the *Primate* and the *Archpoet*. Without doubt they were the greatest poets of the Middle Ages, with all due deference to many a jongleur, and to the poets of the *Romaunt de la Rose* and *Reynard the Fox*.

The *Primate's* real name was Hugh, and he was a Canon of Orléans about 1140. We know further that he studied and taught in Paris, that he was small and deformed, and that the loss of wealth and position made a keen wit more mordant, and a natural taste for wine and women more reckless. Salinbeme terms him "a most amusing rogue and great versifier and extemporizer, who, if he had but turned his heart to the love of God, would have had a great place in divine letters and have proved most useful to God's church." Fortunately, he chose to avoid the narrow path, even as Villon did in a later age, to the great enrichment of literature.

But there was a greater even than he—the *Archpoet*, worthy

---

[1] St. Bernard described Abélard as Goliath; but some writers support the derivation of Goliard from *Gaillard*.

to stand unashamed in any immortal company. His very name is lost, but it seems that he was a follower of Reinald, Archbishop of Cologne, Archchancellor to Frederick Barbarossa. Of noble origin, he was wholly dependent on the bounty of his priestly patron, "soliciting openly and without shame shirt and cloak to hide his ragged nakedness against the keen wintry blasts." He followed his patron to Frederick's court and took part in the Italian campaigns of that monarch. When commanded to compose an epic of the wars, he complained boldly that he could not write on an empty stomach, that the quality of his verse depended on the quality of the wine which he imbibed.

> " Tales versus facio quale vinum bibo."

The masterpiece of the Goliards, the great modern poem of the Middle Ages—the *Confession of Golias*—is attributed to him. It is a song of the open road, of the vagabond life, of taverns and hard drinking, of sport and mocking irreverence, of love, of spring, of gamesters, of poverty, of sorrow and defiance. Its gods are the pagan gods—Venus, Bacchus, and Decius, god of dice. Christianity is all but forgotten.

> In the public house to die
> Is my resolution;
> Let wine to my lips be nigh
> At life's dissolution;
> That will make the angels cry
> With glad elocution,
> " Grant this toper, God on high,
> Grace and absolution!"

Or,

> To my mind all gravity
> Is a grave subjection;
> Sweeter far than honey are
> Jokes and free affection.
> All that Venus bids me do
> Do I with erection,
> For she ne'er in heart of wan
> Dwelt with dull dejection.[1]

[1] Translated by J. A. Symonds in *Wine, Women, and Song.*

Down the broad way do I go,
Young and unregretting,
Wrap me in my vices up,
Virtue all forgetting,
Greedier for all delight
Than heaven to enter in:
Since the soul in me is dead,
Better save the skin.[1]

Here Christianity peeps into the picture, but in a sort of reverse Mass. Note the modern rhythm, the metrical swing, that had no forbears. Nor were these qualities unique in the work of the *Primate* or the *Archpoet*—they permeated the whole mass of Goliardic poetry. Here is a song in a minor key, instinct with the poverty and essential tragedy of the more earnest among the Wanderers:

I, a wandering scholar lad,
Born for toil and sadness,
Oftentimes am driven by
Poverty to madness.
Literature and knowledge I
Fain would still be earning,
Were it not that want of pelf
Makes me cease from learning.

These torn clothes that cover me
Are too thin and rotten;
Oft I have to suffer cold
By the warmth forgotten.

Scarce I can attend at church,
Sing God's praises duly;
Mass and vespers both I miss,
Though I love them truly.

Oh, thou pride of N——,
By thy worth I pray thee,
Give the suppliant help in need,
Heaven will sure repay thee.

[1] Translated by Helen Waddell in *The Wandering Scholars*, Constable and Company, 1927, and reproduced by special permission.

> Take a mind unto thee now
> Like unto St. Martin;
> Clothe the pilgrim's nakedness,
> Wish him well at parting.
>
> So may God translate your soul
> Into peace eternal,
> And the bliss of saints be yours
> In His realm supernal.[1]

Despite the desperate sincerity of parts of this lament, one wonders whether the pious Christian sentiments, the rhapsodic conclusion, do not bear a suspicious resemblance to many a student letter in the formularies, designed to extract the maximum amount of money from an unsuspecting patron. Let us be charitable, however, and trust that the unknown singer received sufficient to clothe his nakedness and withal, enough to wet his gullet.

In a different mood, a rollicking, roistering song of the road and tavern, is the following:

> We in our wandering
> Blithesome and squandering,
> Tara, tantara, teino!
>
> Eat to satiety,
> Drink with propriety;
> Tara, tantara, teino!
>
> Laugh till our sides we split,
> Rags on our hides we fit;
> Tara, tantara, teino!
>
> Jesting eternally,
> Quaffing infernally;
> Tara, tantara, teino!

Then there is the exordium to all good Goliards:

> Some are gaming, some are drinking,
> Some are living without thinking.
> And of those who make the racket,
> Some are stripped of coat and jacket;

[1] J. A. Symonds, *supra*.

Some get clothes of finer feather,
Some are cleaned out altogether;
No one there dreads death's invasion,
But all drink in emulation.

And here is a list of requirements for entry into the Order of Golias, ascribed to the *Archpoet*:

We receive the tonsured monk,
Let him take his pittance;
And the parson with his punk,
If he craves admittance;
Masters with their bands of boys,
Priests with high dominion;
But the scholar who enjoys
Just one coat's our minion.[1]

There was much parodying, too, of the most sacred things. Nothing was too holy, nothing too powerful, for the Goliards' satiric verse: not Popes, Bishops, the Vulgate, the solemn accents of the liturgy, the Lord's prayer, the Mass; not even the Virgin was exempt. The *Verbum bonum et suave* of the hymn to the Virgin became in parody *Vinum bonum et suave*. *Ecce homo, sine domo*, they sang gustily. The Office became a lengthy *Office of Gamblers*, the Mass a *Drinkers' Mass*. The faithful were scandalized by ribald verses following closely the words of the *Sanctus* and *Agnus Dei*. All authority, whether of Church or State, was fit matter for their mocking wit.

Yet it must not be thought that the Goliardic poetry was wholly preoccupied with wine and women and obscenity. There are many lovely lyrics, pure in form and pure in thought. They tell of spring, of a floating cloud, of a field dappled in sunlight, of love:

Oh, tender laughter of those wanton lips
That draw all eyes upon them,
Love's own lips,
Soft swelling
And instilling
Sweets of honey in their kissing
Till I deny that ever I was mortal![2]

[1] J. A. Symonds, *supra*.   [2] Helen Waddell, *supra*.

At length the day of retribution came. Church Councils had thundered in vain against these vagabond scholars. All student excesses, all sacrilegious defiling of altars, all murders and rapes, even the Black Mass itself, were attributed to the *vagantes*.

Finally, in 1231, the Council of Rouen launched the terrible thunderbolt of degradation, a crushing blow to the Goliards, hitherto immune by virtue of the protection of the very Church which they mocked.

Henceforth the *clericus* found wandering was to be *clericus* no more. If captured, he was to be immured in a monastery or the bishop's prison, shaven completely, and cast out without the saving tonsure; a layman, subject to the eager talons of the King's courts; outlawed in very fact.

That was the end. The wandering scholar was now a tramp, a rascal, a vagabond; every man's hand was against him. The Order, if such it could be termed, had fallen on evil days, and had lost the glamorous charm it once possessed. By the end of the fourteenth century the term "goliard" was equivalent to a pimp, a brothel-keeper, and the vilest insult to be flung in any man's teeth.

CHAPTER XXXVIII

Estimates

NOW that the whole vast panorama of the mediaeval Universities has been surveyed, it is time to pause and consider the meaning of this strangely new phenomenon in the Western World, its impact on mediaeval institutions, and the positive value of its educational ideals as influencing its own times and the modern world.

Surveying the Universities from the standpoint of the modern educator, it would be easy to find not only flaws, but palpable absurdities.

For one thing, the principle of authority was made a fetish. Aristotle and the Bible were sacrosanct; so were the Church Fathers, so, in a lesser degree, were Peter Lombard, Gratian, and Averrhoës. Whatever was written in these volumes was holy, not to be questioned or investigated or changed by the tiniest jot. All knowledge was fixed and known in so far as it would ever be given to man to know. The eyes and ears and minds of the world had been for ever closed; observable facts were not facts if they seemed to contradict the voice of established authority. In fact, to the majority of scholars direct observation was a delusion and a snare.

Given the text, it was the Master's business merely to expound and comment upon it, elucidating difficult passages, interpreting and reconciling inconsistencies. It was the student's task to absorb this routine knowledge, and to dispute on set themes, not as original subjects for investigation, but as the pretext for a profuse quotation of authorities. The disputant with the greater number of authorities on his side won the battle.

This method, of course, had fundamental defects. For one thing, it ruled out all practical consideration of the sciences. By their very nature the physical and natural sciences depend on long-continued, patient, open-minded observations of a multitude of facts, to be stored and gradually synthesized into coherent hypotheses and theories, without formal relation to preconceived ideas. The use of authority prevented science from making any material progress until authority itself was swept away in the flood of the Renaissance.

Further, it barred the acute and intellectual thinkers of the Middle Ages from taking wide views and exploring new fields. The mediaeval scholar was restricted to the authorities available. As a result, truly remarkable powers were expended in squirrel-like twistings and turnings within the confining cages of thought. Dialectic was pursued with passionate zeal, until it became the predominant study of the age.

The syllogism afforded a perfect tool for the work required of the scholar. Scholasticism, the method of the Schools, was a matter of disputation by series of related syllogisms, of hair-splittings, of vain distinctions, of futile strivings for victory without regard to truth. In such victory lay satisfaction and triumph for the scholar. The authorities were fixed, immovable. Very well, then: let us see how we can twist them to our needs by verbal subtlety and sophistry.

The Arts Course, the fundamental, primary University course, suffered by reason of the overshadowing prominence of Logic. The classics, and the catholicity that comes from the perusal of noble literature, were scorned because they could not yield to syllogistic methods, because they had no utilitarian value, because the Church frowned on the pagan philosophy.

The utilitarian spirit became the curse of the Universities. In the early days of Abélard the spirit of scholarship was comparatively disinterested; men and boys travelled over half Europe, and willingly subjected themselves to untold hardships, to drink at the mainsprings of intellectual life; but that eagerness for knowledge *per se* died down as the formal Universities rose to power and prominence.

Learning, education, became a matter of achieving a degree, of obtaining a social *cachet*, of opening up paths to riches and fame and easy preferment in Church and State. The sons of the wealthy loved the free, untrammelled life of the University; the parish priests and canons applied for the exemptions that would take them out of their monotonous duties into the varied life of the cities; and the Arts, which should have been the backbone of the University, became a narrowed field, relegated to mere boys.

The true reason for the University's existence was then found in the higher Faculties, the professional Schools. Of these by far the most popular was the Civil Law Faculty. There was good reason for this. The Law Graduate had an unlimited field before him. Private practice was exceedingly lucrative, and all the higher positions in municipality and State, in Parlements and Councils, were open to him. Even in the Church the knowledge of Civil Law was highly advantageous.

Next in popularity ranked the Faculty of Canon Law. The study of ecclesiastical Codes and Law opened the door to rapid preferment in the Church. Every priest, every student, saw rich prizes within his grasp once the coveted degree was conferred upon him.

Both these Faculties, too, were completely amenable to the exploitation of the syllogism, and to respect for constituted authority. They lived and thrived on interpretations and ingenious twistings of what had been said and done before.

Lower in the scale, but still attracting many students, was Medicine. The Doctor of Medicine was normally sure of a good living, a dignified position, and a rich wife. But, unfortunately, medicine is not amenable to the syllogistic method of study. This is why medicine languished during the Middle Ages, at least in Christian Europe, even as did the sciences.

The last of the higher Faculties was Theology. This "Queen of Sciences," in the eyes of the Popes, its godfathers, was the supreme if not the only reason for the existence and continued administration of such a University as Paris. Yet very few students embarked on the long and difficult course, even though Colleges were created to help them through it. The rewards were too remote, and possibly too purely intellectual, to attract the severely practical, utilitarian scholars of the time. It is remarkable to note how little religious instruction the Universities gave, if we except the Schools of Theology. Many a scholar earned his degree without ever having read the Bible or any other sacred writing. The ambitious scholar of Orléans who asked his father for money to buy a Bible and begin the study of theology was advised by his more practical parent to turn to a more lucrative profession.

Because books were few and expensive, the lecture system was inevitable, and this enhanced the power of authority, of *ex cathedra* opinions and the importance of mere memorization. Whole departments of knowledge were left wholly untouched, as though they did not exist.

The professorial system also was eminently unsatisfactory. The teaching Masters were not paid regular and secure salaries. They had to depend solely on their precarious fees. This led to unworthy tricks and popular appeals to obtain pupils, though in Italy, and later, in the Colleges, a system of salaried chairs was established. The Arts Masters were usually young, not much older than their scholars, and they often spent more time in riotous living than in serious intellectual preparation. The dignified Doctors of the higher Faculties were more interested in meddling with the affairs of Church and State, and left a good deal of the teaching work to untried Bachelors.

Yet with all their patent and acknowledged faults and limitations, the Universities of the mediaeval era played a very important part in the intellectual life of the world. Before them were the Dark Ages, when man thought little, and that little crudely. They rode the crest of the twelfth-century Renaissance, and canalized it into fields that the mediaeval man could sow and reap. Without them it is quite possible that the new learning, with Aristotle and Arabic science and philosophy, might have fallen on barren ground and perished of sheer aridity; through them thousands on thousands obtained a glimpse of the life of the intellect, and felt the stirrings of something greater than feudal wars. The Universities cradled philosophy and theology, sired such men as Abélard, Aquinas, Albert the Great, Grossetête, Roger Bacon, Wyclif, Hus, John of Salisbury, and Ockham. Out of them grew the coherent, organic whole of Christian theology, the fabric of philosophy.

They formed a veritable republic of letters, an international exchange, in an era when every village, every feudal domain, was self-sufficient and suspicious of its neighbours. They made learning dignified and respected, and next to the Church, were the great binding forces of Western Europe.

They were the media through which Roman Law survived into modern times, an organized and rounded whole. Through them Arabic culture became a part of the western inheritance. They helped to break down the rigid class lines of feudalism, and made it possible for lads of peasant birth to rise from humble beginnings; they were the great organs of public opinion, and helped to cradle the religious movements. And they were the great beginnings of the far-flung modern University system.

Their limitations were the limitations of their times, their glories superbly their own. What does it matter that eventually they led to sterility, that in their decadence they were blind to the rising star of Humanism and the great Renaissance of the sixteenth century? Unwittingly or wittingly, they had prepared the soil; they had kept learning alive when it might have perished from the earth; they had proved their force in a world too long obscured in darkness.

Great, tumultuous, proud, invincible Universities, with their tremendous privileges and haughty mien, bowing to neither King nor Pope—colourful, magnificent republics—their story remains one of the most fascinating chapters in the history of the human mind.

Bibliography

THE best general bibliography for the mediaeval Universities will be found in the appropriate sections of L. J. Paetow's *Guide to the Study of Mediaeval History* (rev. ed.), 1931. The works appended hereto are those which the author personally consulted in the making of this book.

ORIGINAL SOURCES

Abélard, Peter.   Historia Calamitatum, trans. by H. A. Bellows, 1922.

Bacon, Roger.   Opus Majus, trans. by R. B. Burke, 1928.

Coulton, G. G.   A Medieval Garner, 1910.

D'Andeli, Henri.   The Battle of the Seven Arts, trans. by L. J. Paetow, 1914.

Denifle and Chatelain.   Chartularium Universitatis Parisiensis: 4 vols., 1889-92, supplemented by Auctarium C.U.P., 2 vols., 1894-7.

Dolet, Etienne.   Toulouse in the Renaissance, trans. by J. C. Dawson, 1923.

Duncalf and Krey.   Parallel Source Problems in Medieval History, 1912.

Fournier, M., ed.   Les statuts et privilèges des universités françaises depuis leur fondation jusqu'en 1789, 4 vols., 1890-4.

Garland, John of.   Morale Scolarium, ed. by L. J. Paetow, 1927.

Goulet, Robert.   Compendium on the magnificence, dignity, and ex-cellence of the University of Paris in 1517, trans. by R. B. Burke, 1928.

Haskins, C. H.   The Life of the Medieval Students as Illustrated by their Letters (Am. Hist. Rev., v. 3, pp. 203-229, Jan. 1898).
The University of Paris in the Sermons of the Thirteenth Century (Am. Hist. Rev., v. 10, pp. 1-27, 1904).

Mosellanus, Petrus.   Paedalogia, trans. as "Renaissance student life," by R. F. Seybolt, 1927.

Norton, A. O.   Readings in the history of education: medieval universities, 1909.

Ordronaux, John.   Trans. of Regimen Sanitatis Salernitanum, 1871.

Oxford.   Medieval archives of the university of Oxford, 2 vols, 1920-1.

Sarti and Fattorini.   De claris archigymnasii bononiensis professoribus a saeculo XI usque ad saeculum XIV, 2 vols., 1888-96.

Seybolt, R. F.   Trans. of the Manuale Scholarium, 1921.

Shackford, Martha H.   Ed. Legends and satires from medieval literature, pp. 125-7, 1913.

Sorbon, Robert de.   De consciencia et de tribus dietis, ed. by F. Chambon, 1903.

Symonds, J. A.   Wine, Women, and Song, trans. of Medieval Latin Students' Songs, reprinted 1912.

University of Pennsylvania.   Translations and Reprints, v. II, no. 3, 1895.

Webster, H.   Historical Selections, pp. 579-604.

MODERN WORKS

Azarias, Frère.   Essays Educational, 1905.

Boulay, C. E. Du.   Historia universitatis parisiensis a Carolo Magno ad nostra tempora, 6 vols., 1665-73.

Boyce, G. C.   The English-German Nation in the University of Paris during the Middle Ages, 1927.

Bridges, J. H.   The Life and Work of Roger Bacon, 1914.

Budinsky, A.   Die Universität Paris und die Fremden an derselben im Mittelalter, 1876.

Chiappelli, L.   Lo studio bolognese nella sue origini e nei suoi rapporti colla scienza pre-irneriana, 1888.

Compayré, J. G.   Abélard and the Origin and Early History of Universities, 1910.

Connolly, J. L.   John Gerson, reformer and mystic, 1928.

Crevier, J. B. L.   Histoire de l'université de Paris depuis son origine jusqu'en l'année 1600, 7 vols., 1761.

Crump, C. G., and E. F. Jacob, eds.   The Legacy of the Middle Ages, articles—"Philosophy," by C. R. S. Harris, and "Education," by J. W. Adamson, 1926.

Denifle, H.   Die Entstehung der Universitäten des Mittelalters bis 1400, v. I, 1885.

Dollinger, J. V.   The Universities new and old, 1867.

Dubarle, E.   Histoire de l'université de Paris, 2 vols., 1844.

Emden, A. B.   An Oxford Hall in medieval times, 1927.

Fitting, H.   Die Anfänge der Rechtschule zu Bologna, 1888.

Fletcher, H.   Oxford and Cambridge, 1910.

Franklin, A.   La Vie Privée d'Autrefois, v. II, 1887-96.

Fuente, De La, V.   Historia de las universidades, colegios y demás estable cimientos de enseñanza en España, 4 vols., 1884-9.

Gibson, S. The Congregations of the University of Oxford (Bodleian Quarterly Record, v. 4, pp. 296-314, 1926).

Gross, C. The Political Influences of the University of Paris in the Middle Ages (Am. Hist. Rev., 1901, v. 6, pp. 440-5).

Harris, C. R. S. Duns Scotus, 2 vols., 1927.

Haskins, C. H. The Renaissance of the Twelfth Century, 1927.
The Rise of the Universities, 1923.
Studies in the History of Medieval Science, 1924.

Kaufman, G. Die Geschichte der deutschen Universitäten, 2 vols., 1888-96.

Laurie, S. S. Rise and Early Constitution of Universities, 1903.

Little, A. G. Roger Bacon (Proc. of the Brit. Acad., v. XIV, 1928).
Roger Bacon Essays, Collected and edited by, 1914.

Luchaire, A. Social France in the Time of Philip Augustus, trans. by Krehbiel, 1912.

Mallett, C. E. A history of the University of Oxford, v. I, 1924.

Mansbridge, A. The Older Universities of England, 1923.

Marriott, C. Oxford—Its Place in National History, 1933.

McCabe, J. Peter Abélard, 1901.

Milburn, J. B. University Life in Medieval Oxford (Dublin Review, v. 129, pp. 72-97, 1901).

Mullinger, J. B. The University of Cambridge, v. I, 1873.

Okey, T. The Story of Paris, 1906.

Paetow, L. J. The Arts Course at Medieval Universities, 1910.

Poole, R. L. The Masters of the Schools at Paris and Chartres in John of Salisbury's Time (Eng. Hist. Rev., XXXV, pp. 321-42, 1920).

Post, G. Alexander III and the Rise of the Universities (Anniversary Essays in medieval history, 1929, pp. 255-78).

Powicke, F. M. Stephen Langton, 1928.

Rait, R. S. Life in the Medieval University, 1912.

Rashdall, Hastings. Rise of the Universities, 2 v. in 3, 1895. (This is the most complete and accurate text in English. The author has leaned heavily upon it. A revised edition has appeared in 1936.)

Reynier, G. La vie universitaire dans l'ancienne Espagne, 1902.

Savigny. Geschichte des römischen Rechts, chap. XXI.

Sedgwick, H. D. Italy in the thirteenth century, v. I, chap. XVI-XVII.

Sharp, D. E. Franciscan Philosophy at Oxford in the Thirteenth Century (Brit. Soc. of Franciscan Studies, Pubs. v. 16, 1930).

Taylor, H. O. The Medieval Mind, 2 vols., 1925.

Thompson, J. W.   The Middle Ages, v. II, 1931.

Thorndike, L.   A History of Magic and Experimental Science, 2 vols., 1923.

Thurot, C.   De l'organisation de l'enseignement dans l'université de Paris au moyen âge, 1850.

Tilley, A., ed.   Medieval France, "Scholastic Philosophy and Universities," by A. G. Little, 1922.

Townsend, W. J.   Great Schoolmen.

Vaughan, E. V.   The origin and early development of the English universities to the close of the thirteenth century (Univ. of Missouri Studies, Soc. Sci. Series, II, no. 2, 1908).

Vinogradoff, P.   Roman law in medieval Europe, 1929.

Waddell, Helen.   The Wandering Scholars, 1927.

Whittlesey, D. S.   Life in the Medieval University of Paris—Master's Dissertation, Univ. of Chicago, 1915.

Willard, J. F.   The Royal authority and the early English universities, 1902.

Wulf, M. de.   History of Medieval Philosophy, 2 vols., 1926.
  Philosophy and Civilization in the Middle Ages, 1922.

Young, R. F.   Bohemian Scholars and Students, at the English Universities from 1347 to 1750 (Eng. Hist. Rev., Jan. 1923).

Index